High Tech Holocaust

High Tech Holocaust

James Bellini

A GRAHAM TARRANT BOOK

DAVID & CHARLES

Newton Abbot   London

For Myrto

British Library Cataloguing in Publication Data

Bellini, James
    High tech holocaust. – (A Graham Tarrant book)
    1. Environmental health   2. Air –
    Pollution – Physiological effect
    I. Title
    613'.19   RA576

    ISBN 0-7153-8812-6

Printed in Great Britain
Redwood Burn, Trowbridge, Wilts
for David & Charles Publishers plc
Brunel House   Newton Abbot   Devon

Contents

Acknowledgements

My thanks go to Kareen Marwick for her meticulous help on complex matters of toxicology and biochemistry, and to Jenny Clifford for assistance in seeking out the facts and figures of a contaminated world; to the Environmental Technology Library, Imperial College, London; to the London Food Commission; to the International Register of Potentially Toxic Chemicals of the United Nations Environment Programme; to the producers and researchers of *ECO* at Central Television, especially Vivica Parsons and Paul Cleary, for alerting me to many of the dangers now facing us; to the burgeoning fraternity of environmental institutes around the world whose publications have formed such a vital part of my research effort, not least to Friends of the Earth, Earthscan, Earth Resources Research, Oxfam and Social Audit. And to Graham Tarrant, whose constant encouragement and interest sustained me through many months of mounting anxiety as the true extent of the high-tech holocaust revealed itself. The errors, omissions and conclusions, however, are mine alone.

Introduction
A Pact with the Devil

The high-tech age has given us unprecedented benefits. Without industry, and the sophisticated technologies that it has brought with it, the world would still be living in pre-modern times. There would be no supersonic aircraft, no wonder drugs, no television or video, no skyscraper cities. The popular affluence that we now take for granted in the developed countries, give or take the entrenched problem of unemployment, could never otherwise have been attained. Without industry we would be denied the many and varied benefits of abundance. And humanity would have been spared the horrors of Chernobyl, Bhopal, Thalidomide, acid rain, pesticide poisoning, the health hazards posed by contaminated and adulterated food, the insidious danger of household drinking water tainted by toxic traces, and other unwanted features of life in the late twentieth century.

Poisoned soils, poisoned bodies, a poisoned future. The price of progress is rarely assessed in full. Industrial revolution was welcomed as the catalyst of social and political change, as well as the source of prosperity for many millions. But with it came an unforeseen danger. Under the assault of a rising tide of pollution the nature of this earth was to be changed completely. Now that polluting tide threatens to upset the delicate balance of our own biochemistry. Humanity faces the prospect of contamination overload – the high-tech holocaust.

The coming of industry has changed the character of our habitat for the worst. It reshaped our towns, pushed millions off the land to fill congested urban landscapes. These conurbations developed their own polluted climatic chemistry. A new breed of diseases emerged, diseases of the industrial age that were to be steadily exaggerated over the decades as industrialism transformed the ecosystem. And this Faustian pact with technology brought also the more immediate threat of sudden, unexpected disaster. From Love Canal to Minamata, from Bonnybridge to Canonsburg, from India to the Ukraine, mankind has endured a growing catalogue of toxic accidents, catastrophic explosions and invisible visitations of deathly radiation. All of them are direct threats to our bodily well-being.

Typical of the scale of the problem is the predicament created by toxic wastes from commercial processes in the chemical, petroleum and metal industries. In the United States, for instance, thousands of dump-sites clogged with toxic organic chemicals, dangerous enough to wipe out entire city populations, present the US authorities with a monumental task of disposal. For decades the problem lay dormant, hidden away from an ill-informed citizenry . . . until 1978, when heavy rains pushed leaking drums of deadly substances out of the ground at Love Canal in Niagara Falls, New York. Hundreds of families were driven from their homes for ever. It was not to be the last such disaster in the United States: in 1983 Times Beach, Missouri was turned into a ghost town after the population was evacuated, victims of a massive spillage of toxic waste. And there will be more such cases in the future: since 1950 the US industrial complex has generated some six billion tonnes of toxic waste from chemical plants, refineries, smelters and other installations. Each year yields a further 250 million tonnes of hazardous garbage, with inadequate controls over where, and how, it is dumped.

The situation in the United States is mirrored throughout the world. In the summer of 1984, in the middle of Birmingham, the authorities uncovered a cache of illegally dumped dioxin that was sufficient to kill the entire population of the English West Midlands ten times over.

But toxic industrial waste is only one small part of the threat. The high-tech age has overtaken farming, food manufacturing, packaging, pharmaceuticals, materials, energy production and data processing. In almost every commercial sector the price of material advancement has been the creation of chemical compounds, products or processes that are toxic to man.

High Tech Holocaust charts the steadily growing danger to humanity. It suggests that we have perhaps no more than five years to make a choice in favour of a cleaner, safer world. Failure to make that choice could ensure that mankind is overtaken by a fate more horrific than that of nuclear war, as the contamination of our bodies by a wide variety of toxic elements approaches lethal overload. It is a book written by a non-scientist alarmed at the mounting evidence that points to such a fate. That evidence has been gleaned from both the scientific literature and from everyday news, from the laboratory and from the experiences of ordinary, bewildered people.

Often the evidence is no more than circumstantial. Yet across the world there are thousands, even millions, of individuals who are suffering the consequences of man's decision to make a pact with a devil called industry. After the nuclear accident at Chernobyl, in the Ukraine, in the spring of 1986, we have yet another opportunity to gather circumstantial evidence about the effects of radioactivity on the human body. Only a habit of secrecy will prevent the full truth from ever being known. And not only about the tragedy at Chernobyl: a central feature of the escalating polluting threat to our health is the pattern of secrecy, complacency and lies that has prevented the flow of information to the general public, not only in the Soviet Union but in every country and in every industry where dangers exist.

That habit of secrecy and obfuscation is most apparent in the nuclear industry. But there are many other facets of that diabolical pact that have been similarly obscured from public scrutiny, ranging from chemicals in food to cancer-causing agents in plastic credit cards, from cling film to hair sprays, from pesticides to heavy metals, from acid rain to poisoned drinking water and effluent-choked river systems. But we are reaching a crossroads where the circumstantial evidence will, by its sheer weight, become incontrovertible proof that the world is facing an unsustainable toxic challenge. The high-tech holocaust will be all-embracing, all-pervasive. And time is running out.

1
The Price of Progress

Until 2 December 1984 few people in Institute, West Virginia, had ever heard of methyl isocyanate or the Indian town of Bhopal. Thereafter they would have a terrifying reason for never being able to forget either of these two names. Around midnight on that day clouds of gas leaked out from a Union Carbide chemical plant and fell upon residents of the surrounding shanty town. As injured people crowded into a nearby hospital the company's medical officer, a Mr L. L. Loya, told doctors: 'The gas is non-poisonous. There is nothing to do except ask the patients to put wet towels over their eyes.' Mr Loya was wrong.[1]

The death count in the Bhopal disaster was put at more than two thousand; another two hundred and fifty thousand were injured, condemned to suffer a lingering disease that would kill many thousands more over the years to follow. Nine months later another Union Carbide plant in Institute, six thousand miles away in the United States, leaked an equally toxic gas into the neighbourhood after malfunction in a storage tank. The plant manager, Mr H. J. Karawan, held back from informing local emergency services of the accident because of information flashed to his staff by a sophisticated computerised monitoring system: 'At that time we did not believe the emergency would affect the community because the cloud was hovering over the plant.' The computers – and Mr Karawan – were wrong.[2]

Luck, and a few dollars, intervened to save lives in Institute. About one hundred and forty people were reported injured, few seriously. At least, this was the verdict of doctors at the nearby medical centre. Yet the gas involved in the leak was aldicarb oxime, a powerful constituent of pesticide. It is classified by Union Carbide as among the most toxic of all chemicals, alongside methyl isocyanate, the killer of Bhopal. In testimony to a Congressional Committee in 1983 the company admitted that chemicals in this category can cause cancer, birth defects, genetic damage and irreversible disorders of the nervous system.

Only time can tell what are the real effects of concentrated exposure to aldicarb oxime on the scale seen in Institute in August of 1985. In the meantime, local residents can be thankful that failsafe mechanisms at the Institute plant were in proper working order. The inhabitants of Bhopal were not so lucky. Six months before their catastrophe the vital refrigeration unit meant to keep the gas cool was turned off as part of a cost reduction programme. The saving produced by this step was about $50 a day. This sum represents an infinitesimally small fraction of the profits made each year by the world's chemical industry.

Affluent Effluent

But industry is not a recent invention. As soon as men and women could think rationally they were also searching for ways to conquer Nature. Metal-working was an everyday activity in prehistoric times. Woven textiles were being produced in the Indus Valley of the Indian sub-continent five thousand years ago. The economic value of dyes, ores, crops has been fully understood since before that time. Humans as a species are naturally curious, uncontrollably inclined towards the making of things that can take us beyond what Nature intended. Only now is this talent turning violently back on us to defeat Nature itself.

Planet Earth is being slowly poisoned by the effluent of affluence. The smokestacks, discharge pipes and slurry tanks of a million and one manufacturing plants, power stations and industrial premises across the world have poured out toxic substances for two hundred years; they continue to do so. Other industries have created products that contaminate our insides through the foods or liquids that we ingest or the medications we take; they continue to do so. The creation of new technologies, contrary to expectations that they would lead to a cleaner and safer habitat, has merely added to our ability to generate yet more poisons.

Until very recently the world's atmosphere, and our bodies, could cope with this rising tide of effluent. Now we have passed the danger level. In practically every area of toxic pollution mankind has reached cross-over point, beyond which the natural balance of the earth's chemistry becomes seriously distorted. Sulphur dioxide, for instance, has for millennia been generated by the natural processes of the oceans, forests and volcanoes. Since the beginning of the 1970s the volume of sulphur dioxide produced by man has overtaken these processes, outdoing Nature and taking global SO_2 emissions to such levels that our soils and water supplies are being contaminated by hazardous acidic and metallic substances. The same point of cross-over has been reached in other areas of toxic threat. Our talent for industry has become a self-destructive pursuit.

Seen as individual processes, most industrial activities may appear as necessary and relatively innocent ways to create wealth. Indeed, for many centuries much of the world was engaged in simple manufacturing that posed no real threat to the surrounding community except, in some cases, to those directly employed. Man was certainly aware of the hazards that accompanied the quest for material goods. In the fifth century before Christ the Greek physician Hippocrates was writing of the effects of the working environment on human health; he described cases of lead colic in miners and other occupational diseases.

In the Europe of the Middle Ages a number of learned studies underlined the risks of working with toxic substances. In 1472, twenty years before Columbus discovered the New World, Ulrich Ellenbog in Augsburg had completed a tract on the adverse effects of carbon monoxide, nitric acid vapours, lead, mercury and other metals then in common use. A classic work on diseases in mining was published by Georg Bauer in 1556. It would not be out of place on a twentieth-century bookshelf: it contains graphic details of the silicosis, tuberculosis, lung cancer and other serious illnesses found among Bohemian silver-miners. Nor was this concern limited only to occupational diseases. As early as the 1290s England's King Edward I had decreed that coal should not be burnt while Parliament was sitting because of the acrid smoke that filled the London air.

Perhaps the most prescient observation was that made in the sixteenth century by a Swiss-born physician with a taste for alchemy and the somewhat ornate name of Theophrastus Bombastus von Hohenheim: 'All substances are poisonous . . . there is none which is not a poison. The right dose differentiates a poison and a remedy.' Even four hundred years ago, with the industrial revolution still many generations away, there was an inkling of the dangers to come.

But even the most penetrating Renaissance mind could not have foreseen the all-engulfing transformation of the pattern of global chemistry that would be wrought by the industrial age. The primitive industrial infrastructure of medieval times was spread thinly across a predominantly agricultural landscape. There was not as yet any critical mass of polluting industrial endeavour to match the scale of the German Ruhr, the English Midlands, the congested industrial belt of the north-east United States or the densely packed urban zones of the north Italian plains, south-eastern Brazil or the Japanese island of Honshu. But when, in the 1750s, industrial revolution did trigger off an escalating search for the secrets of manufacturing and an unending boom in factory-building, the warning signs of eventual toxic holocaust quickly became visible for those prepared to see.

Again, the most disturbing evidence came from studies of diseases associated with particular jobs. The eminent English doctor Sir Percival Pott made a pioneering study in the 1770s of scrotal cancer amongst chimney sweeps. The phrase 'mad as a hatter', to be given immortal personification in Lewis Carroll's *Alice in Wonderland*, was born of the early recognition that mercury used in making felt hats invaded the body chemistry of the hat-maker and caused irreparable damage to the nervous system. And the first convincing reports linking defective child-birth to an industrial chemical were produced in the nineteenth century after investigation into the toxic effects of lead. As a result, women were banned from working in many manufacturing activities involving heavy use of this metal.

By the 1880s considerable work with laboratory animals had already been carried out by analysts like K. L. Lehmann in Wurzburg, who tested the toxicity of more than thirty gases and vapours in widespread industrial use. But the conclusions that were reached in all these research projects were seen as important only in relation to the workplace. Thus by the start of the twentieth century there was ample evidence that industry was the enemy of health, though few were ready to agree that the risk went further than the factory gates. They were days of environmental innocence; even the arrival of the motor car, unveiled in 1886, had been greeted as just one more techno-

logical toy for the eccentric rich. As with every other facet of the
factory era, the potential hazards of the combustion engine for
the world at large were never considered.

The Quiet Killer

In some other areas, however, there was concern from the
beginning about the wider long-term dangers. There was a
rapidly growing awareness, for instance, of the impact of
industry on the quality of the air, particularly in countries like
Britain where industrial expansion had already taken dramatic
hold by the end of the eighteenth century. In emulation of King
Edward's initiative seven centuries ago, the British parliament
in 1819 appointed a select committee to inquire 'how far it may
be practicable to compel Persons using Steam Engines and
Furnaces in their different works to erect them in a Manner less
prejudicial to public Health and public Comfort.' Thereafter, the
issue of polluted air was never to be out of the headlines.
Unfortunately, that same unwholesome air was never to be out
of the lungs of the millions of people who poured into Britain's
industrial towns in search of work. For though parliamentary
speeches and crusading newspaper articles highlighted the
problem of contaminated air, it was nearly one hundred and fifty
years before that problem was tackled through the law.

There is a disturbing lesson to be learnt from those first
faltering attempts at curbing the excesses of industry. They
failed because politicians and businessmen wanted them to fail
and because science was slow to supply iron-clad proof of the
risks to human health. This is precisely the case with the
escalating toxic adulteration of the world in the late twentieth
century. Thus the anti-smoke campaign which dominated
British politics in the 1840s was a microcosm of the broad-based
environmental debate that emerged in the highly industrialised
world during the early 1980s.

That 1840s campaign was to last until the 1890s before it
petered out with nothing accomplished. Not for another hundred
years, until the Clean Air Act of 1956, did Britain legislate to
outlaw smoke from its major cities. And by then a host of other
far more toxic substances were beginning to invade our body
chemistry. By the 1980s those substances, the helpmates of a
new breed of high-tech industrial processes, were threatening
an unwitting citizenry with nothing less than toxic overload.
Will we have to wait until 2056 before official steps are taken to

avert the holocaust? If that is so those steps will almost certainly be too late; they may be more than half a century too late.

The British experience with smoke in the early years of industry is therefore an instructive case study; it illustrates how suspect industrial activities can escape prohibition even though they are known to be hazardous. In practically every instance the burden of proof is on those raising the objection, whether they be customers, local residents or employees. And since the objectors are invariably non-specialists they operate from a position of considerable disadvantage. One such pressure group was the Manchester Association for the Prevention of Smoke, created in 1842 and chaired by a Rochdale vicar. They could just as well have tried to extinguish the sun. Smoke was the badge of industry and empire; it would not be prevented.

Thus, the citizen of the early industrial age had no more success than his modern-day counterpart in winning protection from the ravages of progress. The impact of the revolutionary steam engine had been far-reaching for good reason and bad. Textile workers were impelled by commercial pressures to abandon their cottage workshops powered by water wheels and were crowded into immense mills built around steam-driven machinery. The towns they now inhabited bulged with the sudden influx from the countryside. Sanitary arrangements were rudimentary: water had often to be bought from unscrupulous suppliers at profiteering prices. The squalid terraced alleys were riddled with disease. And above them all hung a thick pall of unhealthy smoke. From time to time a combination of climatic influences would drive the dense clouds downwards to choke both the streets and the people who stumbled through them. The larger the town the thicker and filthier was the fog.

The long delay before clean air laws took over is explained by the lack of any firm scientific evidence that smoke was harmful to humans. Most objections were linked not to health worries but to the nuisance factor. One Member of Parliament told the House of Commons in 1843 that a brewery in London's Tottenham Court Road was obliged to change to cleaner anthracite coal after complaints from genteel households in nearby Bloomsbury: 'The gentlefolks in the squares compelled us to do it . . . they said it made so much smoke in the drawing rooms and injured the furniture.'[3]

One causal element in this escalating spiral of harmful pollution was as relevant then as it is now. The thick smoke that belched from the smokestacks and funnels of nineteenth-century Britain was the consequence not of wealth-creation but of waste. An endless stream of specialised witnesses agreed that smoke was merely coal dust that had escaped combustion because of inefficient manufacturing practices. A massively unhealthy contribution was also made by Britain's equally inefficient household grates; in 1880 in London alone there were some 3,580,000 fireplaces. Smoke represented wasted solid fuel, just as so many toxic dangers today – whether radioactive or chemically hazardous – result from the residues and waste by-products of industrial or energy-producing processes.

A belief that this realisation would prompt profit-minded Victorian entrepreneurs to overhaul their manufacturing systems so as to eliminate wasteful fuel consumption, and coincidentally to reduce their emissions of smoke, proved unduly optimistic. Hardheaded mill-owners and factory managers did nothing of the sort. And not only in Britain; smoke remained a major toxic component of everyday life throughout the industrialising world for many decades. Indeed, the nineteenth-century battle for safe air was only the opening chapter in what has become a long and unrewarding saga. In time, coal-generated smoke was to be overtaken by atmospheric lead and sulphur dioxide as the principal causes of poisoned air. Meanwhile, in developing regions of the world today, where smokestack industries are being constructed at an ever-increasing rate, old-style smoke is enjoying a second lease of life.

Significantly, the lack of firm remedial action by nineteenth-century industrialists and politicians to cut down on dangerous pollution was not the result of any ignorance about the hazards to public health. The facts and figures about smoke and human life had already featured in protest literature as early as 1880, without having any real effect on official thinking. The book *London Fogs*, written by the Honourable R. Russell (son of Lord John Russell) and published in the late 1880s, was to be a major source of evidence in the battle against smoke over the years that followed. Russell encapsulated the unarticulated fears of many thousands of city dwellers who had survived (many thousands did not) the choking, filthy blankets of wet dust that fell over their streets at regular intervals. 'It is hard to believe,' he wrote, 'that so harmless-looking and quiet a thing could do such mischief.'

But Russell also put his finger on a vital factor, something that is equally central to the issue of high-tech hazard today. He noticed that disasters which are small in scale but which occur in one place as a single event – such as the tragedy that killed seven space shuttle astronauts in early 1986 – capture public feeling in a way that never applies to much larger catastrophes spread over a lengthy period and dispersed geographically. One thousand times as many people are killed, for instance, on the roads of a medium-sized European country in a typical year, yet there is never the merest sign of national mourning. The same was true of the fog-afflicted society of Russell's day. As he put it, 'a London fog performed its work slowly, made no unseemly disturbance and took care not to demand its hecatombs very suddenly and dramatically.'

Yet hecatombs there were: the week-long London fog of December 1873 is thought to have claimed at least five hundred lives through respiratory failure alone. In all, the death rate in the city for the week was seven hundred above normal. The fog that fell on London in late January 1880 was worse still. In the three weeks up to St Valentine's Day there were 2,994 additional deaths; about two thousand of them were attributed to the fog. In fact, the fatality rate was equivalent to that of a serious cholera epidemic. But while cholera and other such outbreaks had led social reformers like Edwin Chadwick to press, with great success, for radical steps to improve public sanitation, the hazards of smoke created little more than a shrugging of the nation's shoulders. A leader in *The Times* at the height of the 1873 visitation dwelt upon the tragic effects on herds of cattle being kept at an agricultural show in the London suburb of Islington: 'Perhaps these poor beasts may be considered to have been the chief sufferers.'

Efforts to translate Russell's terrible statistics into legal controls over smoke emissions came to nothing. The government's opposition to tough new laws was led by the Prime Minister himself, the third Marquis of Salisbury. Yet another succession of draft laws aimed at smoke abatement – more than ten in all – were presented to parliament by Lord Stratheden and Campbell between 1884 and his death in 1893. All of them were shot down by Lord Salisbury and his supporters. Meanwhile, the death rate from respiratory failure caused by polluted air continued to climb. In 1887 there were ninety-three serious fogs in London; in 1890 there were 156. During a particularly heavy fog in December 1886 the mortality rate was lifted by forty in one thousand, equal to the death rate during the most serious cholera epidemic in recent British history.

Russell's book was the last thorough attempt by a Briton to assess the cost of polluted air until the 1950s, seventy years later, when a series of equally lethal 'pea-souper' smogs engulfed the capital. According to a subsequent Royal Commission report the killer fog of December 1952 claimed roughly four thousand lives. (Coincidentally, the first casualty was an Aberdeen Angus bull brought to London for the annual Smithfield Show, though this time the leader columns of *The Times* avoided comment.)

The 1952 fatality rate was no worse than in Rollo Russell's day, but this time the political consensus was right. Further analysis of the records for earlier years also revealed, moreover, that many thousands more fog-related deaths were hidden away in the dense tables of Britain's public health statistics. The revelations spurred the British government into drastic action, nearly three-quarters of a century after the publication of Russell's *London Fogs*; the Clean Air Act was the result. In the intervening seven decades countless thousands must have succumbed to the lung-destroying legacy of millions of chimneys, both domestic and industrial.

The failure, all those years ago, to act against a self-evident hazard could not be ascribed to a lack of the appropriate technology. Quite the contrary; fuel technologists in the 1880s certainly knew that the pollution was caused by incomplete combustion of bituminous coal and that smokeless fuels burnt in closed or well-designed grates would help reduce household emissions. Comparable changes could also be introduced into factories and on the railways. But the countervailing pressures were considerable. The producers of bituminous coal – in those days a private enterprise – were a very powerful lobby; the major coal owners were Members of Parliament. Many of them were friends of Lord Salisbury as well.

Another major obstacle to clean air laws was the cost to ordinary people. And the coal producers who supplied them with their fuel would never offer to help meet that cost. Hence the prospects for replacing millions of inefficient, open-hearth domestic grates were nil. Indeed, those same polluting grates were by now a national institution endowed with an unwarranted romantic quality. The scientific journal *Nature*, in a special smoke abatement issue in 1882, quoted approvingly the words of the eminent engineer Sir Frederick Bramwell: 'We are strongly of the same opinion . . . that we must have an open, pokeable, companionable fire.'

In this case the price of romanticism and free choice was a 'harmless-looking and quiet' death toll over the second half of the nineteenth century that exceeded the forty-five thousand British losses suffered in the Crimean War of 1854–6. Fittingly, the war ended one hundred years, almost to the day, before the Clean Air Act brought a ray of hope. And by the 1950s industry had invented many other ways to kill and maim us, and on a global scale.

These days 'smoke from coal' takes on quite different meaning. For though the experience of the past hundred years has taught us that burning fuels inefficiently creates serious communal hazards, the lessons have been forgotten. Where once there were the dense urban fogs, now there are equally polluted layers of the upper atmosphere, the result of massive emissions of industrial smoke and car exhausts stretching over many decades. Today the combined efforts of humanity pour some 100 million tonnes of sulphur into the atmosphere every year. This sulphur, with other polluting chemicals, turns the rains to acid and returns to earth as a corroding, potentially lethal influence. And, as we shall see, there is no prospect of a Clean Air Act for Planet Earth this side of the year 2000.

The Age of Plastic

Nothing symbolises the age of affluence better than plastic. In particular, polyvinyl chloride plastic – better known as PVC – came to permeate modern life after 1945 as it took over from a wide spectrum of other materials that had hitherto been used in hundreds of different products. PVC became vital to the manufacture of scores of everyday consumer goods, from household interiors to seat covers in cars, from rainwear to kitchen equipment. It was eagerly taken up by the construction industry, to be used in water pipes, floor tiles and exterior cladding. Credit cards would be less bendy if PVC had never been invented. Because of its resistance to corrosion it is even used as a protective coating on pollution-control apparatus. But the benign countenance of PVC is deceptive. PVC can kill.

On 22 January 1974, the owners of a plastics factory in Louisville, Kentucky, announced that three of their employees had recently died of angiosarcoma, a rare cancer of the liver.

They revealed, too, that a fourth worker had died of the same incurable disease in 1969. The Louisville revelations started a chain reaction. Other plastics companies let it be known that some of their employees had also died of the same illness. Meanwhile, evidence emanating from research laboratories confirmed that tests carried out since 1970 showed that vinyl chloride, or VC – the principal ingredient of PVC – induced a wide range of cancers in animals.

By July 1974 thirteen cases of angiosarcoma amongst US factory workers had come to light. Within a month another twelve similar cases had been reported from places around the world. Nearly all of them involved workers at plants making PVC; of the remainder, one worked at a vinyl chloride plant, another was employed to fill pesticide cans with a vinyl chloride propellant. Two more had died after spending time at a factory manufacturing cloth from PVC sheeting; one of them was an accountant in the executive offices. A major study conducted shortly after the Louisville episode reported that among the thirty thousand US workers exposed to vinyl chloride over the thirty years prior to 1974, sixty-eight were known to have developed liver angiosarcoma.

The relatively small number of fatalities is a misleading index of the lethal nature of PVC. Studies of the US chemical industry indicate that the incidence of angiosarcoma amongst PVC workers could be as much as three thousand times the level normally seen in the general population. The studies also point out that these highly publicised victims were only the early warnings of a massive, global problem. The average development period for liver cancer caused by exposure to VC is about twenty years, so the Louisville cases were only a hint of tragic things to come. Those who were being subjected to high exposures of VC in 1974, when those first deaths were being announced, may not finally fall prey to this terrible, painful corrosion of their vital organs until the 1990s. Already many have died as a result of exposure during the early post-war decades.

In the United States alone the number of those at risk runs into millions; that number is increasing by the year as plastic takes over in other areas of everyday life. The US experience puts the scale of the danger into horrifying perspective. At the time of the 1974 disclosures several hundred thousand US workers were employed either producing VC and PVC or in making products using PVC as a raw material. About four and a half million people lived within five miles of a VC or PVC plant. And in that year alone it is estimated that about 220 million pounds of VC escaped into the air in the vicinity of these plants. Since then the scale of the hazard has spiralled as vinyl plastic has spread even more widely into the western way of life and beyond it into the developing world. It has even caught the imagination of deprived consumers living in economies run on Marxist lines. A highly prized item on the Moscow black market is a plastic shopping bag from any of the major capitalist department stores.

Vinyl chloride is a gas made from petrochemicals and chlorine. It is polymerised into polyvinyl chloride by converting the gas in a reactor. VC was first manufactured in the United States in 1939 and after the war became a vital raw material in the rapidly expanding plastics industry. Because of its versatility, PVC recommended itself for a vast array of products and functions which called for a strong, waterproof, easily cleaned, flexible material. By the time of the Louisville incidents PVC had become the second most widely used plastic in the United States, with annual consumption of vinyl chloride in this one country alone running at nearly six billion pounds a year.

Since then world production of PVC has climbed steadily (in the packaging area alone it has doubled in the last decade) and the range of uses has expanded into every sector of business:

- In building and construction it is used for pipes, floor coverings and claddings.

- In the home it quickly became a favoured material for furniture, shower curtains, paint.

- Electrical manufacturers took it up as sheathing for wire.

- It was widely adopted to make containers for food items, drugs, cosmetics and other commonly available consumer products.

- Pop records were an inevitable market for this flexible but durable material.

- Toy manufacturers enthusiastically welcomed it as the ideal solution, with its apparent virtues as a safe, hygienic alternative for metals and other painted objects.

● The vehicle industry became a major market; PVC was introduced for roofing, upholstery and other coverings.

● Clothing manufacturers began using it for a wide variety of clothing from babies' pants to raincoats.

● Medical suppliers quickly recognised the advantages of PVC for a large number of surgical and nursing devices from blood bags to transfusion tubes.

Perhaps the most bizarre application for PVC, however, was to be in the world of money. When the credit card revolution arrived the banks, card companies and retailers turned to polyvinyl chloride as the raw material for their flexible substitute for cash. Today, hundreds of millions of plastic cards are to be found in pocket-books and purses around the world. PVC has become an essential part of living in the late twentieth century.

Until late in 1973 VC was also widely used as a propellant in aerosol cans for a variety of products from drugs and pesticides to cosmetics. Indeed, even after the use of VC in aerosols was prohibited in the United States following the 1974 discovery of its link with cancer, this did not affect its use in many other parts of the world, apart from the three and a half million cans already distributed throughout the US in homes, stores and such places as hairdressing salons. Tests had shown that VC caused cancer in animals at exposure levels as low as 50 parts per million. Aerosol users might be exposed to concentrations as high as 400ppm.[4]

In view of the central importance achieved by PVC over the post-war period, it seems odd that the cancer-causing properties of VC took so long to emerge into public view. Long before the events of 1974 vinyl chloride was recognised by scientists as a highly dangerous chemical. It is highly inflammable and if concentrated in the air at a rate above 40,000 parts per million it can cause violent explosions. Several workers have been killed by inhaling extremely high doses. Studies show that people exposed to more than 8,000ppm become dizzy and disoriented before finally losing consciousness. Smaller doses breathed in over a normal working day can send the subject into deep sleep. It is hardly surprising that in the late 1940s VC gas was tested as a potential anaesthetic for general use. As it happens, the project was shelved after indications that VC affected the functioning of the heart. It should have been taken as a warning sign, but for unknown reasons no further suspicions were raised. As a result, VC and PVC became an integral part of the post-war industrial miracle.

From 1975 onwards, with research institutes now alerted to the danger of vinyl chloride, the medical journals were to be stuffed full with learned articles on every aspect of VC toxicity. Collected together they tell a harrowing story, all the more disturbing because it should have been told many years earlier, before the events in Louisville. Even then, the upsurge of learned interest did little to reduce the threat; as with the London fogs, nothing was to be done by governments around the world to eliminate the toxic risk posed to humans.

The research findings published over the second half of the 1970s highlighted the potency of VC in invading and damaging the human machine. The risk, as is usual with highly toxic substances, was extreme for people directly employed to handle vinyl chloride. For decades until 1974 many jobs in the plastics industry exposed workers to concentrations as high as 300ppm; as we shall see, this is a dangerous level of exposure if it occurs regularly over time. Records were available which set out the effects of such exposure over periods of months and years. Enlargement and fibrosis of the liver and spleen were common afflictions. There was also a high incidence of Raynaud's Syndrome, in which the victim suffers disorders of the arteries leading, amongst other symptoms, to loss of feeling in the extremities; in serious cases it can produce gangrene. Many workers contracted sclerodoma, a skin condition, as well as acro-osteolysis, a particularly rare ailment where the last bones in the fingers and toes begin to shrink. This disparate range of adverse effects were grouped together by medical specialists under the appropriate name of 'vinyl chloride disease'.

But these were the benefits of scientific hindsight. Though any chemistry student could have testified as to the volatile and violent nature of vinyl chloride, it was not until 1974 that hard evidence emerged that told us that VC is rather more than merely troublesome. Once the events in Louisville had changed the parameters of the issue, researchers began making closer examination of the evidence linking VC and PVC to cancer in humans. What they discovered was highly disconcerting.

One of the first things they encountered was that there were a great number of acute and chronic effects that had not shown up in earlier studies. Arterial problems and fibrosis in certain internal organs, for example, were detectable in microscopic form well before they might produce visible clinical symptoms. Minute scrutiny of liver cells indicated critical changes taking place. Some employees had disorders of the blood or lungs. But these meticulous researches took the medical analysts no closer to answering the question: is PVC plastic deadly?

The answer is that human exposure to VC or PVC creates a real risk of contamination by a proven carcinogen of considerable potency. As early as 1971 the Italian researchers Viola, Bigotti and Caputo had established that VC causes cancer in laboratory animals when ingested or inhaled. In their tests, rats inhaling high concentrations of VC, around 30,000 parts per million, developed tumours of the skin, lung and bone.[5] In early 1974, at the time of the Louisville revelations, this same Italian team produced unpublished evidence for the US authorities showing that rats had contracted angiosarcoma of the liver after inhaling concentrations as weak as 250ppm. Shortly after this, analysts in Illinois produced data indicating that mice had developed the same liver cancers after exposures to VC at levels as low as 50ppm. Thus, the exposure levels of 250–300ppm known to have been sustained by many US chemical workers over the decades up to Louisville could now be put more sharply into focus.

Indeed, two years after the Louisville disclosures, in the autumn of 1976, another Italian researcher disclosed an even more alarming discovery. In the somewhat sinister-sounding 'Maltoni Memorandum', scientist Cesare Maltoni set out the results of inhalation experiments with rats that showed that VC causes liver angiosarcoma – the disease that struck the chemical workers at Louisville – at exposure levels of only 25ppm, and that it produces mammary tumours at only 1ppm.[6]

These varied research projects filled vital gaps in medical knowledge about the carcinogenic properties of vinyl chloride. They also shed light on the underlying causes of the abnormally high rate of liver angiosarcoma in certain groups of workers. Many of the employees who died of this particular type of cancer were found to have been working as cleaners of the polymerisation reactor, the special chamber in which VC is converted, or in other similar functions where exposure to VC is high. The exposure levels under these conditions are thought to range from a peak of several thousand parts per million down to 250 or

300, still well above the levels that produced significant adverse results in rats and mice.[7]

The Louisville incident inevitably sparked off widespread fears about the dangers associated with working with VC and PVC in constricted manufacturing plants. But it did little to build public awareness of the hazards that faced ordinary people. First, local residents living near a VC production plant would be at risk from VC emissions into the surrounding air. Second, there is a constant risk of leakages and other accidental emissions while VC is being transported. In many countries only a small proportion of VC production, perhaps one-third, is polymerised at the original production facility. The remainder is moved to PVC manufacturing sites as a liquefied gas by rail, road, canal barge or ship. All liquefied gases are stored under extremely high pressures and the potential for accidents due to leaks, punctures or explosion is considerable; the location could quite easily be a heavily populated city area. (The same complacency can be seen in the energy industry. In Britain major liquefied natural gas installations are sited at Canvey Island in Essex and at the Isle of Grain in Kent. Both sites are close to the eastern borders of London.) In the event of such an accident involving VC, people caught in the spreading vapour of vinyl chloride could be exposed to concentrations as high as several thousand parts per million. Emergency workers could face exposures many times higher than this. Although these rates of exposure only last for a short time they could easily reach levels of contamination equivalent to those experienced by workers close to the polymerisation reactors; these are amongst the most endangered of all employees in the chemical industry.

Third, because the manufacturing process for PVC, like most commercial processes, is imperfect a proportion of VC stays trapped as a gas in the finished plastic. These residues of toxic gas later escape in the ordinary course of using PVC products. Thus, every building in which PVC floorings, pipes or other construction materials were used is a potential hazard spot because of the risk of contaminated interior air. By being present in pipes, ducts and various utensils elements of VC can escape into drinking water. And if the building happens to catch fire neither the residents nor people who might work there should be under any illusions about their safety; when PVC burns it gives off toxic gases that could be just as damaging as the flames themselves, though the danger in this case would emerge only after the passage of time.

People also risk exposure through ordinary consumer products if these are in any way associated with VC or PVC. Though banned in the United States, VC-propelled aerosols can be found elsewhere, in hair sprays, air fresheners, pesticides, muscular applications and cosmetics. Using such an aerosol in a small, poorly ventilated area such as a bathroom or a garden shed could produce a brief exposure level of around 400ppm. Other cases have involved VC found in rooms that have recently been decorated with certain latex paints. VC leaches into foods and drinks that have been packaged with PVC materials. One only has to inspect the shelves at any local supermarket to realise how widespread the use of such VC-based materials has become for the food-processing industry around the world.

Perhaps the greatest irony is in the risks of VC contamination associated with supposedly hygienic hospital equipment, not least transfusion devices and tubes inserted into the throat to ease breathing. In both these cases if the tubing is manufactured from PVC there would be a high risk of absorbing VC directly into the bloodstream or lungs. Though such matters are regulated in many countries to ensure patient safety, there is no universal rule applied in all medical establishments worldwide. Moreover, the tests upon which these rules are based (which do not necessarily ban PVC items but merely require that those used are tested and approved as 'safe') cannot possibly reflect the long-term effects on people who have been subjected to hospital treatment involving PVC tubing, since the development period of many of the cancers linked to VC can be as long as twenty years, far longer than any test exercise.

It is hardly surprising that studies tell us that citizens of the late twentieth century are absorbing vinyl chloride into their biochemistry at a rate never seen before in human history. One American survey estimated that the average daily intake of VC by normal US citizens through the food they eat, the water they drink and the atmosphere they breathe is around 35 micrograms. As a possible guideline for assessing the level of human exposure that this might represent, in rats a daily dose of 0.9 micrograms of VC is roughly equivalent to inhaling 6 parts per million for eight hours. Although experts point out that there is no reliable application of these figures to give equivalent levels of human intake, a concerned layman would note that the simple, unscientific arithmetic adds up to a level of exposure to VC of 226ppm over eight hours. While the scientific doubts about this comparison offer a degree of reassurance, we can be forgiven our own concern. Even a fraction of this figure would be highly disconcerting; research evidence shows that liver cancer in rats develops after continual doses of less than one-tenth of such an intake.[8]

Meanwhile, research in other fields shows VC to be equally hazardous in completely separate areas of concern. One frightening revelation from tests on laboratory animals is that vinyl chloride is an embryotoxin and a teratogen; in other words is known to cause damage to the unborn foetus. VC has also been found in such tests to act as a transplacental carcinogen, literally a cancer-causing agent that can pass through the womb to the unborn offspring.

The Unquenchable Fire
The record of the past century does not inspire confidence that mankind can deal with industrial hazards quickly and effectively. The failure to curb urban smoke pollution – a proven killer – as the problem escalated in the old industrial world over more than one hundred and fifty years, graphically illustrates the unequal balance of power between industry and the public. The introduction of plastics raised a similar problem, though the adverse side effects on humans in this case are more awesome. Despite considerable evidence as to the toxic hazards of vinyl chloride and products derived from it, plastics have taken pride of place in the commercial scheme of things; their versatility and cheapness recommends them for thousands of purposes, not least in containers and packaging for food.

The most recent revelations about the cancer-causing potential of plastics involve cling film, the see-through wrapping that has been adopted by millions of householders across the affluent world as the answer to short-term food storage in the home. Like most other plastics, cling film is made through combining various chemical constituents with petroleum-based raw ingredients. But many brands of cling film have been developed with the help of an additive called DEHA, and tests in the United States now show that DEHA can cause cancer in mice. The risk to humans arises because of the threat of a migration of toxic substances out from the cling-film wrapping into the food itself. The rate of migration is highest when the film is used to cover fatty foods; many householders would confirm that such foods are precisely the ones for which cling film is used regularly.

But smoke and plastics are only two of an ever-expanding list of hazards that have arrived with the industrial age. Indeed, they are amongst the more straightforward examples. In a disturbing sense they were merely precursors of the emerging high-tech holocaust. As the twenty-first century approaches, the technical sophistication of new materials and complex chemical compounds makes it more difficult still to assess risk and develop rules to protect humans from a terrifying range of consequences. In fact, even in the developed countries, where technological pollution has existed for over a century, the protective backlash is only now catching up with hazards that have been integral parts of the commercial fabric for decades. One instance is PVC; another is asbestos.

Like PVC, asbestos was welcomed by industry as a major breakthrough that opened up endless possibilities in areas of business where a resilient, fire-resistant material is required. It became the first choice for a wide range of construction tasks: roof and flooring tiles, water pipes, fire-proofing partitions and doors. Brake linings for vehicles were an obvious application, as were any household items that were likely to have to withstand strong heat.

Asbestos is a fibrous material made up of magnesium silicate which does not conduct heat and cannot catch fire. Its name is derived from the Greek word for 'unquenchable'. When woven together the fibres form an incombustible material. During the manufacturing or fabricating process large quantities of dust and fibrils, or small fibres, are given off. It is these substances that pose a serious threat to the human body, although it appears that the level of hazard differs widely from one form of asbestos to another. There are three major categories: crocidolite – a blue asbestos – amosite which is brown and chrystolite which is white. Blue asbestos is known to be the most dangerous of the three, with brown amosite ranked closely behind it.

A highly prevalent condition amongst people working with the material or constantly exposed to its more hazardous particles is the disease asbestosis, a hardening or scarring of the lung tissue that results from the inhaling of fine dust and fibrils. Sufferers are afflicted with a debilitating pulmonary condition which eventually can kill. More seriously, asbestos is also known to be a very potent carcinogen. There is reason to believe, for instance, that it plays a role in certain gastrointestinal cancers.

In other fields of cancer research the ominous conclusions about asbestos are much more exact. Research by specialists at the British Medical Research Council has recently produced important new findings about the way in which asbestos invades the bio-system to cause mesothelioma, a rapidly fatal tumour that spreads over the pleural covering of the lung. The MRC studies show that it is the size of asbestos particles that is the most crucial factor. Particles with a diameter of between 0.1 and 6 micrometres were found to be the most dangerous. A rather alarming secondary finding of the research was that identical particles are also found in a number of common substances including household detergents.[9]

The MRC findings were certainly not uppermost in the minds of officials of the British Ministry of Defence in the summer of 1985 when they were confronted with a particularly awkward predicament; the MRC conclusions had not, at that time, been published. But the MOD could have been in no doubt that the many thousands of tonnes of soil contaminated with asbestos at the Faslane nuclear submarine base in Scotland were a highly unwelcome legacy. The inhabitants of a small village near Glasgow told them so. Plans to dump the soil in the surrounding area had to be abandoned after fierce opposition from villagers. Instead, the Ministry decided that about 150 tonnes of asbestos would be treated and made safe in the base by sealing it into glass blocks. The process, known as vitrification, has been developed by the nuclear industry to dispose of radioactive waste. Perhaps the men from the Ministry knew rather more than the villagers; certainly their behaviour did not suggest that the soil they were anxious to be rid of was as pure as Nature intended.

But despite the overwhelming weight of evidence about the hazards of asbestos, both in the workplace and through contact with it in buildings and consumer products, it is still in widespread use in practically every part of the world. US government research, for example, indicates that about two hundred and fifty companies across the country are currently using asbestos in their products to give them fire-resistant qualities and improved wear. Although manufacturers have switched to substitutes in some product categories, asbestos remains a preferred raw material for a host of US construction uses and consumer goods. Annual consumption of asbestos by US companies is currently running at about 240,000 tonnes. As a result more than 800 tonnes of asbestos particles are poured into the atmosphere every year by American industry, either from mining and milling activities or during manufacturing processes. This figure does not include asbestos given off by daily wear on the clutches and brake pads of millions of cars and trucks in US cities.

Yet in spite of the known dangers of asbestos it is still in widespread use in practically every country in the world. Even in the United States, where much of the pioneering legislation in the field of toxic substances originates, the rate of progress has been remarkably slow. The US Environmental Protection Agency, an energetic watchdog body, has failed consistently in its efforts to win government support for tough restrictions. The EPA estimates that a ban on asbestos would, over a period, save roughly two thousand lives by eliminating lung cancer and other fatal diseases linked to asbestos fibres. In May 1984 the Agency proposed to the Reagan Administration that regulations should be brought in to limit the levels of exposure faced by workers and those directly in contact with the material. The proposals, though only for partial restrictions on asbestos stipulating levels of exposure (it would continue to be used by manufacturers) followed closely a decision taken by the EEC. But the government turned down the EPA proposals on the grounds of cost.

A major pressure on the White House that helped produce this negative decision was the reluctance of the US asbestos industry to admit that their material needed any regulation at all. At the time of the government's rejection of the EPA plan there were about twenty-five thousand lawsuits pending against companies in the asbestos-using sector; the cases had been brought by employees and their families in an effort to gain compensation for injuries caused by asbestos particles. Such was the scale of this legal counter-attack, however, that a special Asbestos Claims Facility had to be set up, with offices in Boston and San Francisco. More than thirty manufacturers and twenty-two insurance companies agreed to join the Facility from the outset, thus making implicit admission of blame for the diseases that had overtaken the claimants. The serious nature of those diseases can be gauged from the level of claims being made in the US courts. According to a study by the Rand Corporation, more than $1 billion had already been paid out by corporations and insurers over the ten years up until the creation of the Claims Facility in May 1985. And some five hundred new claims were being filed each month to add to the many thousands of existing lawsuits.[10]

Another source of pressure on the Reagan Administration against an asbestos ban was to be the Canadian government; almost all asbestos used in the United States comes from north of the border. The authorities in Ottawa, mindful of the commercial benefits to the country, are as reluctant as US manufacturers to accept tough restrictions, whatever the implications of scientific research about the threat posed by asbestos to public health.

It was the evidence from many of these civil lawsuits that convinced the EPA of the urgency of drastic action against asbestos, in particular against five major categories of products: roofing felt, flooring felt and felt-backed sheet flooring, vinyl asbestos floor tiles, asbestos-cement pipes and ranges of clothing made from asbestos. The EPA plan would also set strict rules for the steady phasing out of the material in all other products, with a legal requirement to reduce asbestos content by ten per cent each year. And products containing asbestos would now need to carry labels warning of the associated dangers.

The EPA campaign against asbestos nevertheless raises two important issues. The first is in the form of a question. If hundreds of studies and many thousands of medical diagnoses over a long period have linked asbestos to serious diseases, why did it take so long for forward-thinking agencies like the EPA to step in? Certainly, in those countries where the regulatory machinery is less effective it will be many more years before any rules based on US or EEC initiatives are introduced into local laws. One of the most tragic features of most industrial hazards is that preventive laws and controls only evolve from action taken in the more advanced economies. If these countries – principally the United States, Western Europe and Japan – are slow to act, the less-developed areas of the world are left vulnerable for that much longer.

Meanwhile, there are a number of other unanswered questions even in countries where asbestos regulations are already in force. A key concern is over the precise levels of exposure to asbestos fibres that are permitted under these regulations. In

Britain, for instance, occupational exposures set by the Health and Safety Executive stipulate that people should not be exposed to more than 1 fibre per millilitre of air for white chrystolite, 0.5 for brown amosite and 0.2 for blue crocidolite. To the lay reader these limits would have little meaning. Nevertheless, a guide to how much actual exposure to asbestos fibre is permitted by such technically phrased rules is graphically expressed in the recent pronouncement of scientist M. J. Walker of the British Occupational Hygiene Advisory Service: 'It is interesting to note that the occupational exposure limit of 1 fibre per millilitre represents about four million fibres being inhaled by a worker during a normal day.'[11]

The second issue also has a wider import, for it applies to many other kinds of toxic threat. If asbestos is prohibited, manufacturers will be obliged to find substitutes that can deliver the same virtues of fire resistance and durability. Almost by definition these substitutes will be produced through chemical processes, with an equally strong possibility of hazardous contents. One potential alternative is a clay mineral called attapulgite. But it is a relatively unknown quantity, with little data available on its dangerous properties. Then, if a strengthening agent is needed to replace the binding characteristic of asbestos, that agent will almost certainly be another fibre. So the danger of damaging the lungs by inhaling fibres will not be removed. PVC could be used to give added strength, but it does not impart fire resistance. On the contrary, burning PVC produces highly dangerous fumes. Asbestos-cement pipes could be replaced by cement containing cellulose, a carbohydrate that forms the outer walls of plant and vegetable cells; here too there may be other, quite unforeseen hazards. And fibre glass, another potential substitute for building materials and insulation, is still under scrutiny by research laboratories anxious to isolate any dangers that may be lurking in its chemical make-up.

Wealth is Waste
In March 1985 the traditionally constrained pages of *National Geographic* magazine carried the horrific details of events in the small Michigan community of Swartz Creek, a rural settlement sixty miles north-west of Detroit, the unofficial capital of the world's car industry. In 1972 local entrepreneur Charles Berlin and a friend opened an incinerator plant for the disposal of waste materials produced by manufacturing operations in the

surrounding areas. In 1980 Charles Berlin's incinerator business went bankrupt. But the financial collapse was to be only the beginning of the terror for the people of Swartz Creek.

Over the following three years investigators discovered storage tanks and some thirty-three thousand drums of highly hazardous waste collected from chemical plants, car factories, steel mills, refineries and railway sidings. In one tank they found one million gallons of oily waste fluids contaminated with cancer-causing polychlorinated biphenyls, or PCBs. In another reservoir were barrels of cyanide and drums of hydrochloric acid; had the containers leaked and their contents mixed together, a lethal gas would have formed over the site, at the mercy of prevailing winds.

To clean the area, government agencies had to shift more than 120,000 tonnes of earth laced with toxic metals and other industrial waste. But the damage had already been done; Swartz Creek had become a latter-day leper colony, a casualty of public fear about the hazards that had been left behind after the bulldozers had left. One resident summed it up: 'We're prisoners. We can't sell our homes, we're afraid to drink from our wells and our out-of-town friends shy from visits. My sister-in-law won't take gifts of my raspberry jam any more.'

The residents of Swartz Creek were lucky; they, at least, had homes to live in after the incident. In 1983, Times Beach in Missouri was turned into a ghost town after the authorities carried out permanent evacuation of the population following discovery of a major toxic hazard in the area. Ten years earlier dusty country roads in the vicinity had been sprayed with oil containing an exceedingly poisonous industrial waste product.

Even then, Times Beach was not the first township to feel the lethal breeze of toxic debris. When heavy rains pushed leaking drums of hazardous waste out of the ground at Love Canal in New York State in 1978, hundreds of families abandoned their houses to seek refuge elsewhere. Although a subsequent survey by specialists from the Atlanta-based Center for Disease Control concluded that the leak had not caused any observable adverse effects among the local community, few of those living in the district accepted the reassurances. Mothers attributed birth defects in their infants to toxic overspill from the nearby dump. And an earlier report had reached conclusions that were quite the opposite of the Atlanta study, namely that the inhabitants of Love Canal had suffered chromosomal damage.[12]

Love Canal, Times Beach and Swartz Creek are only the beginning. The US Environmental Protection Agency estimates that there may be as many as two thousand five hundred dangerous sites within the country; firm figures are impossible due to the existence of an unknown number of illicit secret sites across the nation. A more alarming figure was published in an article in the *International Herald Tribune* in December 1982 containing leaked details from an earlier, unpublished, report by the EPA. According to the confidential study, there were more than one hundred and eighty thousand surface impoundments of waste materials on 80,262 sites across the United States. About ninety per cent of them were said to pose an actual or potential threat of groundwater contamination. A report published in *The Economist* in September 1984 took this disturbing revelation one stage further when it disclosed that two-thirds of the rural population of the United States are thought to be drawing water from underground sources (chiefly through wells) that harbour bacteria and trace elements leaking from underground dumps.[13]

Each year US industry discards more than 250 million tonnes of potentially lethal garbage. A survey conducted in 1981 revealed that US companies recycled no more than four per cent of their toxic by-products. Between 1950 and 1985 the accumulated total for the United States of hazardous industrial garbage handed over for waste disposal is estimated to be about 6 billion toxic tonnes; most of it has been dumped in or on the land. The vast bulk of this waste contains chemicals that can cause cancer, birth defects, miscarriages, nervous disorders, blood diseases and permanent, possibly fatal, damage to the liver, kidneys or genes. And the same applies for anywhere else in the world where industry has left its mark.

The Toxic Legacy

Industry is a complex mass of processes, technologies and raw materials. And the coming of industry brought with it a confusing array of new dangers for humanity. Nevertheless, a single thread runs through the assessment of that toxic legacy: by far the greatest threat from industry comes not from wealth-creation but from waste-creation. It is perhaps the deepest irony of this consumer age that one of the most serious hazards now facing us comes not from the things we consume but from the things we throw away.

The urban fogs that have killed thousands since the first factory chimneys and household fires belched out their unwanted filth into the air are the result of inefficient fuel-burning devices. While cities in the old industrial countries have been reprieved from the worst excesses of smog by the prohibition of coal-burning processes within the confines of urban areas, these controls do not apply outside the city limits. Coal and oil continue to be burnt by manufacturing industry and power plants across the world, just as inefficiently and on a scale that would dwarf their nineteenth-century predecessors. Hence the global problem of sulphur dioxide pollution that afflicts us today. A long list of disaster areas, from Bhopal, Louisville and the acid-corroded forests of Sweden to Institute, Virginia and Britain's nuclear site at Sellafield all testify to the fact that it is the detritus of industry that invariably causes the damage. It is cast-off vapours and gases, stray chemicals, poisonous dust, hazardous fibres and radioactive left-overs that pollute the air and invade the bodies of the people who are caught in their path.

That list of disaster areas should also include Seveso, a small Italian town that had never reached the headlines until 1976. In that fateful year a factory owned by the Swiss company Hoffmann-LaRoche was rocked by an explosion that scattered the lethal chemical dioxin over the surrounding countryside. The accident contaminated hundreds of acres of land, killed animals and cast doubts over the future health of thirty thousand inhabitants.

The panic that overtook Seveso in the aftermath of the incident was not exaggerated. Dioxin is widely regarded as the most toxic chemical made by man, estimated to be ten thousand times more deadly than cyanide. It was the discovery that this same dread substance had been used on local roads that turned Times Beach into a ghost town. Indeed, since the take-off in toxic chemical usage after World War II, dioxin has been ranked top of the list for danger. Not without good reason are the more potent of the dioxin family classed as supertoxins, threatening dire consequences for the human body. And not without good reason was there widespread public clamour across Europe when forty-one barrels of toxic waste were lost en route from the Seveso accident site to a disposal dump. They were eventually found, in June 1983, hidden by a dishonest disposal operative in a disused slaughterhouse in the French town of St Quentin.

The complicated chemical formulae for dioxin – one of them is 2,3,7,8-tetrachlorodibenzodioxin – has not prevented a great number of scientists from putting this much-feared substance under close scrutiny. One inquiry into the occupational risks associated with the chemical concentrated on the longer-term effects on workers exposed to dioxin during a processing accident at a plant run by the Monsanto company in 1949. It was found that of the 121 employees affected by the incident, nine subsequently died of cancer.

Another series of studies was carried out in Sweden, where pesticides and wood treatments containing dioxins were introduced into farming and the timber industry in growing amounts from the late 1940s. A measure of the speed with which these new chemicals were taken up is the rapid climb in the use of phenoxy acids, a principal constituent of weedkillers. Variants were developed for use as impregnates and other protective preparations for wood. From less than one ton of phenoxy acid in 1947, the level of annual consumption in Sweden (a country of barely eight million people) had jumped to roughly 3,000 tonnes by the early 1980s. A somewhat unwelcome property of phenoxy acid is that it is prone to contain dioxin as impurities.

During the late seventies, Swedish and other researchers began investigating links between phenoxy acids and certain serious diseases. Workers on the Swedish railway system were found to suffer a much higher incidence of malignant tumours; the causes were traced to exposure to amitrol and phenoxy acid. In East Germany an above-average rate of lung cancer was recorded among pesticide workers. Another study suggested a strong connection between malignant lymphoma (in most cases akin to Hodgkin's disease) and exposure to phenoxy acid or other chemicals known to be connected to dioxin.

Elsewhere, a highly varied catalogue of dioxin-related incidents confirm the pervasive potency of this most damaging of toxins. One study describes a case involving dioxin-contaminated chickens. It was found that wood shavings used as bedding for the chickens had been treated with chlorophenols, resulting in concentrations of dioxin accumulating in the birds. The same chlorophenols have traditionally been used in many parts of the world to treat leather and textiles. Dioxin is also found in pesticides such as 2,4,5-T, a weedkiller widely used by farmers and gardeners alike in many parts of the world, despite its prohibition by a large number of governments.

The dioxin danger is an unforeseen consequence of the sophisticated alchemy that has overtaken commerce in the past few decades. But it is only one of hundreds of toxic substances now at the disposal of farmers, raw materials processors and manufacturers. In an advanced economy like that of the United States there are now more than sixty thousand different chemicals in use by corporations. At least one-quarter of them are potentially hazardous. According to author John Elkington, whose book *The Poisoned Womb* charts the increasingly serious effects of this chemical revolution on pregnant women and their offspring, thirteen thousand or more of those chemical substances are thought to lead to genetic damage. Many thousands of them are also linked to foetal deformities (of the kind caused by thalidomide) and cancer.[14]

The spread of new chemicals into every corner of agriculture and industry inevitably means that much of society's garbage is now a cocktail of potentially toxic elements; in some cases the hazard can result from secondary chemical reactions set off between substances within the mass of waste materials itself. These toxic wastes remain hazardous for decades, even centuries. Even disposing of them causes an open-ended danger. If they are dumped in land-fill sites they pose a risk to local communities by contaminating the water supply through leaching into the groundwater system. If they are burnt in incinerators the fumes given off then poison the atmosphere. And if they are dealt with by unscrupulous waste-disposal operators the community becomes an unwilling party to a bizarre game of toxic roulette. The residents of St Quentin can count themselves fortunate that the dioxin drums found in the local slaughterhouse were still intact. All that was needed was a fire, heavy storm or any other incident resulting in the destruction of the containers and St Quentin would never be the same again.

The all-embracing extent of the toxic waste problem can be seen in any country with a tradition of industrial activity. But no country illustrates this point more acutely than Holland, where a vast industrial infrastructure has been created on a tiny, congested, national territory. Nearly one-sixth of the country's industrial output is accounted for by the chemical sector, which disposes of nearly 1.5 million tonnes of waste every year. Until April 1980 most Dutch people were content to accept their industrial past, with its attendant pollution, as the unavoidable price of Holland's enviable prosperity and economic stability. But when a toxic waste dump was laid bare in the Volgemeer Polder, public attitudes began to change very quickly. The authorities found more than ten thousand barrels of dangerous chemical rubbish, including 2 million kilos of waste contaminated with dioxins. Many of the drums had corroded so extensively that they were already leaking their hazardous contents into the ground and surface water. Shortly before the dramatic discovery, Volgemeer Polder had been proposed as a National Scenic Area. Few people in Holland saw the joke.

But there was more. Since the discoveries at Volgemeer Polder more than four thousand other dumps have been found in Holland. More than three hundred and fifty of them posed a certain threat to public health. Recent surveys estimate that altogether more than 8 million tonnes of chemical detritus are buried in soil across the country. At least a third of this huge total is considered 'lost' because of illicit dumping. Most of the sites that are being unearthed were created in the 1950s and 1960s, since when life has continued around (and sometimes on) them by local inhabitants oblivious of their potentially lethal neighbour.

The dump at Gouderak, for instance, was once an inlet of the Ijssel river. After a long period of dumping, during which time the fish in the area were extensively poisoned by leaking drums, the inlet was filled and a housing estate was built on the land. In 1982 it was discovered that land in the district was contaminated with 135,000 kilos of polycyclical aromates, 110 kilos of benzenes, 14,600 kilos of a notoriously dangerous group of pesticides known as 'drins' and another 14,600 kilos of polychlorinated biphenyls or PCBs. The serious hazards presented by this deadly mixture range from cancer to irreversible genetic damage. Residents were put under a state of local emergency. They were advised not to eat their locally grown vegetables; even digging in the garden was strongly discouraged. Arrangements were made to evacuate the inhabitants and pull down nearly one hundred houses.

In Lekkerkerk, in another part of the country, more than two hundred and seventy houses were left empty after a toxic dump was discovered nearby. This time it contained a jumble of toluene, xylene and heavy metals. The first two are solvents that are known to cause menstrual disorders in women. Heavy metals – they include copper, lead, mercury and cadmium – are among the most poisonous substances to be found on this planet, no less toxic because they occur naturally. It cost the authorities about $80 million to clear the site by dragging away thousands of tonnes of contaminated soil, burning it and filling in the scarred landscape with clean sand. Much the same had to be done at Dordrecht, another dump-site, where 35,000 square metres of land were found to be poisoned by xylene and other equally dangerous compounds. More than one hundred houses had to be destroyed.

Even legal activities can raise the spectre of toxic catastrophe if land and industry are as closely entwined as they are in a small country like Holland. Legally allowable emissions of lead and cadmium have permeated vast acreages of soil in different parts of the country. In the De Kempen district of southern Holland, for example, the cadmium levels in the soil are so high that the National Board for Public Health recently called for a massive health check on more than sixty-five thousand local people. Crops grown in local fields are known to contain abnormally high measures of cadmium; specialists estimate that these levels will double by the end of the 1990s.

Holland as a whole is already classified by the World Health Organisation as having dangerously high levels of this particularly dangerous heavy metal. Indeed, cadmium is known to cause a disease that is so painful that it goes by the name of *itai-itai* – a Japanese word derived from the sound uttered by the pain-wracked victims. It is also known that cadmium can cross the placenta, thus entering the foetal support system, and is retained mainly in the foetal liver and kidneys. Tests on rats show that cadmium can cause clubbed feet, cleft palates and malformed lungs.

Nor is the situation any safer across the North Sea in Britain, where an even older industrial history has bequeathed an equally unwelcome inheritance. In June 1985 the newly established Hazardous Waste Inspectorate, set up in the wake of growing disquiet about the issue, published its first report. Bearing in mind the habit of understatement that usually attends government publications on potentially sensitive issues, the report makes alarming reading. It concludes: 'All is not well with hazardous waste disposal . . . there are gross disparities in the standards of hazardous waste disposal operations in different parts of the country . . . disposal site licence conditions are in some cases wilfully breached.'[15]

Like Holland, Britain's industrial structure is strongly rooted in chemicals. Indeed, Royal Dutch Shell, one of the world's chemical giants, is an Anglo-Dutch corporation. Every year British industry overall produces more than 5 million tonnes of hazardous waste. To assist in the disposal of this toxic mountain there are more than five thousand officially recognised sites. There are also any number of illicit dumps around the country where less orthodox disposal specialists have unburdened themselves of a chemical load or two.

The official disposal sector relies on land-fill schemes to bury its hazardous rubbish; more than eighty-five per cent of the total is dealt with in this way. The rest is incinerated, dropped down mineshafts, treated chemically, mixed in with cement and buried in trenches or dropped into the sea. But when officials from the Hazardous Waste Inspectorate began to pay visits to some of the disposal sites under their charge, they received a nasty shock. As they put it in the Inspectorate's report: 'The HWI is in no doubt that the standards achieved are anything but consistent or satisfactory . . . This is a matter of considerable concern.'

This official anxiety could only be made more intense by the realisation that a vast number of illegal dumps existed beyond the official domain. And these would almost certainly be even less well regulated, if regulated at all. Incidents of 'fly-tipping' hazardous chemicals on ordinary urban rubbish dumps are commonplace. A recent episode involved a toxic load being dropped onto the hard shoulder of a major highway. The HWI report itself admits to at least one hundred and fifty such incidents happening somewhere in the country every year. One section of the report tells how inspectors in the Liverpool area are deployed in groups of two or three, equipped with personal radios, in an effort to track down local asbestos strippers and their illicit 'transfer' stations.

Another, rather more alarming, case of improper dumping came to light in May 1974, when it was discovered that the Harwell Atomic Research Station in Oxfordshire had been operating for thirty years as a toxic waste dump without planning permission from the local authority. It was not so much the failure to obtain necessary permits that concerned residents in the surrounding region, but the apparent ease with which such a research establishment could operate a toxic waste facility without any information about it being passed on to local inhabitants. The incident merely put into even sharper focus the lack of effective supervision over hazardous waste that has typified the problem since it first appeared in Britain many decades ago.

To make matters worse, the highly experienced teams of hazardous waste specialists recently built up in parts of Britain by the large local authorities were disbanded with the abolition of the metropolitan county councils in the summer of 1986, thereby interrupting the monitoring of a highly precarious nationwide situation that goes far beyond esoteric substances left over from industrial processes. Apart from hazardous chemicals, Britain has a considerable legacy of run-down industrial buildings containing asbestos. These are now being pulled down as industrial decline takes its toll in many regions. For the past ten years or more the annual total of fibrous and dusty asbestos waste has exceeded 120,000 tonnes in England and Wales alone. The Inspectorate registered its dismay that this waste is not more effectively supervised, with storage bags arriving at disposal sites already broken open because of poor packaging procedures. Large amounts also 'disappear' en route due to inadequate attention to documentation required under disposal regulations: 'The quantities of asbestos notified are often at considerable variance with the quantities received at the disposal facility.'

As if its own national problem of hazardous waste is not sufficient, British disposal companies also operate a flourishing trade in looking after other people's toxic trash. About 5,000 tonnes are brought into the country every year through ports like Fleetwood, Felixstowe, Hull and Newport. A major customer is Holland, which clearly views hazardous waste exports as an attractive option in its continuing struggle to cope with the effluent outpourings of Dutch industry. About 300 tonnes of that total is asbestos, mainly from the Irish Republic. While British disposal specialists are to be commended for their readiness to share the hazards faced by their neighbours, rather less gratifying is the thought of what might happen to offshore waters if a waste-carrying vessel were to sink.

Holland and Britain are, of course, only two examples from Europe's densely packed industrial landscape. Across the twelve countries of the European Economic Community more than 30 million tonnes of toxic waste are turned out every year. A disturbing facet of this immense annual figure is that more than 3 million tonnes of it are transported across the continent to disposal sites in other EEC countries; this amounts to about three hundred thousand lorry loads of hazardous refuse plying Europe's highways every year. With volumes of trans-national toxic traffic like this, it is certain that St Quentin is not the only town in Europe to have an occasional unwelcome visitor bearing sinister canisters to be illegally stowed away in the local slaughterhouse, disused factory, lock-up garage, or wherever else seems a good idea at the time.

Bhopal: Only the Beginning?
But it is not only the over-industrialised regions of Europe, Japan and the United States that have fallen prey to their own toxic legacies. It is an increasingly common feature of the emerging high-tech holocaust that the newly industrialising countries of the poor world are themselves prematurely succumbing to the same toxic fate. The case of India is a strikingly powerful example, for the tragedy of Bhopal was only a foretaste of what could happen on even greater scale elsewhere in the country. Indeed, the Union Carbide plant at Bhopal was probably far better managed and maintained than a large number of other hazardous installations located on the Indian sub-continent.

Recent statistics show that India is now experiencing an epidemic of industrial accidents as the country's headlong dash into mass production begins to have impact on safety performance. The number of factory accidents rose from 5,289 in 1962 to 18,563 in 1984. Out of 8,761 industrial plants recently surveyed across the country, only 2,202 were found to have created pollution control units. This lack of application to basic controls is likely to be mirrored in equally inadequate provisions against toxic accidents. Already this nationwide neglect has earned India membership of the world league of super-polluted countries. Once into this big league, major catastrophes are never far behind; not least in the area of hazardous emissions and toxic waste.

An indication of the failure to anticipate toxic hazards can be seen in the poor approach to ordinary problems of industrial pollution. In Bombay, India's most polluted city, the amount of industrial effluent discharged into the atmosphere has climbed dramatically. In 1973, a study carried out by the National Environmental Engineering Institute revealed that about 1,000 tonnes of polluting particles were poured into the Bombay air during the year. By 1983 this figure had nearly doubled to more than 1,800 tonnes, and has continued rising. In Calcutta, the country's second most polluted metropolis, a research project conducted by the General Electric Company of India in 1983 reported that breathing the city's air was equal to the effect of smoking twenty cigarettes a day.

Meanwhile, the country as a whole is being steadily toxified by emissions of sulphur dioxide from a network of thermal power stations, including seventy-five huge installations dotted around India. They are all coal-fired with local fuel supplies that are high in ash content. Most of them are only fitted with inefficient mechanical dust collectors, so that vast quantities of sulphur dioxide, fly ash and soot are projected into the air. Other sources of toxic pollution include fertiliser factories (fluorine gas, sulphur dioxide, sulphur trioxide, nitrogen oxides and ammonia hydrocarbons), textile mills (smoke, kerosene and naptha vapours, sulphuric acid, chlorine formaldehyde and chlorine dioxide) and an ever-growing population of refineries and chemical complexes, of which Bhopal was one.

The coming of limited affluence to India has also brought a teeming throng of vehicles to the major cities and towns; most of these vehicles are extremely old, badly maintained and built around outmoded engine and exhaust technologies, with the result that urban centres are being choked by carbon monoxide, hydrocarbons and toxic particulates. It is as if India is confronting the entire range of pollution crises that have afflicted the developed countries over two centuries, but this time compressed into a short span of about fifteen years.

Certainly India has not escaped the danger of toxic accidents and the equally disastrous consequences of improperly treated hazardous wastes. Bhopal caught the front pages across the world. But another recent accident involving leakages of ammonia and other gases from a pharmaceutical plant in the state of Gujarat, north of Bombay, went largely unreported. In addition there are chemical companies in Baroda, a few miles south, that are known to keep enormous tanks filled with hydrocyanic acid, considered to be several times more lethal than the methyl isocyanate that caused so much death and destruction in Bhopal. Many Indian corporations also emulate their US and European counterparts in paying scant regard to matters of hazardous waste disposal. One case study relates to the heavily populated district of Chembur in Bombay, where local refineries have been dumping toxic effluent for many years. Sludge removed from crude-oil storage tanks is left to flow into open lagoons, ready for the merest spark to set off a fiery catastrophe. Other reports refer to the marked reluctance of pesticide companies to invest in proper incinerators to allow for safer disposal of their potentially lethal residues.

There seems little doubt, either, that foreign multinationals apply lower standards of safety and waste disposal practice in many of their plants in the less-developed world. Precautions at Bhopal, for instance, appear to have been less rigorous than they would be at a plant run by the parent company, Union Carbide, in the United States or Europe. One excuse offered – that governments in the host country interfere with the flow of management control and therefore dilute carefully designed safety rules – is hardly of value to those families annihilated or maimed as a result of a major toxic incident. In this respect the people of Bhopal are at one with the residents of Institute, West Virginia: in both cases they have placed their trust in the company that has brought toxic danger to their neighbourhood. In both cases, in the old world and the new, that trust was betrayed.

2
Living with the Energy Equation

A favoured method of committing suicide is to sit in a car in a locked garage with the motor running. We know that gasoline kills through its carbon monoxide by-product. Why do we not apply the same reasoning to all other energy sources? In their differing ways they, too, are lethal; proof is there in abundance. Convenience, politics and cost however dictate that we look the other way. But the garage doors are closing fast. Our clamour for prosperity has created an ever-growing hunger for energy. And this hunger has created in turn, a global energy machine that is slowly devouring us.

A random selection of the evidence produces a stark picture:

- Scientists drilling the Greenland icecap have discovered that lead levels in the air we breathe have increased two thousand per cent since the start of the industrial revolution. Most citizens of industrial societies today contain 500–1,000 times more lead in their bodies than did their prehistoric ancestors.[1] Lead too is a poison; there is mounting proof that our brains and nervous systems are being steadily eroded.

- A few years back, on the east coast of Ireland, six young mothers gave birth to mongol children. As teenage friends they had all attended the same Dundalk school at the time when, in the late fifties, fallout from a serious fire at the Windscale nuclear plant in Cumbria across the Irish Sea reached their area. Dozens of similar examples cast a long shadow over the post-war history of nuclear power.

- More recently, in 1984, a fireball engulfed the Brazilian shanty town of Vila Soco after a pipeline ruptured. It claimed five hundred victims, three hundred of them children under the age of five. Religious tradition dictated that the catastrophe be accepted as an act of God. The same year two thousand five hundred people were killed or injured after the dawn explosion of liquefied gas stored near the Mexico City suburb of San Juan Ixhuatepec. 'Madrugo el Diablo' ran the local headline: 'The Devil got up early this morning.' The reality is otherwise; by stealth or by violent death, the energy equation kills and deforms. And it is most definitely an act of Man.

Not only our bodies are at risk. The world's climate, say scientists, is being reshaped by the knock-on effect of chemicals thrown into the upper atmosphere by a hundred thousand power plants sited across the world's landmass. Increasing levels of carbon dioxide are likely to cause a global rise in temperatures, bringing dust-bowl conditions to the great food-producing regions of the US and Canadian grain belt. Significant changes to the world's snow cover and ocean levels could result. The consequences would be serious socio-economic dislocations affecting entire populations.

Already the polluting garbage of world industry is taking savage effect on our habitat. Millions of acres of prime forest are dying as a result of rains turned acid by the smokestacks and exhausts of an immense worldwide energy-producing and energy-consuming infrastructure. Rivers, lakes and oceans have been turned into hazardous chemical solutions in which fish and other marine life can no longer survive. In this way Nature is now paying us back: acid rain is seeping into our biological universe, via the food and water chain, to corrode our own physical architecture.

This disturbing catalogue would be tolerable if the future held out the prospect of significant reductions or at least stability in our habits of energy consumption. The forecasts suggest otherwise. Contrary to expectations the revolution in oil prices of the early 1970s brought no pause in the pursuit of energy abundance. In 1975, on the morrow of the oil panic, as governments across the world pronounced their devotion to energy conservation, a world population of some 4,000 million souls consumed around 7,300 gigawatts of primary energy. UN projections put the figure for the end of the century at 6,370 million people using 18,000 gigawatts.

To satisfy this projected demand will need an increase of more than two hundred and fifty per cent in world energy production in just twenty-five years. And the outlook into the twenty-first century is for continued rapid growth. Total population numbers are expected to reach nine or ten billion by mid-century or shortly thereafter, with most of the increase occurring in poor countries where energy production is likely to be least sophisticated and, more important, least controlled by laws or corporate self-regulation. The future threat thus comes not from esoteric, high-tech forms of energy but from an explosion in power generation using the same old-style energy sources that have fuelled two centuries of Western industrial growth – and in doing so have already poisoned the global habitat to beyond danger point.

The Fossil Fuel Legacy

A hundred years from now roughly four-fifths of primary energy demand will be in areas currently classified as less-developed. Latest estimates put total consumption by then at something approaching 70,000 gigawatts a year, roughly ten times its 1975 level. Practically the whole of it will come from traditional energy sources of the kind that have turned the icecaps into lead concentrate. For despite the political sensitivity and public apprehensions of nuclear power, the world is and will remain a fossil-fuel dependency for the foreseeable future. Though increasing amounts of electricity in the developed world will be derived from nuclear processes, the broader power-generating spectrum will be dominated by fuels extracted from the earth's crust. In this final phase of the twentieth century, ninety-five per cent of our energy needs are still met through coal, oil and natural gas. And these fuel sources are here to stay. Nuclear-electric and hydro-electric methods account for less than four per cent; more esoteric forms such as geothermal, solar, wind and wave power are marginal within the overall energy mix.

This pattern of power production is unlikely to change within the next two generations. Coal is, and will continue to be, a key component of the energy equation, chiefly because of its vital importance in regions now embarked on rapid industrialisation. Nearly fifty per cent of world coal usage is located in the less-developed areas, and though estimates indicate that world coal reserves are limited most experts would agree that there is sufficient to last for the next hundred years or so. Indeed, if reserves were to approach exhaustion sometime in the twenty-first century, the polluting impact would be even greater as power stations and other users would be obliged to fall back onto increasingly impure supplies.

Fossil fuels, coal in particular, are the major cause of the disastrous degeneration, since about 1750, in the quality of the air we breathe in the developed world, with an exaggerated downturn beginning around the start of this century. The by-products that do the damage are lead, carbon monoxide, sulphur oxides and nitrogen oxides; a host of secondary pollutants include cadmium, ozone, asbestos and hydrocarbons. They result from the burning of fossil fuels in power stations, industrial plants and road vehicles. The most pernicious by-product is lead, which enters the body through inhalation and via the food chain; very few foodstuffs can escape its contaminating effect.

Our Leaden Inheritance

Lead poisoning has long been recognised as a hazard in the more everyday sense; an excess of lead in the blood can give rise to clinical syndromes of illness ranging from anaemia to acute abdominal pains. In sufficient doses it can kill almost as efficiently as cyanide or arsenic. The most serious threat, however, is not to our basic organs but to our brains.

Lead is a neurotoxin, which leads to the degeneration of tissue in the central nervous system, acting directly on the bio-chemistry of human intelligence. There is considerable evidence that lead-induced effects on behaviour, learning ability and other intelligent functions are linked to physical changes in brain structure. Such is the toxic power of lead that behavioural changes can occur even at low lead levels; relatively small doses are all that is necessary to inhibit enzymes vital to the flow of transmitters and hence to the brain's information processing activity, at the same time interfering with the regulation of its energy supplies and its control of sensory inputs and be-havioural outputs. In short, the lead-affected brain is a neurotic, unbalanced shadow of its natural self.

One body of research suggests a pernicious, self-reinforcing pattern in lead toxicity. A phenomenon of modern industrial life is the increased reliance on anti-anxiety drugs, including nicotine and alcohol. We commonly attribute this to the high-pressured tempo of the modern age. A more alarming explanation involves the cumulative effects of living in our lead-saturated environment. By raising the levels of amino-laevulinic acid in the brain, lead could serve to increase anxiety levels by suppressing certain of the brain's regulatory functions, in turn increasing the need for cigarettes, liquor and pills.

Other studies show a strong connection between increased

lead levels and conditions such as hyperactivity and hyperaggression, both of which are common ailments of late twentieth-century life. The former is still widely regarded by doctors as a form of mental disorder, especially among children. The latter is invariably explained away as a facet of stress or wider societal decline. Both can be classed as 'diseases of civilisation'. And therein lies the irony; both are attributed to toxicity from lead, the one heavy metal that has been in use since the beginning of civilisation itself. All that has changed is the scale of our lead consumption. In the span of two or three lifetimes the world's lead habit is approaching overdose proportions.

Lead is the most plentiful of the heavy metals, with a record of regular use stretching back to as early as 2,500BC. Thus there has always been a baseline of measurable lead contamination present in the human environment, as demonstrated by archaeological assessments. Further examinations of such media as permanent snowfields, lake and marine sediments and even moss coverings on museum items have yielded a more reliable profile of atmospheric lead pollution over the centuries. The picture they present is less than comforting.

Taking the oldest snow layers as representing the natural lead level, the surveys demonstrate that by the onset of widespread industrialisation in the middle of the eighteenth century lead concentrations had jumped to some twenty-five times above this natural level, even though industrial activity was still confined to limited areas of north-west Europe. By 1940 this factor had increased to about one hundred and seventy-five. Since then levels have risen sharply to five hundred times the natural level. An indication of the man-made contribution to global lead pollution can be gained by ranging the natural emission rate against output coming from human activities; the natural rate is estimated to be 24,500ty-1, that caused by man to be 449,000ty-1 (ty=tons per year).

These measurements nevertheless only reflect the broad, upward curve of lead contamination. There are colossal geographic variations. A key factor is location; in the world's heavy metal hotspots the readings are well above the danger line. These hotspots are predominantly urban sites in the northern hemisphere; in extreme cases, they have lead levels many thousands of times greater than those found in isolated maritime areas.

A recent comparative study highlighted this north-south

contrast. Using a standard measure (ng m-3), a group of 217 urban locations in the United States returned an average rating of 1,100; the figure for Lima in Peru was 493, that for Balboa in Panama just 245. Guayaquil in Ecuador rated 367. The comparison between urban and maritime sites is even more striking: Easter Island recorded a level of 5.7, remote Dickson Island in the Soviet Union only 0.9. Of nearly thirty non-urban locations surveyed none exceeded 160, a fraction of the levels seen in the major northern centres. Salt Lake City, at the extreme, measured 1,346; Miami topped the list with 1,404, though there are many other hotspots that rate even higher.

The neurosystems of people living in the hotspot areas are under constant attack. The food they eat is contaminated: cereals, meat, fish and fruit are at the upper end of the danger scale, with lead levels typically three to four times greater than is found in milk. The streets they walk are toxic viaducts; the motor vehicle is the culprit responsible for ninety per cent of mass lead emissions in the typical developed country. In the world as a whole motor fuels account for sixty per cent of the total, the result of an unprecedented increase in reliance on the combustion engine since World War II. In 1950 the world's motor vehicles burnt 1.4 billion barrels of gasoline a year; by the beginning of the 1980s this already enormous figure had climbed nearly fourfold to around 5.5 billion barrels, with hardly a kink in the steep upward curve to mark the temporary hitch of the oil-price crisis of the mid-1970s.

Added to the cumulative inheritance bequeathed by decades of lead-generating operations, suspended in the everyday air, this toxic diet raises the spectre of neurocide, the widespread deterioration of human intelligence and the escalation of behavioural disorders. The signs of crisis are already visible, though tucked away in obscure medical journals and research reports. Their undeniable conclusion . . . in hundreds of towns and cities across the industrialised world entire communities have already passed the point of safety.

Precise assessment of the scale of the danger is confused by lack of any official yardstick as to what constitutes lead overload. The EEC Commission, for instance, has adopted a directive requiring member governments to apply a sliding scale. Under these EEC rules action is called for when at least half of the population group examined rate above 20ug dl-1 (micrograms per decilitre of blood), with more exacting intervention required in individual cases where the reference level exceeds 35ug dl-1. But national regulations are often at variance with this approach. Under British rules, for example, alarm bells sound when the blood-lead level in a person, particularly a child, goes beyond 25ug dl-1. Most government standards conform to the belief that serious consequences such as dysfunction of the peripheral nervous system, anaemia and kidney damage become very real above a level of 65.

The key point, however, is that these threshold levels are not thick dividing lines between the acceptable and the unacceptable. All lead intake is hazardous. Changes in brain functions, through effects on ALA, the aminolaevulinic acid, begin occurring well before observable clinical symptoms such as anaemia or vomiting appear, at blood-lead levels universally considered as safe. Specialists in behavioural toxicology report that children, by reason of their smaller bulk, can suffer disturbance to their intelligence and behaviour at blood-lead readings only marginally above zero. Recent studies of large groups of New York schoolchildren, for example, have pinpointed significant changes in IQ and personality taking place at levels as low as 5 ug dl-1.

At the upper end, while 65ug dl-1 and above is deemed the red zone for adults, children can show overt signs of clinical lead poisoning at a blood-lead level of 40. A side effect of this is anorexia; it may be no coincidence that this has become a common childhood ailment of the late twentieth century. For unborn children, meanwhile, the hazards are more extreme still; lead is known to have produced imbalance in the neurotransmission processes in foetuses at the minute level of 0.2ug dl-1. Indeed, lead overload could well explain many of the behavioural disabilities usually ascribed to children simply as unfortunate traits of personality, one of the inevitable burdens of parenthood. The scientific explanation could be far more startling: there is growing evidence that minimal brain dysfunction caused by lead toxicity is the real cause of characteristics traditionally associated with 'difficult' children: clumsiness, poor co-ordination and the myriad unpleasant aspects of hyperactivity.

Hyperactivity is itself a poorly understood condition; that there is a strong link with chemical ingestion through food additives is becoming almost incontrovertible. But there is now a widespread conviction that lead, too, plays a role. One study, published in *The Lancet* as early as 1975, tells of the above average incidence of such varied conditions as colic, clumsiness, irritability and hyperactivity itself in a group of high-lead children.[2] Dozens of subsequent studies have echoed this discovery.

A more alarming possibility is that of a connection between high blood lead and serious problems of antisocial behaviour. Follow-up surveys of children originally diagnosed as hyper-active – but who were in fact almost certainly suffering from excess blood lead – have shown that these same children graduate to suffer a higher drop-out rate from school, greater involvement in motor accidents, a greater tendency towards drug abuse and an increased likelihood of ending up in the courts. Indeed sociologists, criminologists and even judges will be highly interested in the increasing amount of evidence that suggests a direct link between lead pollution and the growing incidence of antisocial behaviour, hooliganism and violent crime. Although the conclusions of specialists on the matter are hedged by qualifications, their general arguments have a con-vincing ring.

Lead is known to be particularly hazardous for young children. It is thought to lead to behavioural disorders such as hyperactivity because of its damaging effects on key parts of the nervous system and brain. What has also come to light is that hyperactivity in children affects boys far more than girls. To be precise, hyperactivity is five times more common in boys than in young members of the opposite sex. Recent surveys in London reveal that more than fifty per cent of children living in certain parts of the inner city are either hyperactive or otherwise disturbed. The root cause of most cases of hyperactivity is con-sistent exposure to lead pollution, including in the months before birth. It is equally well known that cerebral palsy and epilepsy can also produce hyperactivity; these are conditions that have been directly linked to lead (indeed, they have been shown to improve by 'de-leading therapy').

These hyperactive children exhibit all the typical symptoms: restlessness and impatience, low tolerance of frustration, emotional immaturity and a tendency towards violent, destruc-tive and over-impulsive actions. Pure hyperactivity tends to fall off during the early teenage years, but in many instances it persists through to adulthood. A survey carried out by two specialists, D. Bryce-Smith and H. A. Waldron, records that in a certain British prison for medium-term offenders nearly all the inmates are classified as hyperactive.[3] As they point out, it is not without significance that the incidence of violent crimes in Britain has been growing strongly in recent years compared to other types of criminal activity. A recommendation of the two analysts may one day have major implications for the operation of penal systems in industrialised countries where lead pollution poses a significant problem. If such common offences as vandalism, mugging and hooliganism are indeed associated with hyperactivity, then a better treatment would be a course of penicillamine rather than prison. Most would agree, in any event, that the latter response has proved entirely ineffective.

An intriguing footnote to these research findings is drawn from recent British history. In England in 1918 there was an epidemic of encephalitis lethargica, a condition similar to brain disorders caused by lead toxicity. A number of those infected subsequently developed antisocial characteristics and went on to commit crimes for which they were convicted and imprisoned. There can be no better illustration than this of a group of people punished for being unfortunate enough to fall ill. How many of today's criminals, languishing in prison, are there for no other reason than being unfortunate enough to be born into a lead-polluted, late twentieth-century society?

The conclusions of analysts working in the newly developing area of behavioural toxicology are highly illuminating in this respect. According to breakthrough research on the link between pollution and changes in human behaviour, lead constitutes the greatest hazard of all toxic substances because of the effects over time of steady accumulation in our blood. Scientists are now convinced that this accumulation is taking us closer to the threshold of potential clinical poisoning than is the case for any other toxic chemical pollutant.

This new research focusses on problems occurring in the nervous system. It is widely known by specialists that the most common kind of injury to that system is a condition referred to as segmental demyelinization; it is connected with deterioration in the efficiency of the peripheral nerves. It has long been realised that conditions such as these are typical manifestations of lead poisoning, but until now it was thought that they were signs that appeared only late in the day after many years of lead exposure. For example, lead encephalopathy, or inflammation of the brain, is a serious late manifestation in adults. A somewhat obscure case study is the abnormally large number of victims among drinkers of moonshine whisky in the backwoods of America. Alcohol, it appears, has the effect of enhancing levels of lead in soft tissue, including the brain. Indeed, the dominant fact that emerges from these researches is that the brain is the main target organ of lead toxicity.

The latest work, however, looks not at the long-term symptoms but at evidence of lead pollution in the human body during the early years. In so doing scientists have produced startling evidence of the damage being done to children and unborn babies, damage that is having disturbing adverse effects on their personality and social behaviour. A key area of research concentrates on a vital component part of the nervous system, an organic acid known as pyruvate.

Interference with pyruvate levels will seriously impair the supply of energy to the brain cells. For young children this is doubly dangerous because, up to the age of four, the oxygen needs of the still-developing brain are much greater than in adults. There is also evidence that reductions in pyruvate leads to the formation of salts known as lactate, which has the effect of producing acute anxiety by cutting down the flow of essential calcium. One other area of major concern amongst analysts is the knock-on effect of all of this in distorting the capacity of the body to deal with fatty acids and cholesterol, which in turn interferes with our ability to synthesise myelin, the white substance that forms the sheath of nerve fibres. If such problems occur at an early age they can lead to grave consequences.

It is clear to experts in neurological disorders that children are the main risk category. The danger appears to be in inverse relation to age; the younger the infant, the higher the risk. The most extensive damage is to the child's cerebellum, the back of the brain, which leads to permanent injury to the neuro-system. A report of the United States National Academy of Sciences offers a detailed summary of the consequences: 'Subtle neurologic deficits and mental impairment are the more common outcomes. These include lack of sensory perception and perseverance . . . Form and proportion are distorted. Motor incoordination and lack of sensory perception severely impair learning ability . . . Such children have short attention spans and easy distractability . . . Many children with documented prior attacks of lead poisoning develop hostile, aggressive and destructive behaviour patterns . . . Although seizure disorder and behavioural abnormalities tend to abate during adolescence, mental incompetence is permanent.'[4]

Another study, from the American Academy of Pediatrics, concludes that at least twenty-five per cent of children with lead encephalopathy will be left with permanent damage to the central nervous system. Many specialists regard this, however, as a conservative view. An earlier report by noted analysts Perlstein and Attala recorded that eighty-two per cent of affected children suffer permanent effects, including frequently recurrent fits or mental retardation.[5]

In the classic research study completed by Byers and Lord in the 1950s a group of twenty children treated for mild lead poisoning were followed over several years to measure longer-term consequences. Nineteen of them were found to be suffering from behavioural and educational abnormalities, even though all had been originally discharged from hospital with a clean bill of health. The educational difficulties were found to have symptoms similar to dyslexia. Other children were hyperactive, with short attention spans. As a result they achieved poor learning levels even when their nominal IQs were high. And many of them had serious behavioural difficulties normally associated with damage to the cortex, the outer grey matter of the brain. Some were prone to impulsive and violent acts.

A secondary finding of the study was no less disturbing. It was discovered that if children who have suffered from lead encephalopathy are again exposed to lead, and suffer a repeat performance of lead intoxication, the proportion of them suffering permanent and severe brain damage rises to almost one hundred per cent. It raises the fearful presumption that such an exposure is almost inevitable for any child living in a high-lead industrialised community, although the absorption of toxic substances in this case will take place gradually over a long time span instead of in a single, readily apparent episode.

The considerable body of research that has been developed on the subject of children and lead has also thrown up a strange phenomenon. It is known as pica and is linked to the uniquely competitive relationship that exists between lead and calcium. Pica is a behavioural disorder in children well known to be predisposed to lead poisoning. It manifests itself in the habit of chewing or sucking toys, soil and other non-food items. Ironically, these are activities that are often dismissed as a quite normal facet of early childhood, and at worst a form of 'naughtiness'.

Although the precise causes of pica are not fully understood it is recognised that a deficiency of calcium in animals has the effects both of promoting pica and of enhancing the toxic aspects of lead. In children, pica has the tendency to produce a craving for lead-rich objects, possibly as a substitute for calcium. Whatever the exact reasons, the discovery adds one more hazard to the list of childhood risks. Certainly, an infant acting under the influence of pica will find little difficulty in finding lead-containing objects in the average home.

The Polluting Stream

Whatever the weight of evidence, both clinical and purely circumstantial, there is as yet no sign of a reversal in the drift towards neurocide. As in so many other areas of the high-tech holocaust, official and medical opinion about the effects of lead concentration is deeply divided. Pressures from the vehicle manufacturers and oil companies, both of them key factors for jobs and incomes in most industrial countries, slow the progress towards a consensus on remedial action. The pro-coal lobbies call for increases in production from the mines. As a result, while the scientists, politicians and businessmen argue the merits of the evidence, the blood-lead readings of millions of highly exposed urban citizens climb ever higher:

- The Frankfurt Blood Lead Study, published in 1980, showed that several categories of worker had levels above the UK 'alert' level of 25ug dl-1. Policemen were most at risk, with levels ranging up to 28, followed by taxi-drivers, street-cleaners and local residents in the investigation area. Frankfurt has in recent years made significant efforts to reduce its lead problem; the majority of industrial conurbations around the world have not.

  Law enforcement seems to be a particularly exposed occupation. Recent work in Rome, for instance, has identified similar problems with the city's police force, no doubt a consequence of their continual exposure to pollutants on the streets and highways. In Denmark, meanwhile, even office-bound police officers have found themselves at risk, but from a more obscure quarter: personnel working in the fingerprint section have suffered white lead exposure caused by materials used in the print-recording process.

- Rapid industrialisation carries its own risks, particularly where the pattern of new infrastructure is concentrated in one or two high-polluting sectors. A revealing example comes from the oil-rich Arab world: a study conducted by the Saudi Arabian Meteorological and Environmental Protection Administration in two primary schools in the bustling port of Jeddah has revealed that lead levels in many children are rapidly approaching danger point. Blood-lead figures exceeded those found in most parts of Western Europe. Meanwhile, the Saudi government presses on with its ambitious development plans, including a massive expansion in the country's oil-refining capacity, a major contributor to local atmospheric problems.

● In May 1982 Dr Fraser Alexander of Newcastle General Hospital in north-east England made public his discovery that since the placenta does not filter lead from the mother, the unborn foetus is at serious risk in high-lead locations.[6] Two months later a circular drafted by the British Department of the Environment advising local authorities to eliminate blood-lead levels above 25 micrograms per decilitre, instead of the existing official limit of 35, was stopped by ministers.

● A host of other specialised studies across the industrialised countries are producing an ever-lengthening list of lead dangers. Household paints continue to be a hazard. Other researchers have identified risks of lead poisoning associated with the drinking of wine – the result of lead arsenate sprays used in the vineyards to control caterpillars. Even tap water has been found to be contaminated to a point of concern; homes with lead-based plumbing are widely seen as high-exposure environments. Correspondence in the learned medical press testifies to professional anxiety over connections between stoneground flour and lead poisoning. Elsewhere studies have focussed on lead-related risks in fruit juices and soft drinks, in evaporated milk, in beef and pork, in vegetables – particularly large-leafed salad produce – grown close to busy roads.

An increasing amount of evidence alludes to the very real health hazards posed by such daily contamination, at work and in the home. The incidence of lung cancer among workers making lead chromate pigment is attracting growing interest. A number of analyses point to dental ceramics and filling materials as the possible culprits in individual cases of severe physical or mental abnormality. Several investigations describe changes in the functioning of the eye and ear due to lead toxicity. Much evidence exists that a condition such as gout is related to lead intake.

For varying reasons Britain has a unique status in the field of lead contamination. The first industrial country, it has for more than two centuries poured an immense polluting stream into the constricted atmosphere of a group of small islands, much of it produced by plant that is old, inefficient and seriously lacking in sophisticated pollution-control technology. There has been very little progress, either, in the elimination of lead emissions from motor vehicles. Hence many of the more disturbing cases of blood-lead toxicity come from British research, not least in the critical area of lead-induced reductions in intelligence.

One survey conducted in the late seventies involved a sample of 166 British children, all of whom had blood-lead levels below the designated EEC alarm rating of 35ug dl-1. The children who recorded levels of 12 or below scored an average of seven IQ points higher than children who rated 13 and above. A curious secondary finding was that within the sample children from better-off social backgrounds had lower blood-lead levels than their less affluent playmates.

It is not difficult to conclude that Britain's high-lead culture is linked to the all-consuming importance of the motor car, with its concomitant role as chief contributor to urban lead concentrations. A study conducted in the late 1970s, for example, looked at lead concentration along the congested North Circular Road in the London suburbs. The guideline adopted by the research team was a government recommendation that 'the annual average concentration of lead should not exceed $2ug/m^3$ [micrograms per cubic metre of air] in places where people are continually exposed for long periods'. The highway in question is used daily by many thousands of drivers, bus passengers and pedestrians and indeed for most of its length the surrounding locality is densely populated. Schools and hospitals are sited along its route.

The study revealed that at its high point lead concentrations reached levels of $5.5ug/m^3$, nearly three times the officially recommended limit. A similar survey in Coventry produced a maximum of 7.2 in the city's Butts Road area; another project in Birmingham yielded a figure of 5.9.[7] Similar results would be found in thousands of congested urban zones across the country. A quarter of a century after Britain's Clean Air Act, sanctioned in 1956 to clean up the cities by outlawing smoke-producing fossil fuels, urban communities stand threatened by an even more pervasive and health-damaging toxin.

Such findings are typical of major conurbations in every

country where lead remains a prime constituent of motor fuel. Because of the financial implications of producing lead-free gasoline, and vehicle engines to match, it will again be the poor regions of the world, unable to meet the costs of building or buying clean cars, that lag behind – the very regions where the next phase of massive growth in vehicle numbers will take place. A glance at the forecasts for the world's vehicle population makes the point eloquently, and disturbingly. At the beginning of the 1980s the global figure stood at 310 million passenger cars. By 1990 this figure is expected to have reached 406 million, rising to about 536 million by the end of the century. Over twenty years, in other words, some 226 million extra passenger vehicles will be added to the world total. Only 75 million of them are likely to be in the major industrial countries that have traditionally dominated the world car market and which are now attempting to come to terms with lead pollution.

Biggest growth will be in the low-income, less-developed countries of South America, Asia and Africa. Together they will see a massive rise in car ownership of around 88 million vehicles. They will also account for a very large increase in the number of commercial vehicles; the figure for less-developed countries is set to grow more than one hundred per cent to 32 million between 1979 and 2000, twice the growth rate for commercial vehicle ownership in the seven major Western industrial economies.

By the end of this century the world will play host to nearly 680 million combustion-engined vehicles. The world's capacity to make those vehicles environmentally acceptable will depend on how much of our resources can, or will, be devoted to the task of eliminating toxic emissions from vehicle exhausts. And this comes down to money. Unfortunately, the surge in world vehicles will be in precisely those territories where money is short, in countries like China and India, where per capita incomes are less than $300. Even at the upper end of the income spectrum in the less-developed world that figure will be no greater than $2,500.

Environmental concern, alas, is a luxury for those who can afford to pay the price of undoing the corrosive, polluting results of a century of industrialism. It is a luxury that can be bought in the affluent countries of North America and northern Europe, where per capita incomes are typically thirty or forty times greater than in the poor countries of Asia. As these poor countries will be the inheritors of the rich world's industrial legacy, just as certainly will they be the world's next generation of polluters.

Fuelling the Inferno

The energy equation nevertheless has its more explosive components which, rather than permeate the human biochemistry by invisible, barely perceptible invasion, wreak sudden havoc without warning. The residents of the devastated Brazilian town of Vila Soco can testify to that; five hundred of their relatives and friends were burnt to a cinder by the fireball that ripped through their makeshift shanty dwellings after a nearby pipeline split asunder in 1984. The poverty-ridden settlement of some nine thousand people, on the outskirts of Cubatõa, was close to a gas depot owned by Petrobras. On 25 February that year highly inflammable gasoline spurted out from a pipeline that had been opened by mistake. Within seconds a horrific fire had consumed eight and a half acres of shacks; the centre of the fire reached a temperature of more than 1,000°C. The coroner remarked that it was strange that no bodies of children under five were ever discovered amongst the eighty-six charred remains found in the burnt-out area. The explanation was simple: their small bodies had been totally cremated. It was later discovered that irrigation ditches around the slums had been filled with the highly volatile gasoline, transforming the unsuspecting township into a time bomb waiting for ignition.

Inferno also overtook the inhabitants of San Juan Ixhuatepec, on the outskirts of Mexico City that year, courtesy of the energy equation. At 5.42am one November morning, a tower of flame surged three hundred feet into the air as exploding gas containers turned the unsuspecting working-class neighbourhood into a fiery hell. Four spherical storage tanks were shattered into fragments, sending out huge splinters of steel that cut through houses like giant grenades. Forty-eight smaller tanks exploded soon after; a fifty-foot-long cylinder rocketed into the air to fall on a house half a mile away, levelling the building. When the flames had abated the tragic cost was counted. More than thirty acres of simple homes were completely destroyed, another thirty nearly so. As victims succumbed to their burns the death toll rose to 365, with two thousand injured; many of the survivors would later die. At the centre of the devastation corpses were discovered carbonised into grotesque rag-doll shapes, beyond identity.

San Juan Ixhuatepec was not the first Mexican shanty town to fall prey to volatile fuel substances that year. In January a 25,000 gallon gas storage tank blew up in Tula in the central region of the country. By luck there were no injuries, but another explosion in Tabasco in June claimed one dead and thirty-three injured. The following week sixteen people in Veracruz were overcome after a pipeline sprang a leak. Again, luck prevented a catastrophe to equal that in Vila Soco. June 1984 was by any account a dangerous month for Mexicans: inhabitants of the luckless San Juan Ixhuatepec insist that around that time their own disaster was forewarned by a fire at the local gas storage depot.

There will be many more such years, and not just for Mexico. The vicious, engulfing fluid that fuelled the flames that November morning was liquefied natural gas. It is growing rapidly as a preferred energy source across the world. Storage sites like those that are terrorising Mexico are springing up on every continent. Liquefied natural gas is a cold, unpredictable killer.

In her book *Frozen Fire*, author Lee Niedringhaus Davis spells out the little-known record of lethal mayhem associated with LNG.[8] The disaster of 11 July 1978, near the Spanish coastal town of San Carlos de la Rapita, which claimed more than two hundred dead and three hundred maimed – practically the entire tourist population of an unsuspecting holiday camp – caught the headlines, but only fleetingly. No lesson was learnt; thereafter the LNG death rate was to climb steadily.

The events in San Carlos followed a typical LNG pattern. At lunchtime a young German tourist heard a popping noise from a large tank trailer on the road nearby. A milky cloud began to drift towards the camp. The young man fled; simultaneously the white cloud erupted into a mass of flames. The fireflash, at least 1,500°C (2,732°F) at its centre, melted the rings and watches of people trapped in its path. More than a hundred of the victims were beyond recognition.

The tanker was transporting propylene, one of a range of industrial gases carried in liquid form for convenience. It was making for the southern Spanish town of Puertollana with 43 cubic metres of gas in its trailer, nearly 11,500 gallons, stored under pressure at minus 47°C (−53°F). Later investigation revealed that the tank had sprung a leak and ruptured; its thin metal skin was not able to withstand the immense internal pressure, not least, it seemed, because too much of the volatile fluid had been pumped into it before it began its journey. The remaining stages in the tragedy of San Carlos followed the pattern of escalation now known to be typical of LNG. The spilled liquid, meeting outside temperatures, vaporises. Moisture in the surrounding air is turned into ice crystals, making a dense, chilling, highly inflammable fog. All that is needed is a spark; in the case of San Carlos one of the many camp stoves in use preparing the midday meal. But it could just as easily be the ignition system of a car or lawnmower, a cigarette, a lightbulb.

Author Davis became increasingly alarmed at the degree of official uninterest that followed the San Carlos disaster. One British official advised her the episode should be treated as a freak accident. Elsewhere governments acted to restrict LNG transports and other hazardous cargoes to major highways away from population centres, but nothing more; San Carlos, they argued, was unique. They were wrong.

Indeed, five days after the fiery obliteration of the San Carlos campsite a gas tanker on the main road between Mexico City and Queretaro skidded, hit a rampart and overturned. It exploded and turned into a ball of flame. Davis records that 'ten miles away at the town of Jilotepec people ran into the streets screaming as flames lit up the sky'. The immediate death toll was ten; of the 150–200 badly injured many were not expected to live. In the weeks that followed argument flowed back and forth as to what exactly had been carried in the tanker; some reports described it as propane, others butane, others as propylene, the gas that killed in San Carlos. The dispute over chemical details matters little. The episode was another frightening illustration of the terrifying destructive power of liquefied gases in all their forms.

It seems strange that public knowledge of the dangers of LNG is so limited, for its history of violent, unannounced death-dealing is long and varied. As early as October 1944, in Cleveland, Ohio, there was warning: a small tank containing some 4,200 cubic metres of LNG ruptured and spewed out its white vapour cloud, which suddenly ignited. Tanks nearby were engulfed, adding to the conflagration. The fire tore through the plant, overwhelming nearby houses. When the flames had abated one hundred and thirty people lay dead, more than two hundred others horribly mutilated. Nearly eighty houses, two factories and several hundred vehicles were totally destroyed; a vast section of the city was seriously damaged. The bill for property alone came to nearly $7 million in 1944 money. By the standards of today's LNG activity the storage tanks in Cleveland were minuscule.

For many years after 1944 LNG was absent from the front pages. But since February 1973, when forty workers were buried alive at the immense LNG plant on Staten Island, New York, the liquefied gas industry has known that widespread public outcry against the danger could only be a matter of time. And yet the opposite has happened. Though there have been sporadic displays of public and official anxiety, LNG has rapidly become a boom sector of the world energy equation, with only the minimum amount of resistance from the conservationist lobbies. These days LNG competes with coal and oil as an indispensable component of the energy spread.

A major reason is the commercial attraction of liquefaction as a profitable means of exploiting natural gas extracted in countries, such as Algeria and Indonesia, that are considerable distances from the big centres of energy consumption in the developed world. Second, liquefaction makes it possible for gas suppliers to store surplus fuel to allow for the peaks and troughs of the annual demand cycle, regasifying their reserves to send out to customers during the colder months. In many cases tankers carry the LNG to sub-stations around the vicinity for speedier delivery to local users. Such was the purpose of the Staten Island facility.

Commercial arguments like these have helped boost the growth rates of the LNG industry, particularly in the aftermath of the mid-seventies oil price hike as industrial and domestic consumers sought to escape from high-cost oil. Within a few years more than seventy plants like that at Staten Island were to be built; the building has continued uninterrupted, producing a global spread of potential LNG flashpoints. The key receiving sites are along the coastlines of the major industrial countries. The first were built on the eastern US seaboard, at Canvey Island and Le Havre on the English Channel, at Fos, Barcelona and La Spezia in the western Mediterranean and at more than half a dozen places around the Japanese industrial heartland of Tokyo-Yokohama. In recent years the global map of LNG storage sites has reached outwards to encompass every corner of the five continents.

And not only on land. The ocean-going tankers that ship LNG around a power-hungry world are gigantic floating danger zones. The largest planned LNG vessel is designed to carry more than 7 billion cubic feet of gas, enough to supply the monthly needs of two and a half million people. It may also be sufficient to fry them to a crisp if frozen fire strikes on such colossal scale.

3
Tomorrow Always Comes

The scene is Canonsburg in Pennsylvania; as one newspaper article put it, 'a small, pretty, clean-living town'. Although its origins can be traced back to the Founding Fathers, Canonsburg could offer no better reason to be included in the history books than the decision of Mr and Mrs Como to settle there and produce a son by the name of Perry. No better reason, that is, until now. For Canonsburg has become a place of death; 11,000 citizens are in no doubt that clean living has not protected them from the peacetime dangers of the nuclear age.

In this close-knit community the mood has changed dramatically as the death rate has climbed. A survey carried out by the *Pittsburgh Press* in 1982 revealed that in the neighbourhood of Payne Place alone, thirty-seven people drawn from three generations had already died from cancer. Another three were found to be suffering from the disease. Since then the tragedy has bitten deeper still. A particularly harrowing case was that of Mark Humble, who died in November 1984 from cancer of the stomach after many months of unsuccessful efforts to arrest the rapid spread of a voraciously malignant condition. Mark Humble was twenty-two years old; he was the eleventh youngster from among 385 classmates at a local school who were known to have contracted the disease.

Two others are already dead. One boy died from lung cancer soon after he graduated. The other needed to have a leg amputated at the age of fourteen after developing bone cancer; at sixteen he was to die from cancer of the lung. Meanwhile, nuns teaching at the town's Catholic school have noticed a marked reduction in the lifespan of women in their order. An established average of ninety years has dropped to sixty. Five nuns have been killed by cancer; their average age was fifty.

Nine more have contracted cancer while another fourteen were to develop cysts and tumours. In 1983 the school was closed down. Meanwhile, Sister Bernadine, the Mother Superior, has developed skin cancer.

Such disconcerting statistics would normally lie buried in the records of local doctors and hospitals, without ever having any impact on public feeling. But this time there was a rare departure from the norm. A Canonsburg resident, Mrs Janis Dunn, increasingly concerned by the high incidence of cancer amongst her relatives, friends and neighbours, decided on a course of action rarely attempted by ordinary citizens when confronted by the harsh reality of the high-tech holocaust. Mrs Dunn decided to go beyond the narrow confines of her own personal tragedy in an effort to discover the true extent of the catastrophe that was overtaking her community. Her own family was evidence enough that something sinister was taking place: her mother-in-law had died of cancer, her sister-in-law had a breast removed and both her husband and brother-in-law had tumours treated by surgery. Mrs Dunn herself had a tumour removed from her uterus, had developed lumps on her legs and throat and suffered from a lung complaint as well as from problems linked to broken blood vessels. But this tragic record was, she found, just one small part of a pattern that was engulfing the entire town.

In forty-five households visited by Janis Dunn in the neighbourhood there were sixty-seven cases of cancer. In one small street of less than sixty residents there were twenty cancer victims. She told journalists: 'The national leukemia rate is three or four in 100,000. I found four cases in one street of only four houses.'[1] She also discovered a far-ranging pattern of other illnesses. Large numbers of young girls had fallen prey to menstrual problems and tumours in the reproductive organs. Lori Ewig was one of them. A classmate of Mark Humble, Lori was diagnosed as having cancer when she was nineteen; one of her ovaries and a Fallopian tube had to be removed. And amongst the townspeople as a whole there was an above average incidence of lung disorders, heart and blood conditions and allergies. This pattern could only be explained by the ominous conclusion that Canonsburg was afflicted by some terrible plague. For most local residents there is no question as to the nature of that plague. They unofficially gave the place a new name; these days they call it Radiation City.

Mortgaging the Future

Between 1942 and 1957 Canonsburg played a quiet role in the creation of the nuclear era. In the depths of wartime, local workers were paid sixty-nine cents an hour to handle radio-active waste from the Manhattan Project, the highly secret American-British-Canadian programme to develop an atomic weapon to defeat Hitler; in the end it would be used instead to destroy Hiroshima. Vast quantities of uranium were carted to Canonsburg to be processed and buried. In time, the land used to bury hundreds of tonnes of atomic debris from the Manhattan Project experiments was designated for normal use by the citizens of Canonsburg. One of the dump-sites was turned into a baseball pitch for the pupils at Mark Humble's school.

Analysis of the Canonsburg soil layer showed it to be dangerously radioactive. All soil is expected to have radioactive traces occurring in it naturally. In particular, radium and uranium would normally be present up to a level of about 2 picocuries per gram. In the Canonsburg samples the readings for radium-226 were as high as 21,800 picocuries per gram; the levels for concentrations of uranium reached as high as 51,000. Radon gas, which is produced by the radioactive decay of radium, also occurs naturally; in a town like Canonsburg it would normally exist at a level of about 0.3 picocuries per litre of air. Buildings around the dump-site recorded levels on average above 100 picocuries. Some readings made by scientists in the vicinity were more than seven hundred times greater than the usual background level.

Canonsburg is only one of more than twenty radioactive waste sites around the United States that have had to adjust to a terrifying legacy. And even these are only one small fraction of the global predicament. Wherever else in the world a nuclear industry is established – whether for energy or for weapons – the same radioactive legacy is being built up. By 1985, forty years after the birth of the nuclear age, there were some 528 nuclear power generating plants in existence or under construction around the world with a capacity for producing more than 400,000 megawatts of electricity.

Only ninety-five of the plants in operation by the mid-1980s, about twenty-seven per cent, are in the United States. The rest are dotted around the globe in some twenty-two countries, including in relatively small economies like Argentina, Korea and Taiwan. Over the second half of the 1980s countries such as

Egypt, Iran, Iraq, Libya, Turkey, Mexico, the Philippines and Romania could join this list if building programmes are completed. Indeed, the figures indicate that the growth of the world nuclear industry is only just beginning to take off.

By 1984 there were 346 nuclear plants in operation worldwide, excluding some smaller facilities. But another 182 were to be built over the period 1985 to 1990, adding another 173,000 megawatts to world generating capacity. This means that the decade of the 1980s will have seen more than 310 nuclear plants added to the world total, more than doubling their number in little more than ten years. Since building more nuclear plants inevitably leads to the generation of more radioactive waste, this huge jump in nuclear processing is creating an unprecedented situation for the 1990s and beyond. And because the health impact of radiation takes measurable effect only fifteen or twenty years after the beginning of the exposure pattern, this doubling of the world's radioactive turnover can be expected to yield a dramatic rise in radiation-related cancers and birth defects towards the end of the century.[2]

The nuclear process creates an open-ended problem that has no parallel in the history of technology. Radioactivity is a highly persistent, long-lived peril; it is profoundly stubborn in the face of efforts to dispose of it. Though vast loads of contaminated topsoil in Canonsburg were carted away and dumped elsewhere, the community itself has suffered irreparable, and incalculable, long-term damage. The peril has invaded their biochemistry, their genes, their future. And many dump-site communities do not even enjoy the advantage of being able to move the offending material elsewhere; it has already spread into the soil layers and sub-strata to percolate into the water cycle and thereby into domestic households.

Like any other energy-generating process, nuclear power plants produce waste. This can be, for example, in the form of spent fuel rods left from the fissioning activities in the reactor itself, or such things as radiation-contaminated tools, clothing, radioactive water pipes, walls, canisters, even vehicles used to transport radioactive material around the installation. A guideline to the amount of waste produced by a typical nuclear plant can be gauged from estimates related to the operation of a 1,000 megawatt pressurised water generator – common in the United States – over a twelve-month period.

About 180,000 tonnes of uranium ore will be used. This will

result in roughly 179,000 tonnes of uranium mill tailings. Then there will be the refining of about 272 tonnes of enriched uranium; this will create some 242 tonnes of refinery waste. Around 30 tonnes of enriched fuel will be needed over the year, resulting in about 29 tonnes of high-level waste in the form of spent fuel rods. A tonne of mixed plutonium isotopes will be used, producing about one-fifth of a tonne of plutonium waste.

Levels of waste produced by nuclear installations vary between types of reactor. In the pressurised heavy water design pioneered by the Canadians, for instance, less uranium ore is used but more reactor fuel is required. Thus, for a 1,000 MW station around 159 tonnes of high-level waste are created each year by this process, more than five times the level for the US-type reactor. On the other hand, only 144,000 tonnes of uranium mill tailings would be produced.

If we apply these figures to the global nuclear industry, assuming that the processes used are similar to either of these two systems, some stark results are obtained. A world nuclear capacity of around 400,000 megawatts could be estimated to produce something between 56 million and 72 million tonnes of uranium mill tailings a year and between 11,000 and 63,000 tonnes of high-level radioactive waste made up of spent fuel.

In addition, all nuclear plants produce waste products such as high-level liquid waste from the dissolving of fuel rods and other procedures as well as radioactive gases. Gases and most contaminated fluids are eventually released into the outside environment. Solid waste and highly contaminated fluids are stored. In both cases, however, the result is the same: radioactive substances are generated that are beyond the capacity of Man to destroy. And so long as they exist, these substances present a mortal danger.

There are three phases in the production of nuclear energy: fissioning, activation and ionisation. Fissioning refers to the splitting of uranium or plutonium atoms. This fissioning process – a violent transformation – produces radioactive fission fragments and activation products. These in turn release ionising radiation. Roughly three hundred different radioactive chemicals are produced by the fissioning stage. They remain unstable for up to hundreds of thousands of years or even longer, as measured by their half-life, which is literally the amount of time it takes for the radioactivity in a particular element to decay to half its original level. Plutonium 239, for instance, has a half-life of more than twenty-four thousand years. In sharp contrast, iodine 129 has a half-life of seventeen million years.

Though the fissioning activities take place inside the enclosures containing the fuel rods, with the fission products trapped mostly inside the rods themselves, activation products can be generated in the surrounding areas – in the air, pipes, water supply system and even in the building itself. After a period of time the installation itself becomes unusable and has to be dismantled, so creating a physically immense problem of radioactive waste disposal. This problem, however, is far greater even than that, for the entire concept of radioactive waste disposal begs a massive question.

To begin with, the term 'disposal' is highly misleading when applied to nuclear waste. It implies that we have the means of storing or destroying contaminated waste matter so that it can never pose a danger of releasing radioactive elements into the human habitat. We do not possess these means. Second, the manner in which we store or dispose of radioactive rubbish leaves serious doubts as to the way the different types of waste are categorised, for these different types pose varying levels of danger to humans and require distinct degrees of caution. What is 'high-level' waste, for example, when it comes to drawing lines of demarcation? Is it merely another way of saying 'a lot'?

Third, there is no universal agreement as to what constitutes a 'dangerous' level of radiation. How, in that case, can we arrive at universally acceptable methods of disposal when we cannot even ascertain to general satisfaction the exact point where a radioactive hazard becomes intolerably serious? There is also the ever-present threat of accidental release of radioactive materials into the local environment from operational plants as a result of leaks or other unforeseen events. Yet despite these uncertainties the world nuclear industry has continued to plan for long-term growth both in the number of installations and in overall electricity output, even though it has established no failure-proof technique for protecting the future. In this respect it shares in common with most other industrial sectors the irresponsible philosophy that when it comes to waste by-products, whether they be smoke or acid rain, toxic chemicals or radioactive trash, tomorrow never comes. Unfortunately, history is already showing this philosophy to be tragically wrong.

The Unthinkable Thought

Radiation has acquired an emotive connotation through its connection with nuclear weapons and the horrors of Hiroshima and
Nagasaki. As a result, the debate on radioactive waste (which is
produced by both military and civilian programmes on a ratio of
roughly 1 to 5) has been curiously distorted. The health risks to
workers in the asbestos, coal-mining and other extractive
industries, for instance, are equally great if seen from the
viewpoint of direct dangers to the individual concerned, either
through industrial accident or bodily pollution. A scanning of
the literature on industrial diseases generally will reveal a
horrifying catalogue of physical and mental ailments resulting
from involvement in certain hazardous activities. Many of these
activities can also have continuing effects on future generations
through genetic disorders or damage to the unborn child during
pregnancy.

Many industrial activities can also cause damage to humans
beyond the confines of the workplace by creating products that
are harmful to the health of the people who buy and use them.
The pharmaceutical industry, for example, can no longer claim
to be hazard-free in the light of the tragedies linked to drugs
such as Thalidomide, Opren and Debendox; the list has leng-
thened rapidly in recent years. The hazards raised by certain
additives in food are still, as yet, unknown, though many of them
have been shown to be cancer-causing to animals in laboratory
tests. In many other areas of economic activity there is a high
probability of risk to the well-being of the wider public. In a
number of key respects health hazards emanating from a
number of non-nuclear sources are, in the short-term at least, as
lethal as anything that could come from radioactive contamination. Nor is there any prospect that they will be curtailed this
side of the year 2000; they are built into the equation of everyday commercial practice. Moreover, most of these hazards –
unlike the relatively esoteric nuclear industry – apply on truly
worldwide scale and increasingly in developing countries where
industrial technologies are only now being introduced in a
comprehensive way.

But radiation is nevertheless different. What sets it apart
from other man-made perils, apart from its seemingly invisible
and all-pervading nature, is its association with nuclear holocaust and the threat of total extinction. Although the bulk of
radioactive waste is generated by the peaceful production of

electricity intended for the creation of wealth and comfort, it stems from an activity that was born of military necessity. Nuclear power continues to be linked in the popular mind with megadeath. It is perhaps ironic that the highest risks from radioactive rubbish come not, in fact, from the weapons programmes but from civilian power-generating operations, which produce potentially the most dangerous forms of radioactive waste.

The other irony is that the lessons learnt from the military use of atomic weapons, on Japan in 1945 and in weapons programmes since then, indicate that fall-out has killed and deformed many more people than were ever annihilated by direct blast. Rosalie Bertell, a cancer research scientist with a long and controversial academic reputation as an observer of the nuclear industry, has published estimates of fatalities that can be linked purely to radioactive contamination from weapons production and tests. While the combined death toll from actual blast following the obliteration of Hiroshima and Nagasaki was about three hundred thousand (both instantly and through injuries that later proved fatal), Bertell calculates that by the mid-1980s about thirteen million people around the world had fallen victim to radiation pollution related to fall-out from weapons programmes developed over the post-war years.[3]

According to Bertell's estimates, by 1985 the global nuclear weapons industry was claiming between seven thousand and fifteen thousand victims a year, or between twenty and forty a day. They have been contaminated, she argues, by radioactive fall-out from either producing and testing weapons or from waste. The figures range from embryonic, foetal and infant deaths to cancer victims and people suffering the consequences of genetic damage, including miners and nuclear workers whose radiation-induced conditions have never been officially recognised. This level of casualties, says Bertell, will continue even if no further weapons tests were to take place. By the end of the century the total number of radiation victims could have reached as high as twenty-two million.

Whatever the accuracy of Bertell's estimates, they are alarming if only because they are restricted solely to weapons-related radiation, since this is only a small proportion of the overall problem. It is true that the fall-out effects from a warhead explosion are more concentrated than those from the continuous emission of radioactive elements from a civilian operation, but only in the short term. Nuclear scientists agree that this difference is more than cancelled out by the slower decay rate of radioactivity produced by a reactor. A striking illustration of this can be obtained by looking at the otherwise horrifying implications of having a nuclear plant destroyed by a nuclear weapon.

Unthinkable though it might seem, analysts agree that an almost inevitable consequence of nuclear war would be the destruction of nuclear power stations. A surface burst on a nuclear reactor of a weapon even as small as 100 kilotons – only five times the size of the Hiroshima bomb and a pigmy compared to major nuclear warheads – would vaporise the entire facility and suck up its radioactive contents with the fireball. This radioactivity would be carried up with the mushroom cloud and absorbed into the overall concentration of fall-out. But here the similarity stops. The radioactivity from the nuclear installation would be different; its rate of decay would be slower, meaning that it would pose a far greater long-term threat.

To be more exact, it is estimated that an attack on a nuclear industry with an installed capacity of 850 gigawatts would result in a residual level of radioactivity one year later equivalent to that resulting from a war in which 30,000 megatons had been exploded – that is, three hundred thousand times the explosive power of the warhead used in the example cited above. The reason is that a bomb creates all its radioactivity in an instant, while a reactor produces it continually, since the decay of short-lived elements amongst the three hundred or so different nuclides usually results in the creation of longer-lived elements that accumulate in the reactor. This process is even more pronounced with waste fuel elements after they have been removed from the reactor and placed in storage tanks. The typical nuclear plant, therefore, can be described as a repository of long-lived radioactive elements waiting for an excuse to escape into the outside environment.[4]

It is for this reason, rather than the threat of regional nuclear war, that nuclear proliferation is a major concern. Every time a small country, with an unsophisticated industrial and technological tradition, decides to embark on a nuclear energy programme the world moves closer to its first cataclysmic radioactive accident. Even major nuclear powers with many years of experience in the construction and operation of reactor sites have difficulty in preventing dangerous leaks or averting calamity. The continuing saga of Sellafield – once known as Windscale – in north-east England is testament to the ever-present hazard of accidental discharges of radioactive elements into the surrounding countryside or offshore waters. The events at Sellafield in early 1986, when a serious leak of plutonium nitrate contaminated eleven plant workers (in one case delivering a dose of radiation equal to the maximum allowed over a twelve-month period), were only the latest in a long line of incidents stretching back to the early 1950s. And the crisis at the Three Mile Island reactor in the United States in 1979, when an average of 30,000 rads an hour were reported inside the containment building, was the closest yet to 'melt-down', or total disintegration of the reactor core. It is worth noting that anyone caught for two minutes inside the building would have experienced an exposure of 1,000 rads, a fatal dose if delivered to the whole body. Then came Chernobyl.

With these incidents in mind it is less than reassuring to learn, for example, that the government of Peru is erecting a 10 megawatt nuclear plant on a site at Huarangal less than twenty miles north of the capital, Lima. The site chosen lies in the middle of the main north-south earthquake zone that has produced so many disasters along the western littoral of the Americas in recent history. Though there has so far been no case of a nuclear facility being destroyed by earthquake, there is no reason to think that the longer-term radiation effects would be significantly different from those brought about by destruction with a nuclear warhead. In the case of Huarangal, hundreds of thousands of people living in the vicinity would be seriously contaminated and a vast acreage of land would be rendered uninhabitable for a century or more. And over that hundred-year period the world would be provided with deadly proof of the potency of radioactive waste, as a concerned planet turned to Peru, as it turned to Japan in 1945, as a huge laboratory test area for assessing the effects of radiation on humans. Except that this time the origins of the death and deformity would be entirely peaceful. Such an exercise, tragic though it might be, would undoubtedly confirm a large number of conclusions about the lethal impact of radiation on the human body.

The ABC of Death

Radioactive elements emit particles known as ionising radiation, an invisible emanation that consists of alpha and beta particles and gamma rays. Ionising radiation has the effect of upsetting or destroying the complex molecular structure of human cells and tissues, leading to a degenerative spiral. Once a human cell has been exposed to radiation its biochemical behaviour changes. The cell may cease to play its proper biochemical role. And though the body's protective mechanism may react to repair the damage, in some cases the invasion of the cell triggers off a chain of adverse effects. This chain may take many years to produce an observable effect, ranging from a skin condition to leukemia or other cancer.

Apart from ionising radiation, radioactive particles can be toxic for quite separate reasons. Radioactive lead, for instance, is associated with radon gas, which is given off during the mining of uranium; radioactive lead can produce lead poisoning and brain damage. Plutonium and radium are attracted to human bone: plutonium collects on the surface of the bone, passing on alpha radiation to the surrounding cells, while radium spreads its effects throughout the bone material and diffuses its impact. Hence plutonium is far more toxic to the human body.

Damage to the cells from radioactive particles that have penetrated to internal areas has a direct effect on organs in the immediate vicinity. Radionuclides reaching the bones can cause damage to the bone marrow and lead to leukemia and bone cancers. Radionuclides deposited in the lungs can produce diseases of the respiratory system. If the whole body is exposed the individual concerned can develop diseases reflecting innate medical weaknesses by accelerating inherent tendencies towards a certain illness. The ageing or degenerative processes can be speeded up.

Alpha and beta particles are the least potent in penetrating the human body. Alpha particles can be stopped by the skin, though the skin itself may be damaged as a result. Both alpha and beta particles find it easier to penetrate cell membranes; thus, ingesting (through food or drink) or inhaling radioactive elements that give off alpha or beta particles will carry them into direct contact with sensitive tissues in the lungs, brain, heart or kidneys. Here they present serious threats to the human bio-system. The most potent elements are neutrons, which are released when uranium atoms are split. Neutrons are microscopically small, but when they escape from a fission reaction they are capable of penetrating the body like invisible bullets; once inside they are amongst the most biologically destructive of all fission products. Though they have a relatively short range, they deserve to be feared to the utmost.

Once embedded within the living cell, ionising radiation is a virulent agent of destruction. Dr Karl Morgan, a noted specialist on radiation effects, describes its impact in terrifyingly simple terms. It is, he says, 'like letting a madman loose in a library'.[5] The result is either cell death or cell transformation; the changes can be either permanent or temporary. The cell may stop replacing itself; it might begin performing a different job, such as producing a hormone or enzyme that wasn't being produced before. It may not be long before millions of rampant cells are running riot in the affected area. One particular mutation highlighted by Rosalie Bertell is the destruction of the cell's capacity to rest, thus generating a proliferation of cells in one place that can lead to the formation of a tumour.

If radiation penetrates the reproductive system to affect the sperm or ovum, subsequent offspring may be damaged. Their children, in turn, will inherit the aberration and so on through successive generations. Eventually the line will come to an end through sterilisation or death; en route there could be horrendously deformed babies. If a pregnant mother is exposed to radiation the foetus itself can be seriously damaged. Radiation can even prevent a woman from conceiving by acting to reduce her fertility.

Research on various aspects of DNA and RNA functions – the fundamental components of living tissue – indicates that ionisation, or the random release into human cells of photons (X-rays and gamma rays) or alpha, beta or neutron particles, can lead to reduced tolerance to challenges to the body chemistry. If, for instance, the DNA of germ plasm is affected by radiation it can lead to chromosome disorders such as Down's Syndrome or mongolism. Hence, studies have revealed an abnormally high incidence of Down's Syndrome in Kerala in south India, a region known to have very high natural levels of radioactivity. In 1983 two women doctors researching into health trends in the Sellafield area close to Britain's troubled nuclear plant, discovered strong evidence linking chromosome abnormalities to man-made radiation. In the nearby village of Maryport they found that the incidence of Down's Syndrome was ten times the average; in every case the babies were born to young women with an average age of twenty-five, well below the age group regarded as at risk from chromosomal birth defects. And in every case the young mother had been either alive or about to be born at the time of the serious radioactive accident at the Sellafield site in 1957.

To convey some sense of the effects of differing levels of exposure to ionising radiation it is possible to tabulate the specific consequences of various doses. The dose levels are measured in rems – a rem being a unit of measurement that reflects both the quantity of radiation received by a person and the quality of that radiation in terms of the biological damage that it causes.

LIVING WITH THE NUCLEAR AGE
Health Effects of Differing Levels of Ionising Radiation

Dose (rems)	Immediate Effects	Delayed Effects
1000 or more	Frying of the brain; immediate death	None
600–1000	Debilitation; nausea; vomiting and diarrhoea. After temporary improvement more serious symptoms appear: fever, bleeding from bowels and generalised onset of haemorrhaging	Death in about ten days
250–600	Nausea; loss of hair; vomiting; diarrhoea; weakness; generalised bleeding from bowels, gums, genitals and other organs and membranes. Menstrual disorders. Serious destruction of bone marrow, lymph nodes and spleen leading to blood problems	Death within six weeks; survivors are seriously affected by tumours and other disorders
150–250	Nausea; vomiting; diarrhoea; skin burns. Later improvement but permanent damage to persons in poor health. If pregnant probable foetal or embryonic death	Susceptible persons will be seriously impaired. Other people may recover but might develop tumours and suffer shorter lifespan. Long-term genetic effects. Risk of deformed offspring
50–150	Acute radiation sickness; burns. Spontaneous abortion	Tissue damage; lowered resistance to infection.

Dose (rems)	Immediate Effects	Delayed Effects
	or stillbirth	Possible damage to offspring; tumours; premature ageing
10–50	Radiation sickness in sensitive people	Premature ageing; genetic effects; risk of tumours
0–10	None	Premature ageing; mild mutations in offspring; risk of tumours; genetic and teratogenic effects

SOURCE: Rosalie Bertell, *No Immediate Danger* (The Women's Press, 1985)

In the light of such details, culled from a variety of research studies (in particular those by Nobel Prizewinner Hermann Muller), it could be expected that governments running a nuclear programme on their territory would, by now, have arrived at a decision about what constitutes a dangerous dose of radiation. In fact, the exact opposite is the case: setting safety standards for levels of exposure has proved an elusive and unsatisfactory exercise. There is still no accepted international view as to where the line should be drawn.

A major problem is lack of precise data about the effects of ionising radiation on humans as opposed to observations made from working with laboratory animals. A recent report from the US National Academy of Science offers a blunt summary: '. . . a major obstacle continues to be the almost complete absence of information on radiation-induced genetic effects on humans. Hence we still rely almost exclusively on experimental data, to the extent possible from studies involving mammalian species [ie mice].'[6]

One approach has been to stipulate a 'permissible' dose, defining this as a level of exposure that produces an acceptable amount of adverse effects on the population. Thus, the code drawn up by the International Commission on Radiological Protection in 1959 put it this way: 'A permissible genetic dose [to sperm and ovum] is that dose [of ionising radiation] which if it were received yearly by each person from conception to the average age of childbearing [taken as thirty years] would result in an acceptable burden to the whole population.' And as Bertell points out, this is not a guideline to safety levels but rather a reference to the economic cost – the 'burden' – that a government is willing to bear for having radioactive pollution. In other words, a permissible dose is one that can be catered for by the nation's health and welfare services; the limit is set by the country's capacity to cope with genetic damage, cancer and radiation-induced ill-health.

As much was implied in other parts of the 1959 report from the ICRP, where it was made quite clear that a nuclear programme will result in radiation-linked diseases, the only thing at issue being the precise scale of the problem: 'The permissible doses can therefore be expected to produce effects that could be detectable only by statistical methods applied to large groups.' There was, nevertheless, an attempt made to set a figure; a further study by ICRP in 1965 concluded that the upper limit for public safety should be an exposure level of 5 rems over a thirty-year period. For workers in the nuclear industry itself the limit should be 5 rems each year. Perhaps the most surprising aspect of these guidelines is not that they are based on inadequate research data but that there is such a massive gap between safety limits proposed for the general public and those for people employed in nuclear plants; to be precise, the one limit is thirty times higher than the other.

There can be no more convincing evidence of the dangers of working with radioactive substances than the string of illustrious victims that have been claimed by ionising radiation. W. K. Roentgen, the inventor of the X-ray, was killed by bone cancer. Marie Curie and her daughter Irene, who led the way in X-ray applications, both died of aplastic anaemia, a condition directly linked to failure of the bone marrow. There were many cases of radiologists in the early days who were forced to have fingers or arms amputated. Even the women who were employed to paint the radium dials on luminous wrist-watches were overtaken by a wide range of ailments associated with radiation. And throughout those early years the exposure limits set by governments and international agencies were fixed by trial and error; there was never any assurance that those limits were entirely safe.

Indeed, as Rosalie Bertell records, the US authorities have consistently lowered the level for permissible doses as more evidence has come to light. In 1925 the limit for ionising radiation was given as 52 roentgen (X-ray) per year. In 1936 the US government dropped it to 36. In 1949, with the evidence of Hiroshima and Nagasaki to hand, Washington brought the limit sharply down to 15 rems per year. In 1959 a 5 rems per year limit was set, with the safety point rising to 12 rems according to age group and the time span for exposure.

The 5 rems limit has become the consensus figure amongst a large number of nuclear officials, although there is still confusion over whether workers should be allowed to face constant levels of exposure over many years. To add further confusion, the ICRP issued, in 1959, a set of guidelines about safe levels of exposure to different parts of the body. The guidelines were nothing if not specific:

- 5 rems per year to the whole body, gonads or active bone marrow
- 30 rems per year to bone, skin or thyroid
- 75 rems per year to hands, arms, feet or legs
- 15 rems to all other parts of the body

There was, nevertheless, a high degree of ambiguity about how these limits should be applied. Some managements have interpreted the guidelines so as to permit workers to receive up to 5 rems internally and a further 5 rems externally over the year. Other recommendations allowed nuclear plant operators to average the doses received from an age baseline of eighteen years, thus making it possible to justify radiation doses considerably higher than those applicable if the calculations were based on a full life-span. Meanwhile, the ICRP recommended that the general public should be exposed to a maximum of one-tenth this figure.

To increase the degree of confusion even more, in 1978 the ICRP, in an attempt to introduce consistency into the figures for recommended safe levels, actually raised the limits. Under their new guidelines the permitted bone marrow dose was increased nearly ninefold to 42 rems. One reason given for this was the rather alarming one of allowing the nuclear industry more freedom; by raising the limits, said the Commission, the industry would be more able to provide economic and social benefits to the community without the constraints of strict safety regulations.[7]

A Matter of Convenience

This confusion over what is, or is not, a safe dose of radiation is crucial to the entire debate about nuclear accidents and nuclear waste. It is obvious that until clearly defined and rigorously tested safety rules are agreed, the industry is operating in the dark and the health of millions is overshadowed by the most sinister threat ever invented by science. Yet even the most recent evidence confirms that the confusion continues. Some of the most damning of this recent evidence has come to light in the course of the public inquiry over the plans to import and build a pressurised water reactor at Sizewell in the English county of Suffolk. Typical of many illuminating exchanges between counsel and expert witnesses is the following (taken from the transcript of the proceedings), in this case involving a government specialist from the Department of the Environment. It deals with the vital issue of the different kinds of hazard posed by various categories of radioactive waste:

Q: 'The position now is, is it not, twenty-seven years after opening Calder Hall, that there are well-established routes for the disposal of what the Department describes as low-level wastes?'

A: 'Yes, though I think one should be aware of circularity in the language. Low-level waste, by our definition, is that of which one can dispose, so it would be equally true to say there are some grades of waste of very limited radioactivity which can now be disposed of and those are, for our convenience, referred to as low-level wastes.'

Q: 'Now, we are getting into an area where confusion is fast reaching chaos, so far as parties to the Inquiry are concerned. It has been brought to my attention that since you gave evidence last week people are now more confused rather than less confused in an area in which I think the Department has said it is essential for the public to understand what is being done . . .'

A: 'First of all, I do not think I can give you an explanation of why the Central Electricity Generating Board or any other part of the nuclear industry uses whatever definition it uses. However, I can talk about the Department of the Environment's definitions.'

The Department of the Environment did, of course, have its own views on the subject of differing kinds of waste, but the lack of broad agreement within the industry itself, as testified by senior civil servants such as the one quoted above, is hardly reassuring. Meanwhile, the Sizewell Inquiry also brought out that the official line is challenged even by other parts of the British administrative machine. Included in the Sizewell evidence was a report prepared by the Association of County Councils, the local bodies responsible for many of the emergency services that would be involved in any radioactive incident. Their report summarised the accumulated doubts of many county authorities across the country:

'Although there is a definition of what is or is not radioactive, there is far less clarity about the precise meaning of low, intermediate and high-level waste. As a result there tends to be a reaction to all such material as a single (and frightening) class of "radioactive".'[8]

The response to this by the Department of the Environment official, meanwhile, suggested that a more precise policy on definitions was almost certainly a long way off: 'We shall need a progressively more exact definition and, of course, it will have to be public . . . but the timing of doing this needs to be judged and one may need to do it by stages and develop the classifications more precisely according to the practical needs of the management operations of the time. It certainly is a job that will need to be done and it will need to be publicly done, but the Department of the Environment has no intention of doing it in the very near future.'[9]

But even more disconcerting was evidence heard at the Sizewell Inquiry of views held by Britain's Central Electricity Generating Board about where the dividing line between differing sorts of waste should be fixed; this divide is a vital ingredient of any sensible programme of radioactive waste disposal. According to Dr Flowers from NIREX, the waste-disposal executive set up by the nuclear industry, that dividing line is blurred: 'The distinction between intermediate and low-level waste is an arbitrary one based on the proportion of radio-active material to non-radioactive material in the waste. It is convenient to refer to that waste that is so dilute that it may be safely buried at shallow depth . . . as low-level waste. In so doing we exclude the even more dilute wastes which . . . may be disposed of as ordinary refuse.'[10]

According to a British government report on radioactive waste management, published in July 1982, the amount of low-level nuclear waste already disposed of in Britain by that time was 35,000 cubic metres. The report estimated that by the end of the century this cumulative figure would reach about 70,000 cubic metres. In the light of this massive increase in the scale of the problem, it would seem good sense that the waste-disposal programme is operated under clear guidelines about categories, methods of disposal and the exact geographical siting of the radioactive dumps. As the published evidence shows most convincingly, there are no such clear rules; Britain's radioactive legacy is dealt with on the grounds of convenience as much as on strict considerations of safety.

More disconcerting still, the figures given for the years up to 2000 are seriously misleading; they omit estimates of the radioactive wastes that will be produced by the closing down – or decommissioning – of nuclear plants. With the older generation of nuclear installations now reaching the end of their active lives, not merely in Britain but in many countries with established nuclear traditions, this decommissioning process will create vast amounts of radioactive debris over the years ahead. Radioactive crunch point is rapidly approaching, with little progress made towards a waste-disposal policy that can protect our future. A more realistic guideline to Britain's future waste problem was offered by a report from a parliamentary committee on radioactive waste published in March 1986. It showed the dominant role in boosting waste volumes played by the reprocessing of spent fuel, giving total figures up to the year 2030.

The Nuclear Legacy
Volumes of Treated Radioactive Waste By Source
(cubic metres)

	Low Level	Int. Level	High Level
Reprocessing	750,000	117,000	2,600
Power Stations	165,000	40,900	—
Research, Medical, Industrial	75,300	31,000	800

SOURCE: First Report of the House of Commons Environment Committee on Radioactive Waste, March 1986

Public ignorance about the issue is heightened by the self-evident complexity of the subject and by confusion over the vocabulary used, as illustrated by the Sizewell example. To begin with, radioactive waste falls into a number of categories. First, it can be classified by phase, in other words whether it is solid, liquid or gas. Second, there is the matter of its origin: is it spent fuel, operational waste from a working reactor or decommissioning waste? Third, it could be classified by its activity –

that is, by the amount of radioactivity per cubic metre. Fourth, what is its radioactive lifetime? And what is its destination in terms of the disposal site ultimately used?

A more common classification, however, is the one already referred to in the Sizewell case, namely a sub-division into low, intermediate and high-level waste. This approach is the one used in Britain, which has the unenviable reputation of having one of the worst safety records of any nuclear fraternity in the world. Certainly, it relies on a hybrid of differing classifications (chiefly activity and destination) to arrive at a decision as to category, without any clear rules about how much weight should be attached to separate characteristics. For this reason, the British experience is an instructive one in highlighting the serious inadequacy of existing techniques for disposing of nuclear rubbish.

Under current British official guidelines, low-level waste is made up of such items as dilute gases and liquids and solid wastes comprising such things as paper, plastic bags, clothing and building materials. Under British practice the gases and liquids may be discharged by nuclear plants directly into the environment. Low-level solid wastes may be buried in shallow trenches or dumped at sea. In addition, some items of very dilute radioactive waste are allowed to be disposed of along with ordinary garbage alongside, say, material from office waste-paper bins.

The intermediate-level category falls into two parts, with differing degrees of hazard. Intermediate-level short-lived waste has a higher level of activity than low-level waste but does not contain a high proportion of alpha-emitting elements like plutonium. This category usually consists of solid and semi-solid materials contaminated by contact with highly radioactive components; it includes glove boxes, process cabinets, resins and other equipment. Intermediate-level long-lived waste is invariably radioactive debris which has been heavily contaminated with alpha-emitting particles such as plutonium and other highly dangerous transuranic substances – the term transuranic referring to an element with a higher atomic number than uranium.

High-level waste, as its description strongly implies, is intensely radioactive. It results from spent fuel taken from nuclear reactors, usually spent fuel rods or liquids left over from fuel reprocessing activities. High-level waste like this produces great quantities of heat and needs to be cooled constantly. There is also a requirement to treat high-level liquid wastes in order to solidify them for greater ease of storage.

Whatever the definitions used, any nuclear programme in any country is likely to generate categories of waste similar to these. In Britain the scale of the problem is made greater however, by the existence of major reprocessing plants which also take radioactive material from other countries. The troubled installation at Sellafield is one such facility. More serious is the accusation that the definitions are abused by diluting higher level wastes so that they qualify under a less hazardous category. The dilution principle is regularly used in British plants to the point where highly toxic materials are mixed in with low-level waste and then discharged into the environment or buried in shallow – many would say inadequately so – trenches in the countryside. The people of Canonsburg, Pennsylvania, can testify to the dangers of this technique.

But definitions apart, the overriding doubts are those surrounding the methods that have been adopted by an increasingly waste-afflicted nuclear industry around the world for the disposal of its hazardous by-products. It is not an exaggeration to say that radioactive waste disposal is the Cinderella of the nuclear business: in no other high-tech activity is such a sophisticated process accompanied by waste-disposal methods of truly primitive proportions. No other hazardous sector of modern industry has waste policies that are so demonstrably insufficient to match the intensity of danger.

For the more hazardous radioactive wastes, those that cannot be simply dumped straight into the environment (although even these wastes give rise to considerable concern amongst many analysts), there are two possible disposal routes, on land or at sea. The more bizarre solution of ejecting nuclear waste materials into outer space has also been considered but, for the moment at least, this path has not been further explored. Considering the likelihood of an accident to waste-carrying rockets on the launching pad or close to earth, this would appear to be a remote possibility, though the thought is a chilling one. Another solution examined has been a rock-melting technique, where hot liquid or solid wastes are poured into cavities or drill-holes reaching down several miles into rock strata; the heat from the waste would then melt the surrounding rock, thus embedding it in the deep subterranean layers. Some specialists have suggested that canisters could be buried in thick polar ice sheets, possibly allowing the hot containers to melt their way downwards.

The existing options are therefore strictly limited, with land-based disposal the more common choice, though the tragedy of Canonsburg has demonstrated the serious risks that attend the burial of radioactive wastes on land. Nevertheless, the practice of land disposal persists, chiefly because there seems to be no alternative. Yet, when the highly disturbing nature of the attendant risks of land disposal are considered, the apparent languor in seeking a safer method seems incomprehensible, if not seriously negligent.

Land-based methods are favoured for the disposal of highly radioactive and heat-generating spent fuel. Before such materials are disposed of it is necessary to allow a long period for cooling; in the US such wastes would be left to cool for at least ten years, in Sweden for about forty. The concept relies on the burying of metal containers in caverns and tunnels, excavated out of deep rock formations using orthodox mining techniques. After the burial is completed, the underground chambers and the access points to the surface would then be backfilled and sealed. The depth would range between 1,600 and 3,600 feet.

How many such underground dumps will be needed is directly connected, of course, to the size of a country's nuclear programme, the state of its decommissioning timetable and the nuclear technology that is being used; all three affect the precise amount of waste produced. There is also the factor of imported waste to be considered. A rough guide comes from comparing Swedish plans with the probable needs of a large nuclear economy. Sweden's relatively small nuclear programme will require about nine thousand waste canisters and one granite-based repository by the second decade of the twenty-first century. Sweden's waste-disposal task is related to a generating infrastructure of twelve reactor plants with a total capacity of about 9,500 megawatts.

The US programme, in massive contrast, relies on more than 130 plants and a total capacity of nearly 130,000 megawatts, almost fourteen times larger than the Swedish nuclear sector. And Britain, France, West Germany and Japan between them represent a combined total of about 175 installations, with a collective generating capacity of more than 128,000 megawatts. The world nuclear sector, meanwhile, has an overall capacity of

403,000 megawatts from nearly 530 nuclear plants, excluding those reactors smaller than 30 megawatts. Applying a very crude comparative yardstick, Sweden accounts for little more than two per cent of the global total of nuclear-generated megawattage. If this country's tiny group of reactors is expected to produce nine thousand canisters of highly hazardous waste over the next thirty-five years, a world figure for this same period (assuming all countries adopt deep burial as the disposal technique) might be at least three hundred and eighty thousand potential nuclear time bombs.

It is these canisters, using stainless steel, copper or lead to separate and isolate the contaminated materials, that will be committed to the earth for eternity. The central principle is that potentially dangerous materials are thereby locked away from living organisms for thousands of years. But while the principle itself might seem, at first glance, to be a sensible one, the geological rationale supporting it is seriously flawed.

To begin with, the safe disposal of radioactive waste underground means that we are trusting that the actions of Nature and of humankind remain stable and predictable for thousands of years into the future. A sense of how great the time factors are in the nuclear issue can be gauged by remembering that the 'natural' nuclear reactors at Oklon in Gabon, made up of naturally radioactive rocks, started generating low levels of power some two billion years ago. The fission reactions involved lasted for more than half a million years producing about 100 billion kilowatt hours worth of energy, all of which was dissipated into the surrounding rock. Such time scales are gargantuan compared to the life-span of the human race on earth. The cultural development of homo sapiens, for instance, began at the end of the Ice Age only ten thousand years ago. By way of comparison, the toxic potency of spent reactor fuel will exceed naturally present radioactivity for at least the same length of time; the radioactive life cycle thus dwarfs the human experience.

So what chances are there that those deeply buried canisters will spill their deadly contents into the soil and thereby into the free environment, leaching into rivers, lakes and oceans and entering the human food cycle? More important, could this occur within a foreseeable period of time, while the wastes themselves are at their most hazardous?

A first observation is that rock strata are not, themselves, impenetrable layers. The kind of hard rock that might be favoured for deep-burial sites – such as granite, volcanic layers and basalt – contains myriad natural fractures, joints and fissures. Sedimentary rocks such as limestone and sandstone, built up over the millennia by deposition, have voids and pores through which water can carry particles in solution. Within these rock layers there is a vast quantity of groundwater, the subterranean part of the natural water system that we usually see only as cloud, rain and surface water channels feeding into lakes and seas.

The second factor is related to this groundwater system. Rock has the property of being able to transmit water through its mass – the so-called 'hydraulic conductivity' effect. Thus, any material introduced into an underground area will, if it is released into open rock strata, be dispersed through the groundwater system of fractures, pores and other conduits. The only way in which radioactive waste could become hazardous to living things is if it is transported up to the surface by circulating groundwaters. And the only way in which the waste itself can be released into the groundwater system is if the canisters are damaged by earthquake, or similar ground movement, or through corrosion by chemicals or other agents. The proponents of deep-burial methods of nuclear waste disposal insist that canisters could never be damaged in this way and that their lethal contents will remain intact for the indefinite future. The evidence of the past few years, however, points the other way.

A Deadly Migration

The waste package is made up of the radioactive waste itself, the canister in which it is stored and the crushed rock or clay which is packed around the canister to fix it into the drill-hole. The moment the canisters are in place, water will begin to penetrate this backfill material. The outer wall of the canister will eventually become saturated. As soon as water comes into contact with the metal outer-casing of the canister it will begin to corrode. The speed at which this corrosion occurs will depend on such variables as the amount of water present, its chemical make-up and the surrounding temperature. But it is inevitable that in time the water will work through the metal and reach the radioactive waste material. The waste, which will probably have been converted into a glassy substance by the disposal authorities prior to its original storage, will slowly dissolve.

The clay layers that are preferred for underground disposal sites will inhibit the flow of waste-contaminated groundwater. With other factors also acting to slow the progress of radionuclides to the surface, it would normally take several thousand years for radioactive particles to reach the outside environment in this way. And it is upon this supposition that official estimates of safety margins are based. Unfortunately, Nature does not always play by the official rules. Sometimes, the unexpected can intervene.

One danger is that a waste depository area could be disrupted by a major fault resulting from a fracture developing along a line of weakness. This line of weakness could have been caused by movements generated during Ice Age readjustments which are invisible to geological examination. If such a fracture were to occur, deep-flowing groundwater would be brought in direct contact with the water system closer to the surface. If any of the canisters had been damaged by the same faulting process, the radioactive debris would be caught up by hydraulic action and introduced into the surface water system which feeds the drinking water supply network.

Besides such geological events, there is also the possibility that deep repositories will be disturbed by earthquake. Such disturbances are frequent occurrences in deep zones of weakness in the earth's crust. Major earthquake belts around the world include the entire western littoral of the Americas, running from the Rockies in the north to the Andes in the south, and a broad band of vulnerable zones stretching from the western Mediterranean eastwards through the Gulf to the Far East, with branches running north and south taking in the east coast of Africa, central USSR, the China coast and down into Australasia.

Even apparently earthquake-free zones are at constant risk. Britain, for instance, is generally considered to be free from earth tremors; this belief is one reason why the anti-waste lobby in the country has not had greater success. Yet the geological data show that many regions of the UK are prone to quite serious earthquakes. In July 1984, for example, the west coast of Britain and the Irish Republic experienced an earth tremor that recorded 5.5 on the Richter Scale. The tremor, described by the Global Seismology Unit in Edinburgh as 'pretty big for Britain', occurred around the same marine basin that also plays host to the major reprocessing plant at Sellafield on the Cumbrian coast.

In addition, there is the risk of underground dump-sites being burst open by meteorites, drilling and tunnelling by unwitting contractors searching for water, minerals or geothermal energy sources, and by an unending list of other human activities ranging from weapons testing to underground exploration. The short life-span of the nuclear waste industry to date has given us very limited exposure to these sundry dangers, yet already there is a track record of alarming proportions. The US experience, for one, shows that deep burial has a nasty habit of rebounding.

Across the United States there are currently fourteen military disposal sites for low-level waste, together with three commercially operated sites. Three other commercial sites have already been closed following worries over safety standards; it is these three cases that give a hint of possible things to come.

● In 1972 the Department of Human Resources in the State of Kentucky discovered that samples of water taken from the area around a low-level waste site at Maxey Flats showed high readings of radioactivity. After a study of the problem the Department decided that no danger existed. These findings were confirmed in a later study by the US Nuclear Regulatory Commission. In 1976, however, after increasing pressure from local residents the State legislature set a punitive ten cents per pound tax on waste being processed at the site; the facility was made uncommercial and was closed.

● In 1975 the New York authorities found increased levels of tritium in water samples after reports of seepage at a nuclear waste-disposal site at West Valley. The site was closed down pending a solution to the seepage danger.

● In 1979 a low-level waste site at Sheffield in Illinois was closed after mounting discontent amongst local residents. The State attorney general accepted local concern about safety around the site.

In all three cases there had been claims by monitoring groups that there had been water infiltration down into the waste trenches from the surface. At West Valley in New York, the clay trench covers were increased from four to eight feet after this discovery. Nevertheless, water continued to infiltrate the waste burial areas. Indeed, the US experience is that water infiltration and erosion are serious whenever sites are located in regions of high rainfall.

More disturbingly, the evidence from the United States indicates that concrete covers fare no better, for as the steel drums inside the trenches begin to corrode and move, the concrete covers collapse downward into the void created. Since steel drums are likely to have a lifetime of no more than between thirty and fifty years (less than one-sixth the hazardous lifetime of the waste stored inside them), this kind of problem will prove to be a constant concern. Moreover, water can enter trenches not only through the covers – clay, concrete or whatever – but through the trench walls. If, for example, the burial medium is intersected by sandy formations, these can act as conduits for large amounts of water flowing into the trench from the sides. The site at Sheffield, Illinois, was closed for precisely this reason after the US Geological Survey found sandy layers running through the area; these layers had not been pinpointed by core drillings made prior to the location there of a nuclear waste dump.

On the other hand, because of its impermeable qualities, clay is attractive to the nuclear industry as a dump-site medium. But the evidence questions this confidence. When the weather becomes abnormally dry, clay can shrink or develop fissures and cracks. More to the point, these channels appear at the upper levels, above the water table that would otherwise keep the clay strata moist. It is precisely at these upper levels that waste deposit trenches are located. Once the clay develops such cracks they may become permanent. Geological studies show that these cracks can run considerable distances vertically, linking up with water-carrying sandy formations to create a vast underground water network along which radioactive migrations can take place.

And it is not only geology that can cause problems of seepage into the environment. The US waste-disposal site at Beatty, in Nevada, was not closed following the revelation in the late 1970s that workers at the site were taking contaminated equipment and tools away from the facility, though in 1979 the site was temporarily closed after evidence that radioactive waste shipments coming to Beatty were poorly packaged. Either way the tale is not particularly comforting.

Many of these issues were to be encapsulated in the saga of West Valley, already referred to as a trouble spot for the nuclear waste industry. It is a saga that illustrates how that industry has evolved by trial and error over the years, despite the serious nature of its task. The West Valley site was originally opened in 1966 for the reprocessing of commercial waste. By 1972, two carbon-steel tanks filled with 600,000 gallons of high-level liquid waste were located there. But from the start the plant was plagued by doubts. First, studies showed that workers at the site were being subjected to dangerous amounts of radiation. Exposure readings reached as high as 7.15 rems, nearly fifty per cent greater than the permissible level of 5 rems per year, which itself is contested by critics as an unsafe limit. Then, a few years later, it became known that the reprocessing plant had been located near an active earthquake fault. As a result, the operating company declared itself bankrupt and abandoned the facility. The huge underground storage tanks were left behind. They are expected to last between thirty and thirty-five years. Unfortunately, the waste abandoned at West Valley is expected to stay radioactive for upwards of several million years.

If either of the tanks had sprung a leak there would have been serious contamination of the surrounding areas. Concentrations of radioactive liquid would have been released into creeks feeding into Lake Erie, upstream of fresh water supplies to about one million residents in the city of Buffalo. In all more than eleven million people in the region would have been at risk from contaminated drinking water. In 1982 the federal authorities began a pilot programme to see whether the West Valley waste could be solidified and carted away to a more secure dump-site. And West Valley, over which there is still a question mark, is only one small corner of a rapidly escalating problem across the world.

At Cap de la Hague in Normandy, on the Atlantic coast of France, events were to be far more dramatic. In 1976, workers at the local reprocessing plant took to fasting in the nearby village church in an effort to draw attention to the mounting hazard posed by apparent weaknesses in the construction of the facility. The dispute had been triggered by fears of contamination, following a gas explosion caused by overheating of water tanks at the la Hague site. The protest cast light on serious radioactive dangers for people living in the vicinity.

The plant had a chequered history of broken pipes, leaking valves and collapsing boilers. The number of cases of contaminated workers rose sharply from 280 in 1973 to 572 in 1975; and these are only the official figures, which exclude unnoticed contamination that may produce adverse effects sometime in the future. In the summer of 1976, there was a serious incident which added further to local fears and increased tension amongst the workforce at the plant. The government reacted by handing the plant over to private enterprise. But the move did not prevent the facts of death at la Hague seeping out to the wider world.

The story of la Hague is set out in clinical detail in Robert Jungk's book, *The New Tyranny*.[11] Jungk had already explored the rise of the nuclear era in a previous work, *Brighter Than a Thousand Suns*.[12] His new study was to make less optimistic reading. Operatives at la Hague testified to the serious health consequences of their employment at the plant. They had dubbed themselves 'radiation fodder' and saw themselves as expendable units in an inhuman industry. They also confirmed the worst fears held by local inhabitants about living next door to the la Hague installation.

Two aspects of the la Hague facility had caused consternation from the start. A 300ft high chimney towered over the land-scape, while a long pipe was known to run out to sea from the inner depths of the reprocessing plant. The tall chimney would disperse hazardous gases into the upper atmosphere, while the pipe would carry dangerous liquid wastes far out into the ocean. That, at least, was the theory. The reality was to prove otherwise.

After an accident in the late 1960s, the French authorities had to buy up all milk supplies in the area. A famous brand of butter produced locally – known as *beurre de la Hague* – took on a totally different brand image and suffered a sudden decline in market appeal. Its name had to be changed to the less evocative *beurre de Val de Saire*. Meanwhile, local fishermen were beginning to notice that their fish were turning black; govern-ment studies revealed that their catch showed five times more radioactivity than fish caught a few miles along the coast. And local residents, by now seriously alarmed, sought help from sympathetic scientists. Their researches showed that land in the la Hague area was contaminated by radiation up to twenty times greater than the legally allowed limit. Other studies pointed out that about two hundred deaths per thousand in the region were due to cancer, a rate that was some fifty per cent greater than in a different region further along the littoral.

Nevertheless, la Hague continues to handle an ever-growing intake of radioactive waste, including increasing amounts from abroad. Like Sellafield in Britain, la Hague is contracted to deal with waste sent from countries ranging from Argentina and Iraq to West Germany and Japan. Large amounts of contaminated debris is disposed of at la Hague by methods now in widespread use throughout the fast-growing nuclear waste industry, namely by packing the radioactive material in concrete and steel containers and then burying it. According to one report, the most dangerous of this waste is stored at la Hague beneath the floor of a low building a few hundred yards from the main installation. Because of the hazardous nature of this repository the drums have to be replaced every thirty to forty years, while the building has to be kept air-conditioned to prevent the steel containers melting to a point where they release their lethal contents. Meanwhile, butter from local dairy farms continues to grace the tables of many millions of households across Europe, though now it carries a more reassuring label.[13]

Such problems are associated with waste emanating from power-generating installations still in current use. An even bigger problem is posed by the legacy about to descend on the international community as a result of nuclear obsolescence. In 1984 it was estimated that there were more than one hundred nuclear reactors around the world close to the end of their productive lives. Over the years to the end of this century, they will be decommissioned and dismantled. This exercise will yield an enormous burden in the shape of highly contaminated buildings and reactor equipment. About twenty test and research reactors now approaching close-down are in developing countries, where facilities for safe waste disposal are even less in evidence.

While the nuclear industry is more than half a century old, it has shown itself inadequate in its capacity to protect us from the danger of radioactivity. From Canonsburg to Chernobyl, from la Hague to West Valley, the construction and operation of nuclear plants have been shown to be less than adequate to the task of keeping hazardous radionuclides away from humans. In the disposal of radioactive waste the failings are even greater. Yet this waste problem is only in its infant stage; we have only seen the merest glimpse of what could lie ahead.

As if in ironic gesture, the fortieth anniversary of Hiroshima and Nagasaki seemed to mark a new chapter in the history of that nuclear danger. As 1986 opened, the Sellafield plant (whose operating company was successfully prosecuted in 1983 for excessive discharges) renewed its claim to be one of the worst sources of nuclear pollution. Within the space of four weeks, there were three serious incidents and a disclosure of alarming details about an earlier radioactive episode. On January 23 a faulty evaporator sent 440 kilograms of uranium into the sea tank and from there into the Irish Sea. In early February there was an 'amber alert' at the plant after a jet of compressed air made contact with liquid containing plutonium, thereby creating a radioactive mist that caught at least fifteen people in its path. Less than two weeks later a pipe cracked; 250 gallons of radioactive liquid poured out.

Assurances from the plant operators as to the minor nature of these events fell on stony ground: they were made as stories appeared in the press that radically changed the facts about earlier leaks at Sellafield. It emerged that between 1952 and 1955 the amount of radioactive waste discharged by the plant was about forty times greater than the level notified to an inquiry team that had been looking into the incidence of leukemia in the surrounding area. It is not so much the fact that this newly discovered detail alters views about the link between radiation and cancer, but rather that the flow of information about nuclear mishaps is seriously impaired. For Sellafield is but one example in a steadily growing catalogue of misinformation, unfounded assurances and cant.

Not without reason was the British nuclear waste industry condemned by a House of Commons committee report in March 1986 as 'amateurish and haphazard', especially when compared with more rigorously administered waste-disposal systems used elsewhere; although these too have their failings. The report described visits by concerned Members of Parliament to the dump-site at Drigg, near Sellafield. There they found rainwater running through trenches filled with radioactive rubbish, and from there into the River Irt and on into the Irish Sea. They also discovered that the waste was not packaged or labelled and that some material that otherwise would fall outside the 'low level' category was buried there, on the principle that it would be dispersed and diluted over a long period if it happened to escape. After more than forty years of experience in dealing with radioactive hazards, such complacency is an alarming indictment of the learning capacities of science.

A Geography of Fear

With the nuclear industry, as with all activities in this industrial age, the most pervasive problem is the problem of waste. And as we have seen, so far the nuclear industry has met the challenge by contaminating the oceans and bequeathing to future generations the unenviable job of standing sentinel over a proliferating pattern of depositories around the world, both underground and offshore. Henceforth, every earthquake, landslip, hurricane, flood and tidal wave has to be looked at with more wary eyes. Has it disturbed a deadly consignment, or ripped asunder a radioactive pile? Every region playing host to a nuclear plant or waste-disposal site must now be classified as having a distinct geography . . . the geography of fear.

Nor is this geography made up only of a number of fixed points spread across the nuclear map. As the dilemma of handling radioactive fuels and waste has intensified it has brought with it another, equally fearsome, possibility. What if there is an accident involving one or more of the rail or road transports that cart nuclear materials and contaminated detritus across the countryside, to the reactor plant, from the reactor site to the reprocessing facility, or from either of these to a disposal area? Considerable quantities of nuclear waste are also transported by sea as part of the international trade in waste treatment and disposal. All these transportation routes are vulnerable to the usual hazards of collision, mechanical mishap and sinking, without even considering the increasingly likely possibility of terrorist attack or hijack. And as the nuclear industry expands into every corner of the globe and the scale of waste disposal increases immeasurably over the later years of the twentieth century, the odds against disaster will shorten.

In France, which has the second largest nuclear industry in the world, the number and tonnage of movements of irradiated fuel have been increasing steadily. Because of the French choice of pressurised water and uranium-enriched reactors as the basis of their nuclear power programme, the irradiated fuel produced as a waste by-product is noted for its high level of activity. It is transported to the much-criticised reprocessing facility at la Hague. Because of the rapid expansion of the French nuclear sector the capacity of the la Hague installation is being increased; by 1991 it will be able to deal with 1,600 tonnes of radioactive material a year, an eightfold expansion of throughput in less than ten years. Since most of this throughput comes from other nuclear reactors, this massive growth in business for la Hague also represents a marked increase in the transportation of hazardous irradiated material around France. French government sources calculate that between 1983 and 1989 la Hague will deal with some 6,600 tonnes of irradiated fuel. Moving this immense radioactive burden requires an average of more than one hundred shipments by road and one hundred and thirty by rail every year. The road shipments involve huge containers weighing up to 80 tonnes, those by rail usually involve one or more 100 tonne containers loaded with 6 tonnes of irradiated fuel. Clearly, as the volume of French nuclear waste increases over the years ahead in keeping with official plans, the number and size of these shipments will grow significantly. And each shipment of hazardous radioactive by-products will be a hostage to fortune.

In the United States, home of the world's largest nuclear waste problem, developments such as the Canonsburg saga have made people doubly aware of the danger. But this concern is likely to grow steadily over the years ahead as the magnitude of the waste-disposal task itself increases dramatically. Until recently, spent fuel shipments in the US were modest, of the order of three hundred journeys a year. This low figure has been due to the reliance on certain practices followed by the nuclear power utilities, as well as the fact that fuel reprocessing in the United States has been at modest levels compared to the widespread existence of this activity in places like Britain. Most commercial spent fuel has been kept in water storage pools at reactor sites. But government officials admit that the evolution of the US nuclear industry is moving towards a massive escalation in the need to transport waste; federal studies predict that the number of nuclear transports will increase from several hundred to many thousands a year by the end of the century due to the expansion of the US nuclear power network from sixty plants to one hundred and fifty. This dramatic rise in truck movements began in the mid-1980s and will, the studies estimate, increase at the rate of around five hundred shipments every twelve months to 9,000 a year by 2005.

Nor is the apparent sophistication of the US system a guarantee that storage and transportation practices are failure-proof. A draft study from the National Academy of Sciences, written in 1981, described US regulations covering movements of spent fuel as 'primitive'.[14] Due to the reluctance of US rail companies to carry spent fuel, most shipments go by truck. The US nuclear authorities have set standards for protection against the effects of rail accidents based on the impact created by a 30ft drop, the equivalent of a crash occurring at 30 mph. But the main weight of waste transportation will continue to be borne by trucks. Indeed, the allegation of 'primitive' standards applied principally to the road-based alternative. And here the outlook is not conducive to public calm.

The 1981 study predicted serious 'impasses' between state and federal authorities as the number of truck shipments escalates. It estimated that some 75,000 nuclear cargoes would be passing across state lines over the medium-term future. The study concluded that without drastic revision of current regulations 'the probability of serious accidents will increase'. One option promoted by some interests, that of a small group of centralised waste sites dotted around the country, would create a complex national map of radioactive waste corridors along which hazardous loads would be transported from a growing number of reactor plants spread across dozens of states. Another option, that of increased use of rail transport, raised the spectre of nuclear accident in the marshalling yards of a major urban rail junction such as Chicago. In a fully operating system based on rail networks it is estimated that hundreds of rail casks would be stored in yards around the United States.

Again, the British example highlights the nature of this risk. According to the Central Electricity Generating Board, which represents only one fraction of the overall nuclear infrastructure, it is necessary to ship fuel elements for the Board's eight Magnox-type reactors from the manufacturing plant to reactor sites around the country. These fuel elements are made up of a bar of uranium encased in a tube of magnesium alloy, called a Magnox. The Board also operates four advanced gas-cooled reactors and for these the fuel elements consist of pellets of uranium oxide in stainless steel tubes, bundled together in groups of thirty-six which are held in a graphite sleeve. These new fuel elements are taken to the power stations by road; at this point they pose little danger by way of radioactivity. But once they have been through the reactor process the situation changes dramatically.

After being used in the energy-producing process the spent elements have become highly radioactive. They are removed and stored in a shielded area at the plant until ready for shipment. They are then put into special flasks and carried by rail to the ill-fated Sellafield site for reprocessing. Since this transportation practice began in 1962, more than seven thousand rail journeys have been completed. The radioactive elements involved range from xenon 133, which has a half-life of just five days, to plutonium with a half-life of twenty-four thousand years. Other hazardous elements in the flasks include (in ascending order of half-life time span) iodine 131 (eight days), ruthenium 106 (one year), krypton 85 (ten years), strontium 90 (twenty-eight years) and caesium 137 (thirty years).

The CEGB is in no doubts about the consequences if an accident were to occur during transportation and radioactive elements were to escape. In their own words: 'If an accident were to occur the public might, in extreme circumstances, have to be protected from inhaling or ingesting these substances . . . Iodine may be absorbed and concentrated in the thyroid gland, while caesium, strontium and ruthenium may be absorbed into various parts of the body . . . Krypton and xenon are gases and are not retained in the human body but, if they are released during an accident, they may cause direct radiation to the public.'[15] Indeed, during the reactor crisis at Three Mile Island in the United States in 1978, it was the release of xenon gases that posed the most serious danger of radioactive exposure to the local population.

The safe track record to date for Britain's nuclear transportation programme is laudable; it also confirms that there is no practical experience gained from handling a radioactive accident of this kind. Thus, emergency procedures are based on scenarios that are inevitably only approximations to what is perceived to be reality. It seems that the first test of these procedures will have to be in a real-death situation. London's Metropolitan Police, for instance, have carried out numerous exercises to assess the difficulties of moving large numbers of people out of an area quickly under panic conditions. They also rely on experience gained in actual emergencies; one example they quote is the evacuation of a district in north London after the discovery of leaking liquid propane gas at a nearby glass company.

But such exercises may underestimate the scale of a radioactive transport accident by a considerable margin. The episode at the glass factory, for example, involved moving 1,500–2,000 people from about 425 households. An impression of the size of an emergency connected to nuclear waste can be gauged from looking at the nature of the cargo being carried. In Britain the flasks used to carry such waste are designed in accordance with standards laid down by the International Atomic Energy Agency, but this does not prevent them from being of fearsome proportions. A Magnox flask is a massive steel box measuring roughly eight feet on all sides. Its loaded weight is 50 tonnes and it carries some two hundred radioactive fuel elements weighing in total about 2 tonnes. A flask for AGR fuel is similar except with a thinner steel skin lined with radiation-absorbing lead. Thus, while the safety procedures for transporting such loads may still be regarded as successful, there always has to be a first time. And when that first time occurs we will learn for certain what 2 tonnes of highly radioactive debris can do when scattered over a neighbourhood; or, in the case of France, what 6 tonnes might do. Even an ounce of radioactive waste can be enough.

That fateful first time could, of course, be the result of a deliberate act. We live in the age of terrorism and sabotage; every gathering point for people is to be regarded as a target. An Air India jumbo jet destroyed by explosion over the Irish Sea, bullets, bombs, missiles and grenades at airports, hijacked cruise liners, suicide trucks in Beirut, besieged embassies; the list grows by the month. With the volume of radioactive transportation now embarked on a sharp upward path, the temptation to attack a truck or train as part of a wider political objective will grow accordingly.

Although the consequences of such an act verge on the unthinkable, expert minds have been turned to the awful prospect. In 1978 the preliminary results of a report commissioned by the US Nuclear Regulatory Commission from an independent research company, Sandia Laboratories, were released. The report looked at the impact on health, safety and the environment of the transportation of radioactive materials. It found that shipments of irradiated fuel rods represented 'the largest single source of radioactivity routinely shipped'. It also reached the ominous conclusion that access to such shipments by a determined person intent on causing damage would be relatively easy. Such an attack, continued the report, would be expected to take place in densely populated areas, where its adverse effects would be most extreme.

In the wake of a sabotage attack, concluded Sandia, the radioactivity released into the vicinity would lead to human deaths within one year numbering in the 'tens'. Within weeks of the event the number of radiation-induced illnesses in the area would rise to as high as several thousand. In the longer term, the death rate from cancer related to the incident would run into the hundreds. All this excludes the direct effects of the explosive blast used by the saboteurs to achieve their end. The exact seriousness of the attack would, of course, depend on such variables as the density of population in the immediate vicinity, the number of casks being carried and how many of these were damaged to the point where leakages occurred. The Sandia researchers therefore set out a range of possibilities linked to various scenarios. At the upper end of their estimates the death rate, both immediate and longer-term, was as high as 7,500.[16] The purely economic costs of an incident of this kind were estimated then as running to more than $2 billion, a figure that would need to be more than doubled today.

Take The A-Train?

Consequence Estimates for Sabotage of Shipping Casks

Source	Population Density (per sq mile)	Early Fatalities	Early Morbidities	Latent Cancer Deaths
3-element truck cask	2,000	0.4/6.3	Not calc.	220/270
3-element truck cask	42,000 to 115,000	26/44	1,000/1,500	450/550
10-element truck cask	42,000 to 115,000	130/1,200	660/7,600	1,600/7,500

*The first numbers represent average values. The second numbers are maximum values.

*Assumed release: 100 per cent noble gases, 1.6 per cent caesium, 1 per cent solids as respirable material.

SOURCE: US Nuclear Regulatory Commission.

The nuclear era dawned, in 1945, with the agony and destruction of two Japanese cities. The revulsion generated by those tragedies, we were told, would make certain that nuclear war would never happen, that the fate suffered by Hiroshima and Nagasaki had made the world forever safe from nuclear holocaust. It is a bizarre twist of history that now, in the late

twentieth century, we face the risk of creeping holocaust, as the
by-products of nuclear energy programmes created to satisfy the
needs of peacetime begin to loom on the horizon as the source of
some future radioactive plague.

After Chernobyl we can now have no doubts about the
inability of man to control our nuclear technology. More terrifying, the disaster in the Ukraine proved that once catastrophe
strikes, the nuclear process is difficult, if not impossible, to fully
contain. It also demonstrates, if further evidence were needed,
that accidents on this scale have no respect for national borders;
the radioactive effects of Chernobyl were felt literally around
the world and, in some places, will continue to be felt for decades
to come.

4
An Acid World

In 1980 an electromechanically drilled core was collected from the icecap in South Greenland. Scientific examination of the core sample revealed startling evidence of the acid fate that is steadily overtaking this planet, the result of chemical emissions pouring into the upper atmosphere from factories, power stations and vehicle exhausts across the globe and then falling back to earth as chemically charged moisture in the form of rain, snow or smog.

This acid fate is destroying our forests, contaminating our water supplies, changing our climate, eroding irreplaceable historic buildings and, we are now discovering, causing the slow wasting of mankind through corrosion of our own body chemistry. Meanwhile the curve of global acid pollution climbs ever upwards:

- In Canada fifty per cent of all car corrosion is believed to be caused by acid rain.

- In Poland the authorities report that because of acid corrosion to the tracks, trains at Katowice are limited to speeds of 40kph.

- Norwegian stocks of Atlantic salmon are now largely extinct as a consequence of the acidification of breeding grounds.

- In India much needed crops are being seriously affected, yields reduced, by acid rainfall.

- Researchers now confirm acid rain in the high Arctic, suggesting unforeseen future changes in climatic trends.

- Swedish surveys reveal that some 18,000 lakes are acidified, 4,000 of them severely; 9,000 lakes have had their fish stocks affected.

- In Norway 13,000 square kilometres of lake are reported dead, with another 20,000 square kilometres on the critical list.

- In the Canadian province of Ontario some 50,000 lakes are thought to be at risk.

- In Italy fifty lakes are acidified, with serious consequences for fish, plant life and local water supplies.

- Right across Europe instances of forest damage and fisheries loss have reached serious levels. Recent developments have seen acid pollution recorded in hitherto unexpected areas of the continent, such as the forests and lakes of the Alpine regions.

- Acid rain has now been confirmed in such places as the Quinghai province of China, as it has in Ireland, the Soviet Union, Yugoslavia, Greece, Czechoslovakia, Japan, Mexico and a growing list of other countries across the world.

- In the United States acid rain and associated spill-over effects have led to red pine die-back in New York State, lake acidification in Florida and ecosystem stress in dozens of other localities. In 1983 a White House science report estimated that crop losses equivalent to five per cent of their cash value were attributable to acid pollution; a multi-billion dollar shortfall.

The Greenland core analysis showed that levels of sulphuric and nitric acid in the world's rainfall have risen dramatically with the onset of the industrial era. From a sulphate level of 22 parts per billion for ice laid down in the sixteenth century, the level had reached 36 by 1900 and had soared to 90 by the late 1970s. Nitrate levels were shown to have risen from around 40 in the 1900s to more than double this by the end of the 1970s, when the Greenland survey was made.

Chemical elements such as sulphates and nitrates are naturally present in the atmosphere through emissions from the sea and soil and from such phenomena as volcanoes, wildfire, lightning and the naturally induced burning of bio-mass. And until very recently such natural emissions were greater than those caused by man's activities. The turning point was the 1960s, when the rapidly expanding world industrial machine took over from Nature as the prime source of acid in the atmosphere. In the space of less than a generation the global chemical balance has been radically altered, giving the prospect of an acid-bath future of uncharted perils. Today the world emits an estimated 100 million metric tonnes of sulphur into the atmosphere every year, the result of man's economic activities. This produces annually roughly 200 million metric tonnes of SO_2, the major contributor to the growing problem of acid pollution. Europe, including the Soviet Union, accounts for some thirty per cent of the total, with North America (sixteen per cent) and China (six per cent) in second and third places.

Latest estimates put the annual damage, to our habitat and health, at levels more appropriate to a major conventional war. The most seriously affected European countries, in the middle of the world's traditional industrial heartland, are believed to be losing crops worth $500 million a year. More than fifty per cent of West Germany's forests are severely affected, with the German fir all but gone (the rate of advance in the German forests is catastrophic: as recently as 1982 the spread of damage covered only eight per cent of forested areas). In Czechoslovakia one tree in ten is already dead; the same is true in Sweden. Half the red spruce in Vermont are dying. In practically no region of industrialised Europe or North America is there any escape from the all-pervading impact.

The acid danger even percolates through the subsoil to contaminate our rivers, lakes and water supplies, in doing so killing fish and other marine life – and, by terrifying implication, placing our own biological security in doubt. Only a lack of official dedication to the task of recording and measuring the exact extent of the acid threat prevents the creation of a more complete, and more worrying, picture.

Nevertheless, the surveys that have been carried out yield a frightening panorama. Again, researchers using dating techniques have traced the acceleration in acidity levels in the worst afflicted areas. Lake Gardsjon in Sweden, for example, afforded comparative readings stretching back to 12,500BC. During a long period of some 14,000 years, until the early 1960s, acidity in the lake remained at between pH6 and pH7, or nearly neutral. Since then acidity levels have risen seventy-fold.

The hazard curve, once again, has taken a sudden and steep upward turn, with every expectation that the polluting juggernaut will continue to sow its acidifying seeds into the distant future. As a 1981 report from the US National Research Council concluded: 'At current rates of emission of sulphur and nitrogen oxides, the number of affected lakes can be expected to more

than double by 1990, and to include larger and deeper lakes.'[1]
Meanwhile, in Europe both official and unofficial reports
suggest that, without significant new controls, the emission of
acid-creating pollutants could increase by about one-third by the
end of the century.

The Body in Question: Acid and Man

The mounting tally of environmental destruction poses an
unparalleled challenge; it is already too late to achieve significant reversal in the pattern of widespread corrosion and contamination before the 1990s, such is the accumulated chemical
dross collected in the world's upper atmosphere. But such a
challenge pales into insignificance compared to the risks related
to the direct impact of acid pollution on the human body. For
there is increasing evidence that the chemical contamination of
water and plants leads to a corrosive invasion of our organs and
bones, with devastating results.

One specialist, Professor John Savory of the University of
Pennsylvania, is convinced, for instance, that there is a link
between acid rain and the rare bone disease osteomalacia.
According to the professor's findings, the major cause of the
disease is aluminium toxicity; a key factor could be the action of
acid rain in releasing aluminium from clay into soil waters and
from there into public water supplies via rivers and reservoirs.[2]

Professor Savory's conclusions have been corroborated by
work carried out in the highly industrialised north of England
by Dr Philip Day of Manchester University. Noticing that the
incidence of bone disease was much higher in the English north
than elsewhere in the country, Dr Day investigated the water
supply from reservoirs in the Pennines, which have for long
supplied the factory towns in the region. He found that the
aluminium level in tap water in Newcastle upon Tyne, for
example, was 1,000 parts per million; in the town of Stockport it
was 2,000 parts per million. The acceptable limit for aluminium
levels set by EEC legislation is 200 parts per million.

Elsewhere studies have established a connection between
higher rates of mortality and periods of above-average acid-
related pollution, in particular the short-term link between
increased sulphur dioxide and nitrogen oxide pollution and
deaths through respiratory conditions. Such a link is not surprising given the degree to which official limits for acid-type
pollution have typically been exceeded in many countries. By

way of illustration, the World Health Organisation has recommended 100–150 micrograms per cubic metre as the highest short-time daily exposure level for sulphur dioxide, above which observable ill-effects can be expected. Deterioration in the condition of patients with respiratory diseases, for example, will set in at between 200 and 250. Yet such levels were, and still are, widely superseded in many parts of the industrial world.

To take the example of a country where pollution issues are taken extremely seriously, surveys of industrial towns in Sweden in the 1970s produced maximum daily averages of around 400. Even concerted efforts to bring down exposure levels proved disappointing when seen against the WHO guidelines: by the early 1980s Stockholm was still recording levels as high as 250. And according to a 1981 study published by the Paris-based Organisation for Economic Co-operation and Development, most European conurbations consistently exceed this figure.

Hence it is that the past thirty to forty years have seen an escalating pattern of assaults on the health statistics of dozens of countries:

● Few now remember the four thousand deaths that were hastened by the 1952 smog disaster in London. But as recently as 1984, some five hundred people in Athens were taken to hospital and an official emergency declared when the city was engulfed in a killer smog just as lethal as that afflicting Londoners thirty years earlier.

● Two years before, in Dublin, an abnormally high death rate from respiratory disorders was recorded, coinciding with substantial increases in levels of sulphur dioxide that took readings well beyond the WHO limits.

● A US Congressional Report prepared in 1982 points out that more than fifty thousand people died in North America in 1980 as a direct result of inhaling sulphur compounds from the air.

● In January 1985 the authorities in the German Ruhr extended their smog alarm to level three, the most serious level there is and one which places in immediate and certain danger infants, the old and anyone suffering from respiratory conditions.

For the general public, unversed as they are in the complexities of biochemistry, these events are usually accepted as part of the inevitable price of living in modern urban communities; rarely, if ever, is a direct causal link established between deteriorating health and the specific issue of acid pollution. Such adverse effects, however, will come as no surprise to anyone familiar with the basic literature of chemistry and toxicity. For while sulphur dioxide in small concentrations is less toxic than such gases as carbon monoxide, our increasingly acid world no longer deals in small concentrations. As the level of SO_2 concentration in the atmosphere rises, our bodies react.

Sulphur dioxide is a highly soluble gas that is easily absorbed into the bloodstream through breathing. As with blood lead, SO_2 intake has effect on the brain functions and senses well before more observable symptoms appear. And as the absorption of SO_2 and sulphate particles passes a certain point a number of physical reactions become readily apparent. Even a moderate case of sulphur dioxide poisoning results in gastrointestinal disorders, anaemia and other irregularities of the blood, conjunctivitis, headaches and conditions such as anoxia, a deficiency of oxygen in the tissues. More acute poisoning resulting from heavy exposure to high concentrations of SO_2 can lead to death due to respiratory spasms and asphyxia.

But the most alarming revelations concern the growing suspicion among scientists that acid rain is posing an unprecedented threat to human well-being by exposing us to the highly hazardous effects of toxic metals. Worse, this toxic metal danger is all the more frightening because its origins are both unpredictable and diverse.

Reports from Sweden, for instance, describe the effects of acid-polluted drinking water in dissolving the surfaces of pipework, thereby elevating the level of copper present in water supplies. As a general observation, acid water tends to prevent the formation of protective coatings (usually of basic zinc carbonate) which would otherwise build up on the inside of pipes. This is known as 'erosion corrosion' and is a key stage in the breakdown of chemical stability in metal conduits, resulting in unexpected consequences for householders – some unfortunate citizens have experienced their blond hair turning green after washing. Research is yet to determine the implications of this for more serious aspects of health, but it has been noticed that copper levels in parts of Sweden have reached 45 milligrams per litre of water in hot-water supplies, far in excess of the WHO maximum permissible concentration of 1.5. It is known that high concentrations of copper lead to diarrhoea in infants and adverse side-effects in susceptible adults.[3] Other dangers may be posed where acid water dissolves the cadmium out of soldered joints in household plumbing.

Indeed, investigations show that there is a general increase in heavy metal content in acid groundwater, much of which finds its way into the water cycle that supplies domestic needs. Surveys in Scandinavia indicate that concentrations of zinc, copper, lead and cadmium in acid groundwaters are between ten and one hundred times higher than the 'background' level found in neutral watercourses. Until now these releases of heavy metals have been acceptable, but the trend is upwards; experts agree that under certain circumstances there will be heavy metal readings above the hygienic limits set by the medical fraternity. This applies especially to cadmium, which in places has already been registered in contents above one microgram per litre.

Scientific opinion in this area increasingly refers to a 'threshold' point for acid values, beyond which hazardous chemical changes begin to occur, leading to excessive levels of heavy metal contamination. Laboratory tests reveal that enormous quantities of such metals, as well as manganese, may be leached out from the enrichment layers of certain soils when the acid level of rainfall goes beyond this threshold.

What Goes Up . . .

Our failure to act earlier to stem the process of acid pollution cannot be attributed to lack of knowledge about the nature of the threat. More than a century ago scientists working in the industrialised conurbation around Manchester discovered a link between acid content in local rain and the sulphur dioxide given off by the area's coal-burning generating plants. By the late 1940s it was widely recognised in Europe that sulphur and nitrogen oxides produced by burning oil, coal, peat and natural gas can become sulphates and nitrates, and then acids, when carried into the upper atmosphere, falling back to earth in snow, hail, rain, fog and mist. The longer these pollutants are held in the upper atmosphere, the greater the concentration of sulphates and nitrates produced.

Most sulphur dioxide, or SO_2, comes from burning oil and coal; in Europe some ninety per cent of SO_2 is produced in this way. Oxides of nitrogen, or NO_x, are also produced through combustion of fossil fuels, both from the natural content of nitrogen in fuels and from nitrogen in the atmosphere. The oxidation of SO_2 is somewhat slower than that of NO_x; airborne SO_2 remains in this state for an average of three or four days compared with only a few hours for NO_x. It is this difference in airborne time scales that explains the fact that SO_2 is often carried aloft thousands of miles away from its source. Hence the tragic visitation of acid overkill on previously unspoilt, rural backwaters of Scandinavia, the result of a bizarre export trade in unwelcome pollutants generated by the industrial regions to the south. Britain is regarded as the main culprit by Scandinavian governments. NO_x, in contrast, creates acid rain much closer to its source, normally little more than a few hundred miles away.

These acids fall as rain when formed into droplets large enough to defeat gravity, sometimes through being dissolved into raindrops present in cloud. On their way down the droplets pick up other acidic substances and aerosols. SO_2 and NO_x are also deposited on the environment in dry form, thereby increasing the overall level of acidity in the landscape.

According to West German biochemist Bernhard Ulrich, a leading analyst of the acid phenomenon, one of the most alarming aspects of acid deposition is its pernicious mode of attack on plant life and soil, producing few negative symptoms until a far-reaching and irreversible havoc suddenly reveals itself. The cycle of destruction, says Ulrich, goes through three stages. First, trees actually gain from the additional nitrogen and sulphur carried in acid rain. During the second phase, rising levels of acidification have the effect of destroying the soil's capacity as a neutralising agent, thus reducing its power to replace lost nutrients such as magnesium and calcium which are essential ingredients of Nature's recipe for plant growth.

As this corrosive process gathers pace, the third stage develops. The sulphur leaches out aluminium traces, turning the soil toxic, while other heavy metals are mobilised by the pattern of chemical interaction. Aluminium is widely accepted as being the most lethal component in the formula of acid rain destruction. Ulrich believes the critical point in this case to be around pH levels of 4.2 or less. There may even, thinks Ulrich, be a calamitous fourth stage in which the poisoned soil begins producing its own acids, thus triggering off a self-reinforcing spiral of acidity leading to the total breakdown of the soil's natural chemistry. Particularly vulnerable are sensitive silty and sandy soils lying on hardier bedrock.[4]

A more precise understanding of the scale of our acid crisis calls for a familiarity with accepted methods of measuring acidity. The most common approach is to express it in terms of pH, a scale built around the negative logarithm of hydrogen ion concentration from 0 to 14; the neutral level is 7, while below 7 is acid and above it is alkaline. Being logarithmic the scale disguises the real dimensions of apparently minor changes in acidity. Each pH unit on the scale represents ten times more hydrogen ions than the unit below it. The equilibrium level prevalent in Nature is around 5.6. Thus, while the pH figures for Britain, for instance, range between 4.0 and 5.0, this seemingly narrow band of variations fails to convey, to an uninformed observer, the true seriousness of the problem. British rain is, in fact, between 100 and 150 times more acid than natural rain.

A glance at recent figures for rainfall acidity in parts of Europe, published in a report prepared for the EEC Commission in 1983, reveals the increasing seriousness of the problem. The table shows north-western Europe to have levels of acidity about five times greater than those produced by unpolluted rain. The report also points out that this has occurred within a very short span of time; in the 1950s the pH level in such countries as Sweden, Norway and the Netherlands was around the natural rate of 5.0.

Europe's Acid Legacy
Average acidity of rainfall in Western Europe

Area	pH	Year
S E England	4.1–4.4	1978
E Scotland	4.2–4.4	1978–80
W Wales	4.9	1981–3
W Germany	4.0	1979–80
Black Forest	4.3	1972
S Norway	4.7	1977
S Sweden	4.3	1975
N Sweden	4.3	1972
N Italy	4.3–5.5	1981

SOURCE: Acid Rain: A Review (EEC 1983)

Similar observations can be made about the Soviet Union and eastern Europe. Soviet emissions of SO_2, at around 25 million tonnes a year, put it at the very top of the world league, an unenviable harvest of chemical by-products that it shares with

neighbouring countries. Soviet emissions are thought to contribute more than eleven per cent of the sulphur pollution
currently affecting Sweden, easily the highest among the
external sources of Swedish acid rain.

SO_2 Emissions: The Big League

'000 tonnes (1980)

USSR	25,000
USA	24,100
CHINA	12,000
BRITAIN	4,700
CANADA	4,500
EAST GERMANY	4,000
ITALY	3,800
FRANCE	3,300
WEST GERMANY	3,200
CZECHOSLOVAKIA	3,100
YUGOSLAVIA	3,000

SOURCE: Acid Earth (Earthscan 1985)

The roots of this Soviet phenomenon lie in the dedication to
electrification that has characterised development programmes
in the USSR for more than fifty years. The massive and
constantly growing demand for electricity has led to the construction of a vast network of thermal power plants that make
use of the country's enormous coal reserves. Soviet plans
indicate a continued heavy reliance on coal for the foreseeable
future.

Ironically, the Soviet Union is now a net importer of SO_2, due
to the outmoded, poorly equipped plants that work to produce
energy in east European countries like Poland and Czechoslovakia. This situation has transformed the USSR into a major
focus of acid destruction, with thousands of lakes and more than
a million acres of forest and farmland seriously affected by acid
deposition. Some analysts have pointed to acid damage as a
possible reason for the consistently poor out-turn of Soviet
agriculture; recent grain harvests, for instance, have been near
to thirty per cent below expectations.

The other major zone of acid destruction is North America.
Here the place of Sweden as the victim of wind-carried SO_2 and
NO_x is taken by Canada, located as it is to the north of the major
US industrial regions. And because the problem is limited to
just two countries the degree of cross-border political invective

has been considerably greater. For the past decade relations between Ottawa and Washington have operated literally in the shadow of the massive acid clouds that drift over the lakes and forests of Ontario and other parts of eastern Canada. During the sixties and seventies, a hitherto tolerable level of chemical emissions rapidly escalated to a point beyond acceptability. By 1980, more than 50 million tonnes of SO_2 and NO_x were being released each year over North America, with the bulk of it coming from factories and power plants in the north-eastern states of the US. Since 1950, emissions from this region have doubled; the outpouring from power plants alone has tripled. With annual total SO_2 emissions of more than 24 million tonnes the US is second only to the USSR as the world's leading sulphate polluter.

The north-eastern states carry most of the blame; ten of them, from Ohio southwards to Florida, account for sixty-five per cent of SO_2 emissions in the whole eastern stretch of the country. They also carry the lion's share of the burden. Throughout the area it is common to experience rainfall with a pH of between 4.0 and 4.5. On several occasions rainfalls with a pH below 3.0 have been noted, many times worse than the figures for Western Europe. In Pennsylvania a pH of 1.5 has been recorded, possibly the lowest figure so far experienced anywhere.

Canada, one of the major victims, nevertheless adds its own contribution to the misery. Indeed, Canadian industry can rightly be regarded as a pioneer in the production of acid rain. In 1886 the Canadian Copper Company set up the first open bed roasting of copper ores at Sudbury in Ontario. By 1916, the Sudbury beds were pouring out more than 600,000 tonnes of SO_2 a year. Today Canada is the fifth largest acid polluter in the world, turning out four and a half million tonnes of SO_2 a year. Nearly two-thirds of it comes from smelters, the copper and nickel smelting complex around Sudbury having the dubious distinction of being the biggest single source of SO_2 in the world, with the nickel smelter on its own pouring out more sulphates during the decade of the 1970s than was emitted by all the volcanoes in history.

This extreme situation brings with it a mounting cost. Damage to the thin or sandy soils in many eastern states of the US is now calculated to run to more than $5 billion every year. According to figures released by the Office of Technology Assessment, the entire eastern water network is under threat: some nine thousand lakes and sixty thousand miles of streams are exposed to acidification. As far west as the state of Minnesota, two thousand miles from the Atlantic seaboard, one lake in six has been damaged. Meanwhile, in the heart of the acid rain belt, in the mountains of New York state, fish have disappeared from the once-idyllic waterways.[5]

As with Europe, North America is experiencing a steady expansion in the geographic pattern of acid pollution, spreading outwards from the old industrial heartlands. Apart from Canada, other regions of the US itself now report a rapidly escalating problem. Acid levels in rainfall in the southern states have been rising strongly since the 1950s. Indeed, one of the lowest unofficial pH levels ever recorded, at 2.0, is accredited to a rainstorm that lashed the town of Wheeling in West Virginia in 1978. In large areas of northern Florida rainfall has become increasingly more acid over the past twenty-five years; pH readings as low as 3.8 have been seen. Even the states of the Rockies, for long renowned for their sunshine and wholesome air, have fallen prey, thanks to massive metal processing developments in Mexico and adjoining US states. Acid deposition in the Rocky Mountains is rising fast; rain collected at sites in Colorado and Wyoming has yielded acidity readings ten times greater than the level for unpolluted rainwater. Thousands of lakes in the upper mountain reaches are now deemed to be in the front line for widespread acidification. In remote upland pools trout have ceased to hatch.

As author John McCormick points out in *Acid Earth*, a survey of global acid pollution, this is only the beginning of the end of the Rockies as a haven of clean air.[6] Most of the SO_2 afflicting the mountain states comes from smelters, the rest from coal-fired power stations. But with projects already advanced for building new coal-burning plants and complexes for fertilisers, synthetic fuels and natural gas, some in the very heart of the Rockies, over the coming decade, the prospect is for even higher levels of sulphate and nitrate emission in the years ahead. One project, the vast new copper smelter at Nacozari, just south of the Mexican border, has been built without adequate controls over sulphur emission. Mexican regulations do not impose the strict limitations applied to US corporations through the Clean Air Act. Together with emissions from another smelter at Cananaea, further along the border, about 625,000 tonnes of SO_2 will be pumped into the atmosphere en route to the once-pure Rocky Mountain region. Proposals are currently in hand to increase the Cananaea plant by two hundred per cent, taking Mexican output of SO_2 to around 875,000 tonnes annually, more than the total output of Belgium.

With SO_2 pouring out from other copper smelters in New Mexico and Arizona (the plant at Douglas being exempted from US controls until 1988 in the interest of preserving local jobs) the border zone is fast becoming one of the world's leading generators of acid rain, much of it drifting north to contaminate the upper altitudes of Colorado. At other times, when prevailing winds dictate, it drifts south over the northern Mexican states distributing its chemical load over the farmlands and villages of the Sierras.

In North America the old, developed world rubs shoulders with the newly industrialised; the first generation of acid polluters co-exists alongside one of the newest entrants to the league of contaminators. And it is the rise of younger economies such as Mexico, with their passion for development and lower regard for regulatory controls, that threatens to turn an already unacceptable level of worldwide acidity – the accumulated dross of a century of profligate old world frenzy – into a truly global eco-disaster.

The case of China offers an alarming illustration of the danger presented by the new industrial countries. Accelerated development of power generation and basic industrial capacity has taken China rapidly up the league table of SO_2 producers. Already it is running at around 15 million tonnes a year, equal to the total of SO_2 emissions for the four major west European economies. Around eighty-five per cent of the Chinese figure comes from combustion of the country's sulphur-rich coal reserves, nearly forty per cent of which is burnt in domestic stoves in rural towns and villages.

Due to the peculiarly high incidence of alkaline elements in the soil (and therefore in the air) in numerous regions of China, pH readings in many areas tend to be very close to the neutral norm of 7.0. But the figures are deceptive; China is a major producer of SO_2 and more searching analysis of the statistics will reveal a picture every bit as disturbing as in other newly afflicted areas like the Rockies. Rainwater in the Beijing area is now showing pH readings of 5.0, in southern China as low as 4.5. Both are comparable to levels commonly seen in Europe. A not untypical report published recently in the Chinese language

Guangming Daily referred to the experience of farmers living
south of the Yangz'te river, whose rice crop planted over a 3,000
acre area had suddenly wilted and died.

China is on course to being the major acid crisis-point in the
twenty-first century as the sheer size of the country's industrialising effort reaches a crescendo. Researchers are already linking
the prevalence of certain health problems witnessed in China
with the rapidly growing emission of SO_2 and other pollutants.
The figures for lung cancer in Chinese cities are well above the
average; at their highest they reach thirty-one deaths per
100,000, compared to four to five in rural areas. One assessment
suggests that polluted air results in the loss of more than three
and a half million working days a year for China's economy.
Some six thousand premature deaths, chiefly among young
infants and the old, are attributed each year to the chemical contamination of the urban environment.[7]

Over a steadily increasing expanse of the Earth's surface the
same evidence is emerging:

- In South Africa SO_2 fall-out in the Johannesburg-Witwatersrand
  industrial belt is running at the rate of 220 tonnes per square
  kilometre. In the highly polluted Ruhr in West Germany the
  equivalent figure is only a little greater at 260 tonnes.

- In Malaysia, rainfall near Kuala Lumpur and in Perak is giving pH
  readings as low as 4.4.

- In Brazil analysts in the congested São Paulo area are reporting pH
  levels of 2.7 to 4.7, far worse than extreme cases in Scandinavia and
  well past the critical threshold described by Ulrich as the turning
  point for serious chemical deterioration in the soil cover, leading to
  the prospect of hazardous aluminium secretions.

- In Thailand, urban areas are exhibiting serious symptoms of air
  pollution, prompting the Office of the National Environment Board
  to establish a monitoring system to track acidity trends.

- In Australia six stations for the measurement of rainwater pH have
  been set up. Around Sydney, low rainfall pH is already being
  reported.

- In the remote Arctic wastes, for long regarded as a paragon of
  unpolluted Nature, Norwegian researchers have discovered SO_2
  concentrations equal to those found in Scandinavia. One major

concern is that the haze created by this pollution could alter the climatic balance of the northern hemisphere by acting as a gigantic atmospheric sponge for solar energy reaching the area during the summer months.

Tomorrow's Acid World

This rapidly growing incidence of acid pollution in the new industrial countries adds a disturbing dimension to a problem that is already a major concern. The old industrial world alone has given us a future of increasing fears for our environment and for our own safety. For there is no real likelihood that the pattern of man-made acid corrosion can be reversed this side of the year 2000.

Most governments in the developed world foresee no reduction in emissions – or depositions – of SO_2 over the next five to ten years. To take Europe, the evidence of surveys by the EEC, governments and energy organisations collectively points to increasing levels of emission and deposition across the continent. Emissions are expected to rise from around 61 million metric tonnes in 1982 to nearly 71 million in 1992, and climbing to about 81 million tonnes by 2002. Much of this increase will come from steep rises in acid pollution generated by smaller countries, which more than cancel out reductions brought about by costly emission control programmes in countries like Sweden and France.

Major culprits will be such countries as Turkey (with emissions rising 200 per cent between 1982 and 2002), Ireland (up 146 per cent), Yugoslavia (up 130 per cent), Greece (up 118 per cent) and Bulgaria (up 108 per cent). Most existing polluters will continue to increase their contributions to Europe's acid future. In real volume terms these increases will be very large. The USSR, for example, will increase its output of SO_2 by only thirty per cent. But this apparently constrained rise will take Soviet emissions from 25.5 million tonnes in 1982 to an even more unwelcome 34.6 million tonnes by the beginning of the next century. As the following table shows, this upward trend is likely to be seen in practically every industrialised country in the Western world.

Europe's Acid Future
Emissions of SO$_2$ in millions of metric tonnes

	1982	2002
Austria	0.43	0.72
Belgium	0.81	0.87
Bulgaria	0.77	1.60
Czechoslovakia	3.37	4.18
Denmark	0.45	0.58
West Germany	3.51	3.93
Finland	0.57	0.63
France	2.89	1.58
East Germany	4.0	4.4
Greece	0.34	0.74
Hungary	1.72	2.17
Ireland	0.26	0.64
Italy	3.07	3.35
Luxembourg	0.03	0.04
Holland	0.49	0.63
Norway	0.14	0.18
Poland	2.5	3.07
Portugal	0.14	0.26
Romania	2.0	3.35
Spain	2.09	3.73
Sweden	0.51	0.36
Switzerland	0.12	0.18
Turkey	0.65	1.97
USSR	25.5	34.6
UK	4.25	5.26
Yugoslavia	0.83	1.91

SOURCE: Ambio Vol 11 No 6

Much of this increase in the global level of emissions over Europe is due to the growing reliance on coal as an energy source. Reserves of coal are ample into the medium-term future, the methods of extracting and transporting it are well known; both factors recommend it as an alternative to oil in countries that are embarked on a trend away from price-sensitive petroleum fuels.

Thus, in Turkey – top of the league for growth in SO$_2$ emissions – coal consumption is expected to rise from 7 million tonnes in 1982 to 22 million tonnes in 2002. Yugoslavia – in second place for SO$_2$ growth – plans to increase consumption from 20 million tonnes to 54 million over the same time span. Europe overall is expected to boost its coal usage by some 540 million tonnes, or fifty per cent, by the start of the twenty-first century. The cost of this massive shift in the balance of energy consumption is a comparable increase in the emission of sulphur dioxide and hence a significant aggravation of the problem of acid pollution. In sheer volume alone the outlook is for an unsustainable level of corrosive chemical effluent in our air, our water supplies and in our bodies.

Much the same outlook threatens the citizens of North America. Although the fact that only three governments are involved – the US, Mexico and Canada – progress towards major reductions in SO_2 emissions has been non-existent. The various industrial lobbies that represent interests in coal, electricity generation and the other sectors most open to emission-control laws are very influential. They trade on the misgivings amongst government officials that tough new rules will seriously affect company profitability, and hence jobs. There are signs that the Canadian government will take its own unilateral steps to cut local SO_2 emissions by giving public funds to control projects. The stated aim is to reduce SO_2 outpourings by fifty per cent in eastern Canada by the mid-1990s. Nevertheless, politics is an uncertain business; these Canadian intentions can be overtaken by new circumstances.

In any event, there are no signs that the US government itself, which presides over an industrial infrastructure responsible for over 24 million tonnes of SO_2 emission annually – nearly six times the total for Canada – is anxious to join its northern neighbour in a crusade against the acid threat. More likely is that any future reductions in emissions by Canadian industry are offset by increases in SO_2 output by US plants, not to mention the notoriously unregulated Mexican enterprises that are now contributing increasingly to the acid pollution overtaking the Rockies.

Successful programmes to combat SO_2 and NO_x are not an elusive dream. No country can be more congested industrially, nor more committed to zealous industrial growth, than Japan. Yet Japan does not figure in the infamous league tables of SO_2. Their policies for controlling emissions of these deadly toxins have succeeded, without detriment to the pattern of economic expansion that has characterised the post-war experience of the country.

In 1968 the Japanese government passed the Air Pollution Control Law. It was amended in 1970 and 1974. The law imposes rigorous limits on emissions of SO_2 and NO_x, as well as on other noxious emissions from industrial premises and from vehicles.

Comprehensive monitoring systems for sulphates and nitrates were put in place, more than sixteen hundred of them. Heavy SO_2 polluters were subjected to a levy, with part of the proceeds going to pay for medical treatment for pollution-affected local residents. Energy consumption was reduced, spurred on by the near-calamitous increase in oil prices in the early 1970s; low-sulphur fuels replaced more highly polluting alternatives. One major component of the policy was a programme for desulphurising oil. The strategy worked. By the beginning of the 1980s, SO_2 emissions had been cut by a remarkable seventy-five per cent against the all-time high in 1967. The financial cost was not inconsiderable. Over the first few years of the 1970s Japanese companies spent more than $4 billion on special equipment to reduce SO_2. From 1975 onwards, all cars were required to be fitted with catalytic converters, adding ten per cent to the purchase price of new vehicles and provoking an immediate fall-off in sales.

The Japanese action proves that rigorous steps can achieve results, though the costs are high. What seems tragic is that Japan's brave efforts are now under serious threat from acid pollution drifting across its islands from mainland China. With China earmarked as the major new SO_2 polluter of the twenty-first century, Japan's success is likely to be obliterated, and its citizens once again put in jeopardy, by the uncontrolled acid outpourings of a neighbour over which it has no control.

5
Heavy Metal Overload

Children born to mothers who have been exposed to large amounts of methyl mercury are likely to be damaged irreparably for life. Most will suffer mental retardation and cerebral palsy with convulsions. Such children will be victims of one of the most terrifying, and the least understood, hazards of living in the late twentieth century, that of heavy metal overload. And they will be the lucky ones who survive, if only as half-humans; in its most serious form, mercury poisoning is fatal.

Heavy metal overload has already claimed the lives of thousands in recent years. But those deaths have occurred in scores of isolated incidents which, because they were geographically dispersed and spread over many years, have never been grouped together and linked to the same dread cause. Now the scientific evidence is beginning to accumulate: we are being attacked on an ever-widening scale by highly poisonous metallic traces building up in the air we breathe, the water we drink and the food we eat.

Yet again, this frightening prospect should not have been unexpected. The danger we face was known to the ancients; for centuries it has figured in dramatic literature and historical narrative as an agent of violent change. Poisoning your enemy has long been regarded as a noble, even romantic, act. But the industrial era has brought with it an alliance with such poisons in order to make possible new processes and materials for the production and packaging of the myriad products that now flood the everyday marketplace.

Essential Poisons
Planet Earth is naturally rich in a vast array of differing metals. Many of them are essential for the maintenance of life forms.

Iron, for instance, is an indispensable part of the respiratory pigment haemoglobin relied on by vertebrates and invertebrates alike. Copper is a major constituent of a substance called haemocyanin, the respiratory pigment of molluscs and crustaceans. Many enzymes, the soluble proteins produced by living cells, contain zinc; vitamin B_{12} enzymes contain cobalt. The coatings of biological ducts such as arteries have significant traces of vanadium.

But there are different categories of metals; each of them have quite distinct properties as far as the human body is concerned. Light metals such as sodium, potassium and calcium are carried about the body in aqueous solutions and would be regarded as vital to health. Then there are transitional metals – they include copper, iron, cobalt and manganese – that are essential to human well-being in low concentrations, but which could be toxic in high concentrations. The third, and most hazardous, category is that of heavy metals. These include mercury, lead, tin, selenium and arsenic. They are not generally needed for metabolic activity (the series of chemical changes central to the maintenance of life) and are toxic to the living cell at low concentrations.

Being naturally present in the earth's crust, these various metals have always been a component of the environmental make-up. But the emergence of industrial processes over the past century has greatly increased the level of metals coming into contact with living things. The annual world production of lead, for example, is now running at more than 40 million tonnes a year. More than 7.5 million tonnes of copper is produced each year for use in the manufacture of electrical items, in alloys and in other forms that find their way into paint, preservatives and such things as algicides. Cadmium – produced as a by-product of zinc smelting activities – has become increasingly popular as an ingredient in plastics, solders, various alloys and in batteries. World production now runs to more than 18,000 tonnes a year. Mercury is widely used in paper production, in the chlorine industry and as part of the mix in pesticides. From a peak in world production of more than 10,500 tonnes in 1971, global output has fallen in recent years; there is nevertheless still a considerable worldwide reliance on variants of mercury. An example is the 'slimicides' used in the timber and paper pulp industries to reduce the growth of fungi.

The contamination of the human habitat by metals from the

natural environment – through erosion of metal-bearing rocks, from gases released from volcanoes, emissions from the oceans and by other means – has existed from the beginning of geological history. But the global eco-system has adapted to this influx over the millennia; so, too, has the human biochemistry adjusted to a constant diet of metal traces. Now, the commercial activities of the human race are adding significantly to this natural contribution. Above all, as we shall see later, the world's hydrosphere – the streams, rivers, lakes, seas and underground flows that together comprise the planetary water cycle – is fast becoming dangerously polluted with metals through waste dumping, accidental discharges from industrial premises, atmospheric pollution (which ends up as metal particles in rainfall) and the contamination of watercourses through run-off from soils heavily treated with pesticides.

Such metals invade the body through the skin, the lungs and through the digestive system as a consequence of eating or drinking metal-contaminated items. Their entry points are many and varied:

- The skin absorbs them via the hair follicles and sebaceous glands, conducting them through the protective layer of the epidermis and into the biochemical system.

- When present in the air as atmospheric toxicants these metals exist as gases or particulates. As gases they can be absorbed by being dissolved in the water of the mucous membranes that coat our internal tracts. As particles they are breathed in and penetrate the lungs; in moderate doses this will produce toxic effects, bronchitis and other conditions. They can also exist in the form of lipid soluble gases: these are absorbed into the blood stream via the lung cavities.

- If ingested through drinking or eating, the hazardous elements are absorbed into the tissues of the gastrointestinal tract, then eventually through the intestinal blood-flow into the liver. En route some metal traces will find their way into the lymphatic vessels and from there into the jugular vein that carries blood from the head.

The scale of biochemical damage depends on a number of factors, such as the rate at which toxic traces are distributed to vital organs and vessels and the length of time such traces are held within the system. These in turn depend on variables such as the action of proteins in carrying toxicants along the body's electrochemical paths and the speed with which invading chemicals are excreted, which in turn is linked to the varying efficiency of such organs as the kidneys. Whatever the variations, the process of bodily absorption brings metal poisons into contact with our internal working machinery. Once active within the system the symptoms of heavy metal toxicity begin to appear. These symptoms differ according to the metallic source involved, but share the same awful characteristics.

Lead is probably the most prevalent heavy metal confronting us. In the words of the recent British Royal Commission on Environmental Pollution, 'it is now one of the most widely dispersed of environmental pollutants'. But its dangers are also among the most widely documented, due to its association over many years with the broader issue of air quality and vehicle emissions. Lead apart, it is mercury that poses the most significant threat because of its seemingly all-pervasive presence in critical areas of our daily environment, particularly in food items that are widely considered not merely safe but even health-promoting. And mercury is also extremely lethal.

The effects of mercury poisoning in man are an instructive illustration of the pernicious and potentially deadly nature of heavy metal pollution. To begin with, the symptoms may occur weeks or even months after an acute exposure to toxic concentrations. These include numbness and tingling of the lips, hands and feet, irregularities in control of bodily functions, disturbances of speech, impairment of sight and hearing and emotional imbalance. With severe intoxication the adverse effects are irreversible. A key factor is the possibility of methyl mercury accumulating in the brain, leading to brain cell damage and hence the loss of control over co-ordinated muscle movement. The precise pattern of symptoms depends on the organs that are affected and the areas of the body that are invaded.

Adverse effects from other heavy metals follow a similar course. Lead poisoning gives rise to several clinical syndromes of illness: acute abdominal colic, anaemia, disorders of the brain and disruption in the operation of the nervous system leading to such conditions as paranoia and hallucination. In severe cases the marrow and central nervous system are damaged resulting in mental retardation and death. The chronic effects of copper poisoning include pathological liver cirrhosis, enlarged spleen, fibrosis and cysts in ductless glands and brain cell damage.

The danger is even more extreme for unborn babies. In the

case of mercury the human foetus acquires far greater concentrations of the metal than does the mother. There are many instances in which children with congenital brain damage have been born to mothers who have shown no symptoms of mercury poisoning. Methyl mercury penetrates the placenta with little difficulty, producing a concentration of mercury in the baby's blood that is some twenty per cent higher than in the mother.

How Much Kills?

The true extent of the heavy metal danger is obscured by the complex scientific and medical data that surround the subject. The methods of measuring exact metal levels in foodstuffs, water and in the air are, as in other areas of environmental study, based on meticulous statistical analysis. For metals these levels are expressed in terms of parts per million; inevitably this leads to extremely fine variations that disguise very large differences in metal levels, differences that can be the vital margin between life and death.

The extreme toxicity of mercury has been well known for centuries. The otherwise quaint expression 'mad as a hatter' in fact relates to the prevalence of mercury poisoning, and hence to mental disorders, among nineteenth-century hat-makers who used mercury in certain processes involving felt materials. The consensus amongst the medical fraternity is that clinical signs of mercury poisoning in man are produced with an intake of between 1 and 2 milligrams per day. Fatal doses vary from 3 to 30 grams.

A dose of 1 to 2 mg of methyl mercury is equivalent to eating 200 grams of fish a day with a mercury content of between 5 and 10 parts per million. The comparison with fish is not without its relevance; the biggest single disaster in the post-war period involving mercury poisoning was linked to fish and shellfish eaten by the inhabitants of a Japanese coastal community in the early 1950s. That disaster was to become the opening chapter in a saga of environmental hazard that is still to be fully recognised by the world at large.

The citizens of Minamata Bay, like many millions of their Japanese compatriots, had for centuries enjoyed the benefits of the plentiful fish and shellfish to be found in the inshore waters of their islands. Until the 1950s, when in a short space of time 111 people were killed or seriously disabled after eating fish contaminated with mercury flowing into the sea from a nearby chemical plant. Forty-six of them died. It was found that waste from the plant contained up to 20ppm of mercury, twice the level accepted as a danger point when present in fish.

Had those hapless citizens the benefit of knowing the intricacies of the biochemistry of fishes, they would have understood the causes of the disaster that had befallen them. Researches show that fish and mercury make a lethal combination. It seems that whatever the nature of the mercurial pollutant, a methylisation of mercury compounds takes place in the fish itself (or, as in the case of Minamata, research suggests that micro-organisms in coastal sediments can convert non-toxic mercury into lethal methyl mercury, which is subsequently absorbed by fish). Swedish studies of the northern pike, for instance, show that its mucus is able to convert inorganic mercury almost completely into methyl mercury, the most toxic form, within two to four hours.

The Minamata incident introduced a new phrase into the medical dictionary. Minamata Disease is a condition caused by the ingestion of large amounts of fish and shellfish contaminated by alkyl mercury compounds from industrial waste. But that terrible episode was not to be the last. In 1965, in the Japanese community of Niigata, twenty-six people were taken ill with mercury poisoning; five of them died. Analysts discovered they had regularly been eating fish containing 5ppm.

In 1969 a family in New Mexico was struck by heavy metal overload. Three of them were disabled after eating pork from pigs that had been fed on grain treated with a mercurial fungicide. The story triggered off a widespread concern about the effects of eating crops grown from seeds dressed with small quantities of methyl mercury. Methyl mercury is a highly toxic substance that is known to cause damage to the nervous system as well as producing chromosomal aberrations and horrible deformities to the foetus.

But the New Mexico and Minamata experiences, ironically, do not bring home the reality of the heavy metal threat. For it is not the headline-grabbing catastrophes that should trouble us; they are merely isolated, though tragic, examples of the extreme case. What is more alarming is the imperceptible, but inexorable, build-up of heavy metal contamination in our bodies resulting from constant exposure over many years to metal poisons that register, at one point in time, only modest readings on the scale of lethality. Closer examination will reveal, in any event, that Minamata was not the result of sudden mercury excesses. The offending industrial plant, at Chisso nearby, had been using mercury in varying processes since 1932. In the thirty-six years up to 1968 it is estimated that more than 80 tonnes of mercury, nearly half of it in the form of highly toxic organic mercury, was discharged into Minamata Bay. It is probable that fish-eating communities along the littoral had been suffering varying degrees of mercury poisoning for twenty years before a major, and for many fatal, outbreak overtook them.

Indeed, fish-eaters everywhere should begin to ask themselves whether the apparently wholesome diet they favour is quite as innocent as it seems. A growing amount of research is showing that fish and crustaceans – including those, such as oysters, crabs and lobsters, that are considered luxuries – are particularly doubtful when it comes to heavy metal contamination, not only by mercury but by copper, itself an extremely toxic element. A recent report by the British Ministry of Agriculture, Fisheries and Food is representative of a great number of studies that point to the danger posed by metal contamination in fish and crustaceans.[1] The conclusions of the report are particularly alarming on the subject of copper.

British regulations set a recommended limit for copper in food of 20 milligrams per kilo, and of 2 milligrams per kilo for beverages. The limit of 20mg/kg in food has a long history; as long ago as 1949 it was laid down in statute as the legally permissible limit for tomato ketchup. With these guidelines in mind the Ministry analysts examined a wide range of some one hundred and fifty foodstuffs regularly eaten by the British public, from drinking chocolate to beer, from pickled eggs to canned snails. Their analysis indicated striking differences in copper levels between various food items and, more disconcertingly, readings for some categories of food which placed them well above the 20mg/kg safety limit.

Shellfish yielded results that give rise to serious concern. Dried oysters returned figures that reached as high as 440 mg/kg, some twenty-two times greater than the officially recommended level of intake. The lowest reading in the sample was 150. A can of fried oysters was found to contain 310mg/kg. Fresh clams recorded levels up to 230mg/kg, more than ten times the recommended copper content. The mean reading for the whole sample of clams was 36, still nearly double the acceptable limit. Brown crab meat yielded readings as high as 150mg/kg with a mean of 49, two and a half times the safety level. White crab meat produced figures that ranged up to 89; those for dressed crab reached 55.

In associated research focussed specifically on fish and shellfish from waters around the British Isles, and published in the report, the conclusions were no less daunting. High readings were linked to samples of whelks, which reached levels of 220, and to crabmeat with levels of up to 230. In both cases the mean reading was several times greater than the official guideline. More disconcerting still were the findings for lobsters. Not one crustacean in the sample registered lower than 65mg/kg, more than three times the advisable limit. And the mean level for copper content in the total lobster sample was 220.

The report also highlighted the danger of indirect copper intake through eating the organs of animals raised on metal-contaminated feedstuffs. It was this very hazard that claimed the lives of the unfortunate family in New Mexico, though in that case the offending metal was mercury. In the British survey, examination of a very large sample of pigs' livers produced readings running as high as 280mg/kg of copper, although the mean for the sample as a whole was 18, marginally the right side of the safety divide. For lambs' liver, however, the analysis produced unacceptable mean readings of 35, with individual samples giving results up to a level of 140. The figures for calf and ox liver were equally disturbing.

To appreciate the significance of these results it is necessary to compare them with other food items examined by the Ministry scientists. Biscuits produced mean readings of just 1.3 mg/kg; the highest recorded was 1.6. Camembert cheese returned a mean of 1.0, canned soups just 1.1. The only non-fish food items that approached the recommended limits were curry powder and pectin (used as a setting agent in jams and jellies) with 12 and soya protein with 11. The samples of ketchup, subject of the earliest controls, returned figures of 10.

The analysis of beverages, meanwhile, produced findings that were even more worrying. It transpired that the country's near-sacred national brew was not quite as benign as it seemed. Against the much lower recommended limit for beverages of 2mg/kg, the government chemists discovered that tea dust, the raw material of tea-bags, recorded copper levels of up to 69, with a mean for the sample of 44 – making it the most highly contaminated item in the entire survey. Cocoa had a mean level of 32, leaf tea one of 23. Coffee made from beans, as opposed to instant, registered upper levels of 14, seven times the limit, with a mean of 13. Malted drinks showed levels of 5.5, still considerably above the margin of safety.

In comparison, alcoholic drinks, for other reasons condemned as extremely harmful, proved themselves almost entirely free of this particular hazard. Beers, ciders, wines and liqueurs were found to have copper levels no greater than a mean of 0.2. And carbonated drinks, the essential ingredient of so many alcoholic mixes, registered the minuscule reading of 0.05.

Vegetables, whether fresh, canned or dried, featured well below the 20mg/kg limit for foods as an overall average, but in some cases yielded quite high figures: some samples of fresh vegetables, for instance, recorded copper levels up to 19mg/kg. Fruits in various forms returned mean readings below 2. Sugar products ranked well down the scale. Milk yielded a reassuring figure of 0.1, only one-twentieth the recommended level for beverages. Derivatives such as condensed and evaporated milk, however, encouraged no such comfort: they returned readings as high as 6.7, nearly three and a half times greater than the officially recommended borderline. Although these products are usually consumed after being diluted with water, such excessive copper levels are hardly encouraging for parents using them in desserts for children.

A Self-Inflicted Eco-Threat

The ever-growing risk from copper is just one facet of the heavy metal danger that is now adding yet another dimension to the spectre of global catastrophe, both to our external habitat and increasingly to our own biochemistry. Lead, mercury and other toxic metals are also invading every corner of our natural and personal environment. And, as with many other aspects of the approaching hi-tech holocaust, the root cause is an unholy and unhealthy partnership between Nature and technology, between a hitherto unspoilt world and a humanity relentlessly searching for more affluence, convenience and comfort.

For example, the reasons for the wide variations in copper content between items of food and drink commonly found side by side in the typical shopping basket come down to a complicated mixture of chemistry, geography and commercial practices. The high readings for animal offal, particularly in liver, are linked both to copper content in animal feedstuffs and the activities of internal systems associated with metalloenzymes and proteins.

The same observations can be made about fish. Surveys in Aberdeen on the north-east coast of Scotland, for instance, have confirmed that fish caught in the Firth of Clyde, the Bergen Bank and the Bressay Bank fishing areas contain up to ten times more copper in the livers than in the filleted flesh. The origins of this copper contamination is almost certainly a mixture of metal traces naturally existing in the offshore seas, together with toxic elements contributed by the many industrial activities that surround this congested area of north-west Europe. Similar results can be found in comparable offshore areas of the Mediterranean, the eastern seaboard of North America and offshore Japan.

On land a key factor is the copper content of soils, which may result in certain foodstuffs returning abnormally high results. Soils exhibit marked variations in copper levels, ranging from 2 mg/kg up as high as 100 in normal environments, with much heavier readings in highly metalliferous regions. The use of copper sprays or sewage sludges can also push up the figures. Plants themselves react differently to traces of copper in the soil. Nevertheless, the risk of copper contamination is ever-present. In this respect the bland conclusion of the British government report, referred to above, on the issue is chilling: 'It is unusual for the concentration of copper in the edible portion of plants to exceed 20 to 30mg/kg (dry weight).' Three pages earlier the same report confirms the same government's recommendation that 20mg/kg should be regarded as the limit for healthy eating.[2]

Water, too, is a potential carrier of copper traces. This has much to do with the recent realisation amongst scientists that acid rainfall can leach out certain metals from the soils, sending them into the water cycle for eventual human consumption. Additionally, where local water supplies are soft and/or acidic, copper can be stripped from the piping that traditionally has provided domestic plumbing in many countries.

The small town of Gusum in southern Sweden offers an object lesson. A long-term study, the 'Gusum project', was started in 1972. Its object was to measure the impact of heavy metal pollution on a local forest. The findings were less than comforting, confirming as they did that copper is a deadly visitor that acts by stealth on an unsuspecting and unprotected Nature.

Close to Gusum is a brass-works which has been in existence since 1661. It is the only industrial plant in the district and gives off emissions of copper, zinc and moderate amounts of lead. The smokestacks are not very tall, which means that emissions are deposited heavily within the immediate vicinity. Since there is no primary smelter (crude metals are imported from other areas) the levels of acidic compounds such as sulphur dioxide in the local atmosphere are practically zero. Gusum, in other words, is a self-contained environmental laboratory for the assessment of heavy metal damage.

The Gusum project has confirmed a pattern of significant heavy metal contamination of trees, soil and water supplies. Lack of good historical data makes it impossible to gauge the effects of metal pollution taking place there in previous decades or centuries, but the impact of more recent emissions has been nothing less than calamitous. Between 600 and 700 tonnes of emitted metals are present in the topsoil alone over a radius of five kilometres. Nearly two-thirds is zinc, one-third is copper and a small percentage is lead, together with traces of nickel, vanadium and cadmium.

The local vegetation has been transformed as a result of this onslaught. Lichens and mosses have steadily disappeared, leading to major changes in the composition of the forest floor. This in turn leads to greater vulnerability to drying out and erosion. The quality of the substrata changes. The make-up of the soil is affected, with vital fungi destroyed. These fungi would otherwise play an essential role in the cycling of chemical elements and compounds. Various soil animals such as earthworms, important agents in the mineralisation process, have been eliminated. Without such activities the forest ecosystem begins to die. Thus it is that the Gusum conifer groves are deteriorating fast. The vegetation of the forest floor has been killed off by heavy metal deposition. Most of the conifer regrowth, indispensable to future survival of the forest, has also perished, leaving only a sparse cover of birches and old pines.

The Gusum study provides telling proof of the voracity of heavy metals in devouring and distorting the natural ecology. It takes only the smallest act of imagination to comprehend the wider consequences for the human ecology of heavy metal pollution on a global scale, of the kind now being produced by the ever-growing reliance on such metals by the world's commercial system.

The residents of the mining district of Konnerud, a few hundred miles away in Norway, will need little help in making that act of imagination. Very recently, examination of their household water supplies revealed unnervingly high levels of heavy metal contamination. It is thought that metal traces from mining districts in the ore-rich parts of the region have been carried by irrigation systems onto agricultural land and into the domestic water network. Whatever the explanation, the levels of contamination recorded by analysts came as an unpleasant shock. Samples from water sources used to provide local households showed levels of cadmium, which is poisonous even in small amounts, measuring as high as 0.013 parts per million. This is almost three times the tolerable limit of concentration in drinking water. It needs to be stressed, in any event, that cadmium is highly lethal, especially when associated with foodstuffs, such as rice, that are very efficient in absorbing such pollutants. In a particularly tragic episode of cadmium poisoning in Japan some years ago, when heavy metals from a sulphide mine polluted irrigation waters used in local rice paddies, killing or seriously affecting a number of people in the area, the streamwater concerned was found to contain only 0.0006 to 0.0066ppm of cadmium.

Some wells in Konnerud were also found to have very high levels of other metals. Zinc concentrations of 2.8ppm were found; the tolerable concentration limit is 0.3. And Konnerud is not alone. Many other ore-bearing regions across the country face the same hazard of contaminated water networks. Asterudtjernet in eastern Norway relies on water polluted by a disused nickel mine to irrigate farmland over a wide area. Analyses of water sources have revealed high concentrations of nickel as well as other elements. In Drammensfjorden and Drammenselva, the water sources supplying local intensive agriculture have been exposed to industrial effluents for some years. Only a lack of precise knowledge about the chemical composition of the area's water system prevents more unsettling details coming to light.

How many other communities like Konnerud, Asterudtjernet and Drammensfjorden are there around the world, living under the shadow of heavy metal overload? Or, put more simply, how many similar plants, working with toxic metals and emitting poisonous effluents into the atmosphere, are there dotted across the globe, pouring their unwelcome copper, mercury, lead, cadmium and other dangerous pollutants into our lives?

The answer is not so simple. It has to do with the worldwide pattern of metal usage in primary raw material processing, manufacturing and farming, and in such secondary aspects of commercial activity like packaging and canning. An instructive exercise is to take a brief look at the evolution in the use of one particularly dangerous heavy metal, mercury, in the United States, the world's largest consumer.

It has been estimated that since 1900 more than 200 million pounds of mercury have been consumed in the US, with an acceleration in the rate of consumption since World War II. At the beginning of the 1970s, annual consumption was running at nearly 6 million pounds. This high rate of mercury usage was linked to its importance in the chlorine-alkali industry and in the fast-growing electrical sector, above all in the production of fluorescent lights, switches and batteries. Mercury has also been widely used in paint, as a way of inhibiting mildew, in the manufacture of instruments and in farming as a key ingredient of fungicides. Other uses include acting as a catalyst in the production of plastics, as a pharmaceutical preparation for the treatment of skin diseases and in dentistry. It has for many years been commonly used in laboratories.

This pattern of mercury consumption has been repeated elsewhere. After all, mercury has proved itself a valuable partner in a large number of commercial areas.

- Mercuric cyanide, which is highly soluble in water, has been used as a diuretic, an antiseptic and as a disinfectant for surgical instruments.

- Mercuric nitrate, a soluble salt, recommended itself in the manufacture of explosive caps and in the medical treatment of certain skin diseases.

- Organic mercury compounds were to be adopted as a major ingredient in a wide range of herbicides and fungicides, in medical preparations for both animals and humans and to control slimes in paper mills. The waste waters discharged from such mills could well be heavily contaminated with mercury. In some countries legislation has sought to eliminate the use of paper containing mercury in the wrapping and packaging of foods and beverages. But many other countries have taken no such steps.

● Phenylmercuric acetate has been used extensively as a herbicide for the control of crabgrass.

● Methyl and ethyl mercury compounds have been used as liquid seed dressings in places like Sweden and Canada. They have thereby added their own lethal contribution to the vast array of chemical and metallic armaments that the modern farmer now uses to 'protect' his working capital out in the fields, and incidentally to destroy millions of birds and other wildlife that happen to feed on his land. This is not even to raise the issue of the hazards that face us, the consumers, who eat his contaminated harvest.

Because of the nature of most of the commercial and medical uses for mercury, the risks of incidental release of toxic heavy metal traces into the environment are high. Most industrial plants, for instance, rely on water flows to cool, irrigate or transport raw materials; eventually these water flows have to be discharged. Hence it is that the files bulge with cases of serious mercury pollution of rivers, lakes and offshore areas, not least because many installations using mercury are actually sited close to water. Mercury production in Canada, for example, was for long located at the one site of Pinchi Lake in British Columbia. The chlor-alkali plants owned by Dow Chemical on the St Clair river, by Lake Huron, contributed greatly to serious mercury pollution of the waterway through releases from leaking tanks; similar plants operated by the Wyandotte Chemical Company on the Detroit river polluted the surrounding waters by discharging the toxic metal when ventilating the otherwise closed system. In Europe the Saale river is one of many that have been found to be carrying abnormally high levels of mercury.

Much the same observations can be made about copper. Like mercury, it was to become a key element in a broad array of industrial, agricultural and medical activities. Copper is commonly used in metal extraction, electroplating, ink manufacture, fabric dyeing, printing and photographic processes, tanning and in the pigment industry. It is employed in fungicides, bactericides, algicides and insecticides, as well as in medical treatments. And, as with mercury, man has been less than careful in preventing it from seeping into our everyday habitat.

A disturbing case study is that of the Rhine river. Being the crucial waterway of the world's major concentration of industrial infrastructure, coursing as it does through the heartland of Western Europe, the Rhine is massively polluted with chemical wastes. A recent assessment recorded two thousand separate chemical pollutants in the river, many of them the result of discharges by immense complexes run by companies like Ciba-Geigy, Hoffman-LaRoche, Sandoz, Bayer and BASF. The Rhine also supplies drinking water to about twenty million people.

In 1980 it was discovered that Bayer had been given permission by the Dutch government to dump more than half a million tonnes of acid waste a year into the sea close to the Dutch resort of Scheveningen. Analysis of these wastes revealed that they contained numerous carcinogens such as chloroform and carbon tetrachloride . . . and enormous quantities of heavy metals, including copper and mercury. On reflection, it seems strange that the Bayer company had, as its corporate logo, a linden leaf with the motto 'Bayer research for a clean environment.'

6
The Last Refuge

When the French cargo ship *Mont Louis* collided with a car ferry off the Belgian coast on the last Saturday of August 1984, the innocuous news bulletins belied the reality that lay beneath the ship's decks. By the following Monday, however, the awful truth began to emerge. The *Mont Louis*, it was discovered, was carrying 450 tonnes of uranium hexafluoride gas in thirty containers and 250 kilogrammes of plutonium, en route to the Soviet Union for reprocessing.

Because the shipwreck happened at the weekend it was more than twenty-four hours before the owners of the *Mont Louis*, the Compagnie Generale Maritime, could release details about the nature of the cargo. Not even the crew had been told they were carrying radioactive materials. An additional reason for the secrecy about the journey could have been that the ship also had on board French-made electronic equipment bound for Soviet customers, in possible contravention of the western embargo on technology sales to the Soviet bloc. Whatever the Machiavellian circumstances, the world was slow to learn the true facts about the sinking. Meanwhile, it was fast becoming clear that the North Sea had entered a new age in the history of pollution.

Salvage operations were interrupted by continuing bad weather, sometimes reaching force nine gales. Floating debris crashed through the ship's deck, freeing some of the other cargo. A huge floating crane, with a lifting capacity of 1,200 tonnes, had to be towed out into the rough waters to assist in the rescue efforts. Great care had to be taken to ensure that none of the uranium hexafluoride came into contact with the seawater, since if it did so a violent and toxic chemical reaction was likely to result.

On 11 September the *Mont Louis* broke in two. Already an

empty uranium container swept from the ship's hold had been recovered. In the meantime, the French Commissariat à l'Energie Atomique had let it be known that the containers would stand up to immersion in the sea for at least a year, and would cause only minimal pollution if they were to leak. In the light of a chequered post-war history of radioactive accidents and lame official explanations, these reassurances attracted widespread scepticism.

By early October all but one of the thirty barrels had been recovered by divers; one of them had sprung a leak while being craned up onto the salvage vessel. But the incident quickly slipped from the headlines and the busy flow of North Sea traffic returned to normal. Yet it was one more step towards global contamination of the high seas, this time with a radioactive twist. Unfortunately, it was hardly an exceptional event. Radioactive seas are the latest addition to the catalogue of man-made catastrophes that are turning our most precious resource into a quagmire of toxic substances.

The waters of the world are our last hope in the struggle to avert biocide. Yet while the oceans, rivers and lakes represent a vast, essential natural inheritance nearly 1.5 billion cubic kilometres in volume and far greater in size than the land-masses that they surround and irrigate, they too are beginning to fall prey to human profligacy. We have, perhaps, half a century before this last refuge from the high-tech holocaust is also claimed by the polluting flotsam and jetsam of civilisation.

The hydrosphere is the third component of the biosphere, along with the air, or atmosphere, and the lithosphere formed by the earth's crust. To understand the accelerating crisis of hydrospheric pollution it is necessary to view these three elements not as distinct ecosystems but as interdependent links in an ecological chain. Contamination, once it is set running by human activity, passes within and between all the parts of that chain. What makes the world's hydrosphere a more powerful actor in the global ecological drama is its capacity to permeate, to erode and corrode, to dilute, to travel and carry toxic substances over immense distances, even to change the chemical make-up of elements by mixing its own chemistry with those of its new companions.

The world's waters form a dynamic system, with the hydro-logic cycle operating through the evaporation of liquid water that is transported up into and through the atmosphere. And while this atmospheric vapour is but a tiny fraction of the entire water system, it is utterly indispensable both to the temperature balance of the globe and to the replenishment of fresh water needed for human drinking and for agriculture. Key to understanding the precarious nature of this fresh-water system is the basic fact that almost ninety-five per cent of the world's water is not fresh but saline. Moreover, most of the earth's precious flow of fresh water is locked away in polar ice and below ground in soils and rock strata. A measure of how inaccessible this tiny supply is to humanity is its so-called 'turnover rate', the length of time needed for each part to be exchanged in the hydrological cycle. For groundwater it takes around five thousand years to complete this exchange; for water frozen in polar caps it takes eight thousand years.

A starting point in assessing the growing crisis of global water pollution is to recognise that chemically pure water has never existed in Nature. Water is a powerful solvent that washes a wide range of chemicals and other substances out of the earth's crust; all waterways, even without the intervention of man, carry considerable amounts of chemicals, trace metals and other particles. Studies of unpolluted rivers and streams indicate the presence of such chemicals as calcium, magnesium, sodium, potassium, sulphates, bicarbonate and chloride, with lesser amounts of nitrates, carbon dioxide, ammonia and iron. Trace metals found in natural river water include heavy metals such as zinc, lead and copper, as well as several other metals in minor quantities. These elements have found their way into the groundwater system from the surrounding rocks and soils due to erosion and leaching since the beginning of geological time.

From the earliest years this near-pure hydrological system has been under threat from humanity. Sewage, discarded materials, carcasses and a wide assortment of debris have, by long habit, been consigned to the waters by way of disposal. But until very recently this approach to waste management posed few problems. Humanity was too small in number, its activity too innocent and the universe of water too immense, to pose any threat to rivers, lakes or seas. Only with the rise of modern industry did the balance begin to tip towards calamity. Within the space of little more than a century, we have transformed the hydrosphere from a wholesome, cleansing medium into an increasingly poisoned one. We now stand within sight of hydrospheric catastrophe.

Most industrial activities, even the most simple crafts, contribute toxins and other polluting substances to the water system by a variety of means. Water is an essential factor in almost all commercial operations for cooling, washing, mixing, diluting or carrying away wastes. A glance at the processes used in basic activities like brewing and textiles, two of the earliest modern industries, will show the vital role played by water, and the consequences for the water network. Even the innocuous-looking neighbourhood laundry contributed its share. The emergence of other industrial sectors expanded this role and thereby broadened the consequences. And as the pattern of basic industrial production has spread outwards from the older developed economies to the far corners of the world, an inexorable, ever-growing burden of pollutants has come with it. The net result has been an increasingly greater degree of contact between a once untainted water cycle and polluting elements that range from nitrogen fermented starches to dyes and alkalines. Paper, for instance, one of the most innocent-seeming products of all, is manufactured by a process that involves contaminating the surrounding water system with effluent from an enormous array of ingredients, some six hundred in all, including dyes, fillers, plasticisers, preservatives and other agents such as formaldehyde, a substance known to cause cancer in animals. This example is all the more pertinent because paper is a major component of twentieth-century life, essential to a thousand-and-one commercial activities from packaging and printing to bank notes, household decorations and toilet rolls. The level of paper consumption by a national economy is one of the key measures of degree of its economic maturity. Over the next century the world production of paper will expand to many times its current volume, with a comparable increase in its contribution of pollutants to the hydrosphere.

The greater part of the contamination from paper-making comes from the pulping process, when raw materials are broken down into a fibrous pulp by machine or by chemical action. Whichever method is used, a range of chemicals is employed to digest the wood chips so as to produce a manageable mixture. These chemicals include such agents as sodium hydroxide and sodium sulphide. The spent chemicals, together with organics from the wood, form a black liquor. The treatments applied to this liquor results in the emission of volatile and ill-smelling gases such as hydrogen sulphide. Further treatments are then introduced which yield a green liquor, followed by other processes involving the addition of substances such as calcium hydroxide, resulting in a white liquor. At each stage a variety of pulp-mill wastes are generated. The actual quantity of such pollutants delivered to rivers and to the atmosphere via chimneys depends on the age of the plant and the type of technology used, but the entire process relies on a constant flow of water passing through screen wires, showers and other parts of the paper machines as well as through beaters, regulating and mixing tanks, and other screens. This contaminated water eventually ends up in the outside environment.

Poisoning the Last Refuge
Water Pollution by Industrial Processes

Industry	Origin of Contaminant	Type of Contamination
Food		
Canning	Preparation of fruit and vegetables	Organic matter suspended solids
Dairy	Milk dilutions, buttermilk	Organic matter: protein, fats
Brewing, distilling	Grain, distillation	Dissolved organics, nitrogen fermented starches
Meat, poultry	Slaughtering, rendering bones, fats	Dissolved organics, blood, proteins etc
Sugar Beet	Handling juices, condensates	Dissolved sugar and protein
Yeast	Yeast filtration	Solid organics
Pickles	Lime water, seeds, syrup	Suspended solids, dissolved organics, variable pH (measure of acidity)
Coffee	Pulping and fermenting beans	Suspended solids
Fish	Pressed fish, wash water	Organic solids, odour
Rice	Soaking, cooking, washing	Suspended/dissolved carbohydrates
Soft Drinks	Cleaning, spillage, bottle washing	Suspended solids, low pH
Pharmaceutical		
Antibiotics	Mycelium, filtrate, washing	Suspended/dissolved organics
Clothing		
Textiles	Desizing fabric	Suspended solids, dyes, alkalines
Leather	Cleaning, soaking, bating	Solids, sulphite, chromium, lime, sodium chloride

Laundry	Washing fabrics	Turbid, alkaline, organic solids
Chemical		
Acids	Wash waters, spillage	Low pH
Detergents	Purifying surfactants	Surfactants (surface-active agents)
Starch	Evaporation, washing	Starch
Explosives	Purifying/washing of TNT and cartridges	TNT, organic acids, alcohol, acid, oil, soaps
Insecticides	Washing/purification	Organics, benzene, highly toxic acids
Phosphate	Washing, condenser wastes	Suspended solids, phosphorus, silica, fluoride, clays, oils, low pH
Formaldehyde	Residues from synthetic resin production and dyeing synthetic fibres	Formaldehyde
Materials		
Pulp and Paper	Refining, washing, screening of pulp	High solids, extremes of pH
Photographic	Spent developer and fixer	Organic and inorganic reducing agents, alkaline
Steel	Coking, washing blast furnace flue gases	Acid, cyanogen, phenol, coke, oil
Metal plating	Cleaning and plating	Metals, acid
Iron foundry	Various discharges	Sand, clay, coal
Oil	Drilling, refining	Sodium chloride, sulphur, phenol, oil
Rubber	Washing, extracting impurities	Suspended solids, chloride, odour, variable pH
Glass	Polishing, cleaning	Suspended solids

SOURCE: M. Lippmann and R. B. Schlesinger, *Chemical Contamination in the Human Environment*

The emergence of more sophisticated industrial processes in the second half of the twentieth century has meanwhile added even more hazardous elements to the equation of risk, ranging from highly dangerous chemicals to the radioactive by-products from nuclear reactors. These, coupled with the significantly greater volume of sea traffic, the rapid growth of offshore industries and the sheer immensity of the effluent flow from major industrial hinterlands around the world, have taken the steadily increasing pressure of hydrospheric pollution beyond fresh-water systems on land into the oceans themselves. Such is the scale of this development that the world's seas are now under threat from the same man-made agents that have already wreaked havoc with many parts of the land itself.

The Degrading Prospect

The global industrial machine never ceases to pour out its unwanted rubbish, increasing amounts of it into the waterways; the creation of wealth demands the constant devouring of raw materials and the transformation of crude ingredients into energy and products. This mammoth exercise will grow in size, complexity and geographic extent into the indefinite future. So great is the volume and variety of waste already produced by the world's wealth-creating edifice that waste has itself become a science, with its own vocabulary and formulae, epitomised in new studies such as *Marine Pollution* by R. B. Clark.[1] It is a science that offers a guiding hand through the otherwise bewildering morass of effluent pumped into the rivers and seas by an oblivious humanity.

The greatest volume of waste discharged into coastal waters and estuaries, as Clark points out, are degradable substances, chiefly organic material that is vulnerable to attacks by various bacteria and thus can eventually be absorbed by this process back into the natural environment. The term 'degradable wastes' covers a wide spectrum of household and industrial activities. It includes the greater part of urban sewage as well as a broad range of wastes from agriculture, including animal excreta. This latter has been increased greatly in the developed economies by the advent of factory farming and agribusinesses. It also encompasses refuse from food-processing activities that cover everything from slaughterhouse and freezing operations to oil-seed pressing and sugar-cane pulping. There is, too, the large number of activities outlined earlier, ranging from brewing and distilling to paper and wood mills, chemical installations and oil refineries and terminals. All of them make an unwelcome contribution to the mounting tide of marine filth.

A vital consideration, when surveying the problem of degradable wastes, is the speed with which bacteria can encourage the decay that is essential if these waste products are to be reabsorbed. Because if the conditions are wrong or, more important, if the flow of effluent is too great, then the degrading process is interrupted or distorted; the waste is not reabsorbed but instead produces further unwelcome by-products, while also setting off a destructive chain of events affecting flora and fauna. This, in turn, leads to further deterioration of the surrounding environment and the process of destruction is reinforced; a vicious circle of waste-induced degeneration is set in motion. In short, an excess of waste – over and above the capacity of the marine habitat to cope with it – leads to a steady disintegration of the hydrosphere and the prospect of serious long-term problems.

Other kinds of waste have varying degrees of impact and have to be dealt with by the hydrosphere by means other than bacterial degradation. There are, to begin with, 'dissipating' wastes, industrial discharges that have effect only in the immediate sea area and only for a comparatively short time. Acids and alkalis pumped into seawater are counteracted by the buffering capacity of saltwater. Even poisons such as cyanide, a commonplace waste product from the metallurgical industry, decompose in seawater and are believed to have only limited effect in the locality near to the discharge zone.

Inert particulate waste material, however, poses a different kind of problem. This category includes such things as fly ash from coal-fired power stations, colliery waste, clay and silt from various extractive operations, dredging spoil and a vast range of man-made items, invariably plastic in origin, that end up in river systems and eventually in the sea. These wastes have varying impact on the marine balance but in one particular regard can lead to serious consequences for marine life: they can cut out light penetration and thereby reduce or eliminate photosynthesis processes in plants, can clog the feeding and breathing capacities of sea animals and in time can change the very ecology of the seabed. There is also the ever-present problem of heat, one of the major by-products of industrial activities. The variation in temperature above the norm is usually about 10°C; while this is of little consequence in cooler climes, such an increase in tropical waters can take the temperature above the death point for living marine organisms. In this case, industrial heat wastes are a significant long-term threat to the balanced evolution of the marine system.

But amongst the more serious kinds of waste are those that are inherently harmful yet are neither reduced by bacteria nor dissipated by sea action. They fall into three separate categories: heavy metals, halogenated hydrocarbons and radioactivity. It is these forms of marine pollution that represent the most disconcerting threat to the wholesomeness of the hydrosphere, and therefore to the longer-term health of humankind.

The Effluent Juggernaut

As in most other aspects of global pollution, the contribution of man needs to be seen within the context of a world ecosystem which itself produces large amounts of naturally created contamination. One example is sulphur dioxide; until very recently planet Earth was alone in producing many millions of tonnes of SO_2 each year in the form of natural emissions. Now, the world's industrial machine has overtaken this natural output, thereby more than doubling the global level of sulphur dioxide emissions and creating an unprecedented degree of acid pollution. The same is occurring in the hydrosphere. Indeed, acid pollution itself is a major contributor to our worsening marine situation. But there are many others, as we shall see.

Most of the polluting substances examined in this chapter already exist in Nature. There has, for example, always been a constant flow into the oceans of organic material that has then been degraded by the action of bacteria. There have, too, always been offshore areas where oil has found its way into the coastal waters from onshore deposits, and where materials such as coal have been carried into the marine environment by erosion. Inhabitants of the coastal regions of California and the Gulf of Mexico, for instance, can testify to the long history of naturally induced oil pollution affecting their seashores. And inhabitants of certain parts of the Brazilian littoral, and of coastal stretches of south-west India, are no strangers to seawater contaminated by spontaneously produced radioactivity. But these instances are minuscule alongside the juggernaut of man-made pollution that is now close to running off the road completely, turning the world's water into a threatened medium.

A major source of marine pollution is sewage, which is poured into watercourses, river mouths and coastal seas by a rapidly growing world population and an equally fast-growing worldwide industrial infrastructure. People produce excreted effluent; industry produces a lengthening list of chemical waste of an increasingly hazardous nature. Human excrement can hardly be classified as a high-tech danger; the danger comes instead from our failure to meet the increasing scale of this effluent challenge. This facet of the emerging holocaust comes not from technical exuberance, but from neglect. We have preferred instead to apply our new technologies to the creation of immediate wealth, leaving our refuse to take care of itself. While much of the sewage sludge generated by modern sewage treatment methods is applied to the land as fertiliser, there is a limit to how much is needed for this purpose. And as the world's output of sewage steadily rises over the years to come, a growing proportion of it will have to be found an alternative outlet. The inevitable choice as dumping destination is the hydrosphere.

The scale of this human waste-making machine is already incomprehensibly large. By way of illustration, there are nearly five billion people now living on this planet, more than three times the number that existed a century ago. It is estimated that forty people between them produce about one tonne of solid waste in a year. Applied to that global population figure, this would mean that humanity currently produces about 125 million tonnes of solid waste every twelve months, or nearly 2.5 million tonnes a week. And the prospect is for an escalating output of such wastes in the years to come, as world population climbs ever upwards. The United Nations has forecast that by the end of this century at least another one billion people – and therefore another 25 million tonnes of excreted waste a year – will have been added to these statistics. Most of the growth will be in developing countries where sewage treatment technologies are often rudimentary and in most cases cannot even manage to deal with existing levels of effluent.

When sewage is introduced into the hydrospheric network a chain of chemical reactions is set in motion. Bacterial decay sets in; through a process of oxidation the molecules in organic substances are turned into stable inorganic compounds. To achieve this the bacteria present in water use up quantities of oxygen – the O in H_2O. In turn, the receiving water replaces its lost oxygen by taking in extra oxygen from the outside air. So the hydrosphere is assisted by the atmosphere, in what is a good example of the integrated global ecosystem at work. This, at least, is the theory.

Every delivery of sewage to a body of water thus demands an expenditure of oxygen found from within the chemical make-up of the water itself. Analysts talk of 'an oxygen budget', the relationship between the inflow of sewage into a water system and the capacity of that water to offer sufficient oxygen to deal with the intruder and then to replace the oxygen that has been lost. Put simply, it means that water can only handle a given amount of sewage; above that level the chemical balance of the water is thrown into confusion.

One important stage in this pattern of chemical adjustment is referred to as 'oxygen sag', in effect the temporary reduction in oxygen availability due to the demand placed on the water's oxygen content by an arrival of waste material. When the amount of waste delivered to a watercourse is considerable, the oxygen sag can be correspondingly great, leading to anoxic conditions in which a severe lack of oxygen places any living organisms in dire peril. In a typical case, a congested river estuary surrounded by heavily populated land areas will be unable to cope with the magnitudes of waste being received. The oxygen sag will be so marked that the estuary is turned into an anoxic zone; most living things will be killed off, the waters become foul-smelling and fish that would normally swim through the estuary as part of their migratory pattern will be unable to cross the zone. Their natural cycle – particularly that of new offspring – will be interrupted and the entire fish community endangered, if not destroyed completely.

At the more extreme end of the effluent spectrum, large amounts of sewage being discharged into a river system can pose very serious and direct threats to public health. All human sewage has significant amounts of enteric bacteria (originating in stomach linings) as well as disease-producing agents, viruses and the eggs of intestinal parasites. Some of these remain active even in crude sewage and sewage sludge. Thus, any development which allows these various organisms to enter the accessible water system is increasing the risk of disease from contaminated water. An obvious example is bathers swimming in polluted coastal waters. Another is the irrigation of crops with river water polluted with sewage containing parasite eggs, though, as the experts somewhat ominously point out, the risk is greater with salad crops than with vegetables 'because the eggs are destroyed in the course of cooking vegetables'.

It is no secret that sewage contamination of public water supplies is an everyday problem in most poor regions of the world. To take the well-publicised case of India, the situation is deteriorating by the month. Scientists at the country's National Environmental Engineering Institute have recently revealed that about seventy per cent of available water in India is polluted. Three-quarters of this pollution is from the community wastes of human settlements. Indeed, one estimate is that more than sixty-five per cent of all illness in India – mainly typhoid, infective hepatitis, cholera, diarrhoea and dysentery – are directly attributable to this source. To take one instance amongst many, studies show that the city of Varanisi, about six hundred kilometres south-east of Delhi, pumps 25 million gallons of untreated sewage every day into the River Ganges, the principal waterway system of the Indian sub-continent. In spite of the fact that some two hundred million people inhabit the basin of the 2,525km-long river, in the mid-1980s it had no fully operational sewage treatment plants. And of the fifty largest cities and towns along the edge of the Ganges, only ten have closed sewers; in eight of these ten, fewer than half the households are actually served by a sewerage system.

Now the evidence increasingly shows that in many parts of the developed world, that has for so long proudly boasted of its efficiency in handling a vast flow of human effluent, the authorities are failing to keep up with the problem. Already, some of the major cities of the rich world have encountered localised ecological breakdown linked to excessive output of human solid wastes into the natural water system. Much depends in each situation on local factors of geography, not least the precise mechanics of river networks and offshore marine currents. A key element in creating such a breakdown is the development of a thermocline, a condition of the water layers that separates cold, dense bottom water from warmer parts closer to the surface. When a thermocline sets in, the bacterial degradation of organic wastes on the sea floor produces a severe drop-off in the availability of oxygen, with destructive consequences for the surrounding marine ecosystem. Another vital factor is money; cleaning up a sewage-contaminated river course is almost prohibitively expensive and takes many years. In many afflicted cities the response to hydrospheric crisis has been too little, too late. Elsewhere, the day has been saved, for the moment at least, although only long-term scrutiny will tell us whether more serious, irreversible damage has been caused to the offshore marine balance.

In New York City, for instance, sewage sludge from twenty sewage treatment plants around the metropolis has been poured into the New York Bight off Long Island since the nineteenth century. At its high point, about 10 million tonnes a year were being dumped. In the vicinity of the dumping zone marine life has been severely affected. More seriously, the contamination has spread out from the Bight into nearby offshore areas. Contaminated sediments have drifted into the Hudson Trench at the mouth of the Hudson River. As an indication of the volume of waste built up over the years, in the spring and summer of 1976 a massive area of the Middle Atlantic Bight was overtaken by environmental crisis as oxygen depletion engulfed some 12,000 square kilometres of the sea floor. The worst affected spot was at least 100 kilometres south of the New York dumping site. Analysts estimate that over the summer of that year about 143,000 tonnes of the clam *Spisula* were killed as a consequence. A similar fate would have befallen other living organisms in the area.

In mid-1982 a similar crisis developed over a wide area off the German and Danish coasts. Fish were killed in their millions; millions more abandoned the region to escape the toxic waters. Fauna previously flourishing at the lowest depths were wiped out. Much the same kind of marine disaster occurred in the Heligoland Bight in 1975, after years of sewage sludge dumping by the city of Hamburg. And, as R. B. Clark records, London said goodbye to its indigenous river salmon as long ago as 1820, when sewage from the rapidly growing capital began to be discharged into the Thames. Even twentieth-century technology could not keep up with the burgeoning output of human waste. By the 1950s some twenty miles of the river through London were anoxic during dry spells. Only a massive investment programme in sewage treatment works could reverse the downward trend.[2]

Such massive investment was not to be available for the Mersey estuary, one of the most polluted waterways in the Western world and a case study widely used by marine specialists. The River Mersey passes through a series of huge industrial conurbations, including Greater Manchester and a coagulated mass of cotton towns such as Oldham, Bolton and Rochdale, before reaching Liverpool with its immense hinterland of factories and refineries. Unlike most other major industrial estuaries, therefore, the Mersey is already heavily charged with effluent before it arrives at its congested meeting point with the sea. From Warrington, many miles inland at the upstream head of the estuary, down to the sea there are a great number of effluent discharge zones where the waste inputs are invariably untreated. In Liverpool alone there are twenty-six sewage outlets. And the Manchester Ship Canal, built in the 1890s, by-passes the upper and middle stretches of the river, thus bringing very little fresh-water relief to the estuary itself. Even the tidal surges that would otherwise help to cleanse the estuarial water network merely succeed in pushing back the fresh-water stretches into the ship canal, which then overflows and dumps more effluent into the estuary further upstream. As a result, the Mersey estuary is seen by specialists as an extreme example of river death. The upper estuary becomes anoxic in summer. The mud banks along the entire length of the estuary are seriously contaminated by heavy metals. Along the lower estuary there is a constant problem of visible solid wastes, which drift ashore at holiday beaches at places like Crosby, Formby and New Brighton.

The Politics of Waste

The extreme conditions of the Mersey estuary have earned it a unique place in the annals of water pollution. Ironically, the situation would have been even more intractable had not the industrial momentum of the area – and hence its waste-making capacities – been severely curtailed by the collapse of the region's economic vitality. As it is, even in its half-active state the Merseyside hinterland, covering some three to four million people, has continued to lead the world in effluent excesses. In 1983 Britain's then Minister for the Environment, Michael Heseltine, condemned the locality as 'an affront to the standards of civilised society'. Almost 2 million tonnes of sewage sludge were at that time being dumped in the seas around Liverpool Bay.

Under a new plan, it is intended to build a series of sewage works along the banks of the river to cut down the volume of untreated human waste and toxic industrial refuse pouring into the estuary. But there is a downside cost to the project: under the proposals the actual volume of sewage sludge to be dumped will double to around 4 million tonnes a year, the greater part of it ending up in the Irish Sea. There is also a very large question mark over the long-term financing of the scheme. Public spending is under increasing fire from British governments; added to this uncertainty is the prospect that Britain's water authorities are to be sold off into private ownership, thus imposing a more commercially aware management regime that may view such expenditures as unprofitable and therefore unnecessary. Besides these factors, the Liverpool city administration has itself fallen into serious financial difficulties in recent years, not unconnected with the chronic unemployment that has overtaken the once-prosperous metropolis. With these imponderables at work the ambitious plans for cleaning up the Mersey may never be completed.

But the holidaymakers who frequent the resorts close to Merseyside are not alone in having to face the perils of sewage-infected waters. For several years the signs have indicated that hundreds of beaches around the British Isles are turning into cesspools. Scientists have become increasingly concerned at the deteriorating condition of the seas around the country's major vacation towns. They have regularly pointed to evidence that the quality of bathing water at Britain's top resorts, including heavily patronised places like Blackpool and Scarborough, is known to fail standards set by the Common Market Commission in Brussels.

Not untypical of the constant reminders of Britain's beach problem was the revelation in June 1982 that schoolchildren swimming in Swansea Bay, in South Wales, had contracted infections thought to be linked to human effluent; a marine biologist at the town's university college advised people to stay well clear of the polluted waters, which form part of the Bristol Channel that runs out to sea from the River Severn. There were to be many more such scares around Britain over the months that followed, so many in fact that by July 1985 ministers at the Department of the Environment were obliged to order Britain's ten water authorities to act positively to deal with the growing danger. The department ordered that two hundred British beaches should be sampled during the summers of 1985 and 1986 to test their bacteriological quality. Water experts were not optimistic about the outcome: studies by the Welsh Water Authority involving one hundred and twenty beaches had already shown eighty-two of them to be below EEC standards. Meanwhile, as if in ironic welcome to the ministerial initiative, the sewage system feeding the Bristol Channel struck again just weeks after the word had gone out from the Department of the Environment. Water scientists announced that an outbreak of diarrhoea and stomach pains that had afflicted more than one thousand people in the south Bristol area in July 1985 had been traced to the amoeba *Giardia lamblia* that had been found in local tapwater supplies. Analysts believed the organism entered the water system after broken sewers had leaked effluent into soil around a reservoir operated by the local waterworks company.

Within two months of this announcement, further evidence

emerged casting doubt on the purity of Britain's drinking water.
The annual report of the Institution of Environmental Health
Officers, published in September 1985, drew attention to the fact
that more than a quarter of all samples of private water supplies
tested by health officers had failed to reach the required EEC
microbiological standards. And scrutiny of public water supplies
showed that one sample in eight out of a test group of 18,000
samples failed to meet those standards. The danger of effluent
contamination, it seems, is an all-pervasive one that, by
percolating into the groundwater system and via this into
reservoirs, now affects fresh water in the home just as much as
saltwater at the seaside.

Efforts to raise the standards of bathing water around
Britain's beach areas, meanwhile, are not helped by a habit of
bureaucratic secrecy and awkwardness. As long ago as 1981, the
journal *New Scientist* described how the British government and
the water authorities (many of them run by traditional and
authoritarian cliques) contrived to define bathing beaches in
such a way as to exclude from official EEC scrutiny such
heavily used resorts as Brighton and Blackpool, precisely the
locations giving most reason for concern. As the journal
surmised, beaches in places like this 'might not have met the
bacteriological standards set by the EEC for "designated
beaches"'. The device used by the British ministry involved in
the affair was to affix the term 'designated' only to a beach on
which, on specific days, at least one thousand people could be
found on a stretch of coastline one kilometre long. This approach
was far more restrictive than guidelines set elsewhere in the
EEC; it had the effect of eliminating many beach areas that
otherwise would have merited close attention.[3]

Indeed, the British authorities have been in the habit of
publishing bacteriological data on a national basis for only
twenty-seven beaches; even these were made public only in
response to a 1980 EEC directive on bathing water. In this
respect, British foot-dragging over the new EEC policy is fully in
character. France, in contrast, has designated thousands of
beaches, including those on inland river banks. In the autumn of
1984, the European Commission instigated steps to take the
British government to the European Court of Justice to obtain a
ruling forcing Britain to meet the requirements of the EEC
directive.

Again, the decisive factor is money. Practically nothing has been spent on the maintenance and improvement of Britain's sewerage infrastructure since it was first laid down in the late nineteenth century. It has never been a national political issue; few politicians have ever seen the benefits of building their political careers on such an unpleasant subject. The guiding rule has been the maxim applied to the entire spectrum of waste hazards: 'out of sight, out of mind'. Much the same outlook has been applied to dealing with the consequences, even more so in this age of public frugality. It is estimated, for example, that cleaning up Blackpool beach alone so as to meet EEC rules would cost at least £30 million. A thousand British beaches would thereby represent a potential cost of around £30 billion, more than a tenth of the country's entire national output for a year.

British reluctance should nevertheless not obscure the parlous state that also afflicts Europe's most popular vacation sites around the Mediterranean littoral. For many decades this almost landlocked sea has absorbed an ever-growing flood of wastes from coastal zones overtaken by belated industrialisation, rapid population growth and an unprecedented tourist boom. Coupled with the fact that the Mediterranean does not have the advantages of a tidal regime to clean and replenish its waters, this surge of human activity along its shores has taken this ancient expanse of water to the edge of the abyss of dangerous contamination; in some areas the situation has passed beyond that point.

A measure of the problem posed by human effluent can be gained by reading a study produced recently by the UN Environment Programme on microbiological pollution of the Mediterranean by sewage. Its findings, drawn up in collaboration with the World Health Organisation, were alarming enough to dissuade even the most adventurous gourmand from eating in the otherwise charming restaurants that nestle in the many harbours and bays of Europe's southern coastline. Only the diplomatic sensitivity of United Nations officials, acutely conscious of the potential impact on tourism of any negative comments, prevented the naming of specific resorts and eating-places. The report found that only between three and four per cent of fifty unnamed sampling locations in four unspecified Mediterranean nations were suitable for the direct consumption of shellfish. Because of the ingestive mechanisms of marine forms such as oysters, clams and mussels, which work on a filter principal, these shellfish build up concentrations of bacteria and viruses from sewage during feeding. Hence the consumption of raw or partly cooked shellfish caught in congested coastal waters raises considerable risks of contracting viral diseases like hepatitis. There is also great likelihood of a connection between bathing in sewage-polluted waters and the incidence of respiratory infections and gastroenteritis, better known as 'holiday tummy'.

The UN/WHO study also revealed that the Mediterranean has a beach problem every bit as serious as that found in Britain. Applying EEC criteria, two-thirds of the beaches looked at in fourteen separate countries around the Mediterranean coast were found to be the wrong side of the safety divide on grounds of effluent pollution. Swimmers were especially advised to avoid drinking seawater.

Similar evidence of serious damage to water systems can be found in almost every other region of Europe where industrial development and fast population growth have taken their toll. In Poland, for instance, the problem has become so severe that many large water pipelines have to stop working from time to time, or the supply of drinking water reduced, because of excessive pollution. The Vistula river, downstream from the city of Cracow, is described in some reports as being so infested with wastes that it cannot be included in any pollution classification.

Elsewhere the true dimensions of the crisis are obscured by lack of data or straightforward bureaucratic misrepresentation. Water authorities across the world have proved to be exceedingly slow to react to the growing threat. In view of the mounting proof that sewerage systems are failing to meet the challenge of effluent overload, this is a deeply perturbing development. It is even more disturbing when it is realised that household sewage is only a small fraction of the total flow of toxic substances. The crux of the problem is the rapidly escalating outpourings of poisons by world industry.

A Lethal Solution

A team of US scientists from the University of Western Illinois recently published details of a research project that examined drinking water taken from a reservoir in the state. The findings showed that chemical waste being washed into the water by rains were mutagenic, capable of producing genetic changes in living things. Their unadorned revelations need no further embellishment as yet another warning signal of the emerging crisis.

Using a method called the 'Tradescantia' micronucleus test, the scientists exposed plant cuttings to the water and followed through by subsequently examining the young flower-buds for signs of abnormality. The tests proved positive; toxic substances present in the water were producing genetic mutations to the plant forms. Further studies revealed that the micronuclei causing the genetic damage were far more prevalent at certain times of the year. To be precise, water taken from the lake in July (over two successive years) was found to produce nearly three times more abnormalities than would otherwise be expected. This peak period coincided with an increased run-off of chemicals from surrounding industrial land brought about by heavier summer rainfall.[4]

The scientific literature now paints an increasingly alarming picture of a pollution-induced transformation of the marine habitat, both offshore and in the fresh-water networks that provide us with drinking supplies. As we have seen, organic sewage from households and industry has made a large contribution to that degeneration. But the major problem stems from other kinds of refuse, from toxic chemicals and radioactive wastes dumped on Nature's doorstep by factories and nuclear installations. Directly or otherwise, these toxic substances find their way into the hydrosphere. The oil industry, too, makes a massive contribution to that plight through discharges and accidental spillages that have spread millions of tonnes of petroleum (itself a densely-packed mass of potentially danger-ous hydrocarbons) across the waters, most of it without any regard for the outcome. Now the consequences of this wanton-ness for plant life, fish and sea-dwelling mammals around the world are slowly becoming clear. It will not be too long before the effects on humanity are only too apparent.

Already there is weighty testimony as to the effects of advanced pollution on certain kinds of sea animal. Baltic seals, for instance, have suffered a dramatic fall-off in numbers due to reproductive failures related to high levels of DDT and PCBs, two of the more lethal ingredients in pesticides. The endangered white-tailed eagle has been caught by a similar reproductive failure, this time linked to the laying of thin-shelled eggs as a result of eating fish contaminated with PCBs and heavy metals. Spawning areas in certain stretches of the Baltic have been

disturbed because of entrophication caused by excessive pollution. And anecdotal evidence concerning the destruction of
inshore fishery zones is legion. This evidence is now being
increasingly supported by thorough scientific analysis. An
extensive fish kill observed in July 1980 in a creek near a small
community in the north of Sweden was traced to leakage of a
fungicide containing chlorophenols from the premises of a
sawmill company, where it was used for wood impregnation.
Further investigation revealed that the leakage was no
accident: a hole had been drilled into the drum to facilitate its
slow, preferably unobserved, disposal into the watercourse.

The chlorophenols were found to have spread through more
than fifteen kilometres of the river-lake system connected to the
creek. Examination of the affected fish showed that death had
been caused by direct toxic effect on their livers, the first and
major target organ for chemicals after entering through the
gills. Researches elsewhere into similar incidents confirm that
discharges of toxic substances such as pesticides produce
contamination of both fish and water for some considerable time
after the discharges have stopped. One study found that
pentachlorophenol still persisted in the sediments of a fresh-
water lake two years after a spill, and there were traces of PCP
still present in fish six months after the same accident. Indeed,
PCP levels actually rose in later months due to leaching out of
the chemicals from contaminated areas by heavy rains.

Such inshore catastrophes can be a precursor of more widespread fishery collapse, affecting much larger nearshore areas.
From the Pacific and Atlantic coasts of the United States to the
congested coastal waters of Europe such indigenous fish as
salmon and sea-run trout, for instance, have vanished from
streams where once they flourished in abundance. Elsewhere,
the complex ecosystem around such phenomena as coral reefs
and mangroves are at serious risk from river-carried pollution
that can disrupt the food-chains that have sustained life forms
for thousands of years, leading to permanent destruction of the
underwater balance.

Most of these instances of species death are linked to
pollutants that can also harm people. All that is required is an
increase in pollution to levels that are beyond the boundaries of
human safety. This would mean lifting the pollution readings
from levels, for example, that are already producing genetic
mutations in plants, to levels that will produce the same

horrifying effects on humans; or from levels of pesticide contamination that are known to kill fish by destroying their livers, to levels that will produce an equally lethal reaction in people. It is nothing more than a matter of degree, of raising the quantities involved; the flow of toxic substances into our water systems is, after all, well under way.

It now seems certain that we are in sight of this calamitous goal. The surge of chemical and radioactive effluent that has been let loose on the marine world over the post-war years, and that has accelerated ominously since the 1970s, is now carrying the dials that measure toxic danger towards red alert. One of the more disconcerting developments taking us towards this unwelcome eventuality is the dramatically rising index of heavy metal contamination that is steadily poisoning vast expanses of the world's water. This danger alone is serious enough to warrant an international response of the utmost urgency.

Heavy metal contamination of groundwater, as we have seen, is now recognised by an increasing number of scientists as a serious by-product of acid rainfall. Precipitation infused with chemical particles that have been emitted by motor vehicles, power stations, smelters and other industrial operations is now known to have a leaching effect on soils and rock layers. The result is that highly dangerous metals like mercury, copper, lead and cadmium are being progressively carried into the water network and therefore into rivers, lakes and offshore areas and, more alarmingly, into domestic water supplies. Industrial wastes add further to the contaminatory flow. Run-off from pesticide-covered agricultural land raises that toxic flow even more.

The crucial factor is the man-made increment in metal levels over and above natural inputs. It is, of course, axiomatic that this planet is endowed with immense quantities of metals of every description. For eons they have trickled into the marine environment. It is estimated, for instance, that about 325,000 tonnes of copper flow into the world's waters every year as a result of erosion of mineralised rocks. About 3,500 tonnes of mercury come from the weathering of mercury-bearing rocks. In addition an indeterminate amount is released each year into the atmosphere as gases from volcanoes and other vents in the earth's crust. But the contribution of humanity is rapidly overtaking these quantities. The 7.5 million tonnes of copper used annually by world industry is more than twenty times the natural input. The amount of mercury coming from rock erosion is little more than half the quantity used each year by manufacturing enterprise.

Cadmium is a particularly telling example of the cost to human well-being of man's growing courtship with heavy metals. It gained notoriety following discovery of its causal involvement in an outbreak of 'itai-itai' disease in Japan soon after the tragic episode of mass mercury poisoning in Minamata. This second metal-induced tragedy claimed more than one hundred lives, ample testimony to the lethal potency of this little-known element. Victims who are unlucky enough to survive suffer a degeneration of their bone consistency to the point where limbs break like dry twigs.

Though cadmium is readily found in the earth's crust, it is closely associated with zinc and is made available to business users only as a by-product of zinc smelting. Total world production now amounts to some 18,000 tonnes a year, with most of it going to companies making plastics, solders and other alloys; it is also used in batteries and in some electroplating activities. But only a very small percentage – less than ten per cent – of cadmium used in these processes is recycled. Practically all of it is discharged into the environment. In addition, there is a steady flow of cadmium into both the atmosphere and the hydrosphere from other industrial operations. These include fumes and dust from lead and zinc mining, rinsing water from electroplating, cadmium lost from various galvanised metals through corrosion, and cadmium released through wear and tear from zinc oxides used in automobile tyres. Overall, it is estimated that about 8,000 tonnes of cadmium ends up every year in the oceans; about half of this input originates from man-made sources.

These metals react to their marine surroundings differently but all, in their various ways, pose an immediate threat to living things. Mercury, for instance, usually becomes attached to the surface of other particles rather than being taken up in solution. In its organic forms, mercury can be converted by microbial systems into highly toxic methyl mercury, which can in turn be accumulated by organisms such as shellfish. The rate of absorption of mercury by fish of the swimming variety differs as between species and according to the level of contamination of their home waters. Most kinds of fish from oceanic waters have a mercury content of about 0.15 parts per million. Fish taken from areas closer to industrial sources of heavy metal pollution will have significantly higher readings. Cod found in the strait between Denmark and Sweden, for example, have been recorded as having nine times the oceanic level. In contrast, cod caught off Greenland, where industrial and other sources of heavy metal are minimal, show readings as low as 0.01 parts per million.

In the case of cadmium, more than one-third of the metal accumulates in bottom sediments, most of it on the continental shelf. While cadmium is not readily taken up by fish and sea mammals, it does build up in plankton close to the surface. Here it is consumed by petrels and other sea birds; as with other species, the offending poison accumulates in the vital organs. Petrels have been found to contain nearly 50 parts per million of cadmium (dry weight) in the liver and 240 parts per million in the kidney. More seriously, very large concentrations are found in molluscs, with cadmium readings reaching as high as 2,000 ppm in the liver. Tests on types of oceanic squid have yielded figures of around 1,900ppm. Very high levels have also been found in whelks; one study of molluscs in the Bristol Channel off south-west England produced cadmium readings as high as 38ppm. Meanwhile, an investigation of oysters from the Derwent estuary of Tasmania – set in train after an outbreak of nausea and vomiting among people who had recently eaten them – revealed concentrations of cadmium as high as 173ppm.

Copper, though also extremely toxic to humans, is an essential element for the sustenance of life for most sea creatures. High concentrations are to be found in a wide range of marine inhabitants from shellfish to octopuses, many of them figuring amongst the delicacies on any restaurant menu. Again, excesses of the metal collect in the liver and other vital organs; one study recorded as much as 4,800ppm in the livers of octopuses and 2,000ppm in the innards of lobsters. Some types of oyster can build up exceptionally high concentrations; their blood cells have been found to contain upwards of 20,000ppm of the metal. Copper is nevertheless highly toxic to a large number of other marine life-forms, a quality that recommends it to manufacturers of paints and other preparations designed to prevent encrustation and fouling of boats and marine structures. More popular still as an anti-fouling agent is tin, which has become a preferred ingredient in paints used by boat operators to reduce the problems caused by barnacles and weeds. As a result, a new source of metal pollution has evolved, with reports of growing harm to marine organisms such as oysters.

Even a cursory examination of the media in recent years will reveal a steady accumulation of evidence about the toxic threat to people posed by this increasing contamination of the world's water by metals, above all the threat linked to such poisons in our drinking supplies. Contamination of the oceans, after all, is in large part the result of wholesale metal pollution of onshore fresh-water networks. But because there is only a limited awareness amongst the general public about the nature of this new threat, the widely dispersed media references go unnoticed:

- In May 1982 more than half a million Brazilians were left without drinking water after the dyke of a storage lake burst and toxic mud flowed into the Paraibuna river in the heavily industrialised state of Minas Gerais. Following the disaster the river contained twenty times the permitted maximum levels of cadmium, zinc and lead. Cattle and other animals drinking the water were found dead on the river bed; millions of fish were killed. Other animals and fish survived, posing a serious threat to people in the area who may eventually eat them. The Paraibuna river supplies about fifty Brazilian towns with drinking water and delivers a significant volume of water to the South Atlantic.

- According to a study recently completed in Finland by three Finnish universities and the national Water Board, a large number of the country's lakes are now seriously polluted with mercury. Pike in forty per cent of the ninety-three lakes examined in the study were adjudged unsuitable for breeding.

- In October 1984 a conference in Bremen of environment ministers from major West European countries was given information disclosing that up to 22,000 tonnes of mercury, lead and cadmium are dumped in the North Sea every year. Much of this toxic effluent comes from the Rivers Elbe, Rhine and Meuse.

- A meeting of the International Water Tribunal held in Rotterdam has considered forty complaints against major companies accused of dumping unacceptable quantities of heavy metals and other hazardous pollutants in the seas and rivers of Western Europe. Among the toxic substances being dumped were cadmium, mercury and arsenic.

- Recent studies in the Scottish towns of Glasgow, Renfrew and Kyle have shown that at least seventy per cent of the people in some districts could be drinking water containing levels of lead above the safety limit set by the World Health Organisation. In the town of Ayr on the coast south of Glasgow more than ten per cent of water samples had ten times the levels of lead deemed to be safe; some households had twenty or even thirty times the safety level. These Scottish figures have to be seen against a national problem of metal-polluted water that has already reached serious proportions. A report published in July 1985 pointed out that some seven and a half million people in Britain could be at risk from lead poisoning linked to contaminated water supplies.

● Limpets found on the Californian coast near San Francisco can contain lead levels as high as 100 parts per million as a result of atmospheric fall-out, leading to contamination of offshore areas.

The Mundane Killers
As if this escalating confrontation of the hydrosphere with human effluent and toxic metals were not enough to condemn the world's water resources to eternal contamination, there are other polluting pressures bearing down on the purity of our rivers, lakes and seas. Chief among them are hazardous chemicals, oil and radioactive waste. Individually they represent serious dangers to the natural environment and, through Nature and the water cycle, pose potentially intolerable challenges to our own biochemical security. Acting in concert, they add yet another ominous dimension to the equation of human risk.

Pollution of the water system by chemicals is the inevitable outcome of a massive world dependency on high-tech solutions to problems arising in every facet of late-twentieth-century commercial activity, from agriculture and mining to food processing and pharmaceuticals. It is calculated that the advanced nations now manufacture some 70,000 different chemicals for industrial and agricultural customers; most of these substances have not been properly tested for signs of longer-term danger to humans. One reason is the obvious one that there has not been sufficient time to assess that danger.

These chemical compounds, developed for an ever-expanding list of functions, eventually enter the hydrosphere, either by atmospheric emissions, waste discharges, dumping or run-off from the land. Unlike metals, which exist naturally, a great number of these compounds are man-made. On the other hand they share with metals the capacity to remain as permanent additions to the environment. The world's press is replete with coverage of incidents involving chemical waste; few people take the time to gather them together to create a global picture. If this were to be done the results would be horrifying. Typical of that news coverage is a story from the *Corriere della Serra* in February 1985 pointing out that Italy's Adriatic Sea is polluted by more than 14,000 tonnes of phosphorus every year; a third of it comes from household detergents, one-fifth from agricultural activities. There are hundreds of similar stories worldwide reported every year.

One important category of chemicals is that of halogenated hydrocarbons, characterised by their low molecular weight; the category includes a wide range of industrial agents, amongst them vinyl chloride, dichlorethane, carbon tetrachloride, perchlorethylene and chlorofluorocarbons. The complicated names disguise everyday purposes, most of which would be widely regarded as indispensable components of modern living. They make it possible to make such mundane items as dry-cleaning fluids, aerosol propellants, foamed plastics, coolants and a host of basic products. They also include amongst their number some of the most viciously damaging substances known to medical science; vinyl chloride, for instance, is a proven carcinogen of considerable potency. At least 35 million tonnes of such chemicals are produced worldwide each year; almost all of it ends up in the outside environment.

Then there are the chlorinated hydrocarbons (which have higher molecular weights) that include the more troublesome pesticides and polychlorinated biphenyls, or PCBs, that now feature so regularly in the literature on hazardous water pollution. This category boasts some of the more notorious contaminants produced by human inventiveness this century, among them DDT, lindane, benzene hexachloride and the infamous 'drins' (pesticides such as aldrin). Such is the pervasive energy of these compounds that they have taken up permanent residence in the biochemistry of late-twentieth-century homo sapiens, chiefly through residues on food and through the water cycle. Thus, cancer-causing chemicals, including PCBs, are to be found in ninety-nine per cent of all Americans. According to the US National Cancer Institute, US citizens have a thirty-one per cent chance of contracting cancer before the age of seventy-four; most of the causes are environmental contaminants such as toxic chemicals.[5]

One of the most exhaustively researched on this list, as far as marine pollution and the human food chain is concerned, is DDT. It is known that when DDT enters rivers it is consumed in small amounts by millions of tiny fish. Instead of being excreted by these minnows, the chemical lodges in their fatty tissues. And as these small fish are eaten by bigger fish, and these are eaten by birds, so the ratio of DDT to body weight increases. Eventually the concentration of hazardous pesticide arrives on the dining table, in the shape of fish, fowl, game or other relevant animal, ready for human consumption. All of these pesticides have been in copious use since the start of the postwar period. Though many of them have since been outlawed by concerned governments, vast amounts are now lodged in the soil cover and in the sediments of estuaries and watercourses across the developed world, from whence they can continue to contaminate water supplies and fishing areas for some considerable time to come. More seriously for the future, such chemicals remain in common use in less rigorously regulated regions of the developing world. The highly toxic DDT is a clear example: though banned for use in the United States, US chemical companies still produce more than 18 million kilograms of DDT pesticide every year. Most of it is exported to less sophisticated economies in South America, Africa and Asia; in such places the era of danger is just beginning.

A striking example is India, which figures so regularly in assessments of the emerging threat to the younger industrial economies. It was no accident that the tragedy of Bhopal occurred on the Indian sub-continent; in its enthusiasm for progress the authorities in Delhi have welcomed every instrument of high-tech expertise, though not always with adequate attention to the consequences of the unfettered use of hazardous compounds. In doing so they have made India vulnerable to the ravages of the high-tech holocaust, not least in the domain of water. A recent assessment of the dramatic deterioration in the quality of Indian fresh-water systems included a survey of four of the major river networks; because of the impoverished state of India's public infrastructure such natural river systems are critically important to many millions of local inhabitants. Yet all of these vital rivers are falling victim to unsustainable chemical pollution from pesticides and industrial chemicals:

● The Ganges river system, which drains about one-quarter of the
  country's land surface, is seriously polluted by wastes from

tanneries, DDT manufacturing plants, paper and pulp mills, petro-chemical and fertiliser plants and textile mills. One exercise in the study discovered that a show factory and distillery alone discharged 250,000 litres of unprocessed waste into the waters every day. So toxic was the river that fish placed in the effluents of the shoe factory died within forty-eight hours.

- The Hooghly river, a tributary of the Ganges, is seriously polluted even by Indian standards. A major cause is the massive amount of waste produced by the teeming industrial districts of Calcutta: more than one hundred and fifty factories regularly dump their toxic refuse into the river.

- The Yamuna river which passes through Delhi, is estimated to pick up nearly 200 million litres of untreated sewage and 20 million litres of industrial discharges every twenty-four hours.

- A tributary of the Yamuna, the Chambal river, receives the wastes of a fertiliser complex, an atomic power station, a thermal power facility and a cluster of industrial establishments around Kota.

Elsewhere in India researchers found blatant disregard for the hazards posed by carelessly dumped chemical waste. In Vapi, in the industrial state of Gujarat, chemical debris was discovered piled high on open land. When the monsoons set in, the rains wash lethal pesticides from the dump into the groundwater system and thereby into local drinking supplies; the use of dangerous pesticides such as the organochlorines, for instance, is permitted under Indian law. It is hardly surprising that Indian health statistics perennially include a significant number of pesticide poisonings.

Yet India is just one corner of the developing world. Imagine how prevalent, and how dangerously toxic, is this same degree of chemical pollution in other poor regions of the planet. Most of these regions are as yet uncharted by analysts of the man-made chemical catastrophe that is rapidly overtaking our water resources. One area that has been studied is the basin of the River Bogotá in Colombia; the findings are a dramatic warning of what probably awaits researchers of other river systems in the developing world. Because of the comprehensive scale of human and industrial pollution in Colombia, it is estimated that only one citizen in four has access to unpolluted water. Along the banks of the Bogotá river itself the figure is almost zero. A dense expanse of industrial plants, together with the daily effluent flow from more than five million local residents, has turned the waterway into an open sewer. And the toll of human health confirms the heavy costs of such a crisis: the small town of Tocaima, totally dependent on the river for water for its homes and farmland, has Colombia's highest rate of infant mortality. In the second half of the 1970s this death rate climbed by nearly seventy per cent, with other effluent-related infections of the population jumping by a third.

A New Black Death

The explosion of world industry would have been impossible without massive expansion of the world energy industry. In particular, two new energy forms have burgeoned in the twentieth century, both of them bringing in their wake stark challenges to the earthly habitat and to the people it sustains. Oil is a child of Nature; nuclear energy is an infant of pure science. Yet in their different ways they have turned on their creators, to become unwelcome – and even deadly – intruders on man's territory.

Oil pollution of the seas and rivers is not a recent phenomenon. From the earliest days of the world oil boom the warning signs were there. One concerned writer penned these words in 1926: 'Of recent years pollution by oil has assumed grave proportions. Oil has fouled beaches . . . destroyed the amenities of many seaside resorts . . . been the cause of fires in harbours . . . numerous birds have perished miserably . . .' The words were both prescient and, unhappily, excessively optimistic. The oil threat to the hydrosphere has become so severe that we are now in sight of marine catastrophe affecting vast areas of ocean and nearshore waterways, with serious consequences for human health.

Being a liquid, petroleum is a difficult prisoner. It escapes with ease from even the most meticulous guardianship and flows freely on the waters when it encounters them. Accidental loss from refineries alone is estimated to contribute some 200,000 tonnes of oil pollution to the oceans every year. From a typical effluent source such as a major estuarial city, oil and grease make up one of the most significant categories of polluting waste. In the offshore dumping sites south of New York, for example, this type of effluent amounts to nearly 900 tonnes a day, second only to outpourings of carbon-type wastes. There are discharges and spills from oil tankers at sea, as well as oil-polluted washing water poured overboard after the ships' tanks are cleaned out. And there is a constant flow of oil into the marine environment from tankers that have sunk as a result of storms, collisions or enemy action. The Persian Gulf has become a tragic example of oil-induced asphyxia as a result of continual discharges and spills from refineries and tankers, the latter source being massively increased by leaks from vessels damaged by fighting in the long Iran-Iraq war.

Crude oil is a mixture of hydrocarbons, sulphur, oxygen, nitrogen and certain trace elements. During refining very large amounts of steam and water are used for heating, distilling and cooling. And various acids and solvents are used in the treatment stages. All these elements, as well as hydrocarbon products, concentrate in the waste water that is constantly being discharged by refinery complexes. Unless treated to remove these pollutants, this waste water adds yet more chemical toxicity to the waterways. Oil and oil fractions are unwelcome visitors to the marine habitat, where they cause distortions in the growth patterns of plankton and other living forms essential to the development of the underwater ecosystem. Serious oil pollution will probably kill many categories of sea vegetation, thus upsetting natural protective mechanisms vital to the longer-term wholesomeness of the hydrosphere.

But beyond the damage wreaked by oil on the hydrosphere there is a potential risk to humans. Some petroleum hydrocarbons are toxic to man; more seriously, some polycyclic aromatic hydrocarbons are known to be cancer-causing agents. Though there is little firm proof, some scientists believe these substances can concentrate in the tissues of marine organisms and that these concentrations build up to hazardous levels at the upper reaches of the food chain, thus posing a danger to human beings who consume the contaminated fish. Whatever the current state of proof, there is no questioning the reports of fish afflicted with tumours and fin erosion in places like the Brittany coast after massive oil spills (in this case after the wrecking of the giant tanker *Amoco Cadiz*). It is also known that concentrations of a very potent oil-related carcinogen, benzo[a]pyrene, are found in clams, shrimps, crabs, plaice and herring taken from polluted waters.

The intensity of the oil threat to oceans and fresh-water systems is denied recognition by the general public for the simple reason that oil-spill disasters are inconsistently reported and rarely, if ever, viewed as an accumulating catastrophe. The moment news details of a spill leave the headlines the matter passes into oblivion rather than into a ledger of escalating marine pollution. Yet each and everyone of these news stories is another assault on the purity of the hydrosphere, and therefore on the safety of the human habitat. A random reading of the press in the 1980s reveals a depressing pattern:

- In May 1980 a US publication, *Oil Spill Intelligence Report*, reveals that 'loss of oil' figures for 1979 were fifty-six per cent higher than for 1978. It records that 328 million gallons of lost oil resulted in the deaths of 250 people, 270,000 fish and 50,000 birds. In June the same year, a report of the UK Advisory Committee on oil pollution of the sea discloses that a record amount of oil was spilled onto the oceans in the previous year. One single incident in the Gulf of Mexico, the blow-out of the well Ixtoc 1, resulted in 140 million gallons of oil being released into the sea.

- In July 1983 the World Wildlife Fund claims that oil pollution from damaged oil wells in the Iranian Nowruz field, running at twelve hundred barrels a day, has reached 'catastrophic' proportions, with a heavy death toll amongst turtles, dolphins, fish, sea snakes, birds and sea cows. Other estimates put the spillage rate as high as six thousand barrels a day. The oil disaster expert Red Adair, noting that the spills are coming from at least eight wells in two offshore oilfields, puts the spill rate at more than ten thousand barrels per day.

- In June 1983 a report commissioned by the municipal council of Aviles, a town on the north coast of Spain, reveals that the estuary on which the town is located is one of the most polluted in the world because of the effluent flowing from an immense steelworks nearby; most of the effluent is oils and greases.

- In September 1984 a state of emergency is declared on the Danube river after petrol is released from a Hungarian tug after a collision with a Czechoslovak cargo vessel. Wells are closed and precautions taken to stop the pollution entering a nuclear power station at Paks.

- In September 1984 serious pollution occurs in the Gulf of Bothnia off the Swedish coast after a Finnish cargo ship runs aground and leaks heavy fuel oil into the water, which then drifts through the nature reserve at Vaasa. A Finnish government official estimates the incident to be the country's most expensive oil disaster ever.

● In August 1985 poor weather impedes the clean-up of Denmark's worst-ever oil pollution disaster after a twelve-mile slick from a West German tanker threatens an important nature reserve.

The Ultimate Hazard

The threat from nuclear energy is, however, a totally different issue. Radioactivity, unlike oil-related pollutants, is a unique category of hazard. And as the world nuclear industry burgeons, so the danger of radioactive water grows ever greater. As with most large-scale industrial processes, nuclear energy requires considerable volumes of water. This water becomes contaminated by radioactive elements; much of it is then released into the water system. In addition, there is the practice of dumping radioactive waste materials at sea. A third source is the fall-out from weapons tests. In combination they are helping to push the Geiger counter readings of marine contamination steadily upwards.

Seawater has naturally present measures of radioactivity, mainly through the existence of potassium 40, with other natural inputs helping to maintain a constant radioactive content. Heavy radionuclides dissolve poorly in water; they accumulate instead on the surfaces of particulate matter. Marine sediments are therefore major gathering points for radioactive elements. Marine sands, for instance, typically have as much as thirty times the level of radioactivity found naturally in oceanic seas; with coastal muds the readings can be up to eighty-eight times higher. This helps explain certain naturally occurring regions of abnormally high radioactivity around the world; the best known are areas of Kerala in south India and the coastal districts of Espirito Santo and Rio de Janeiro in Brazil.

To this natural level is now being added a constantly rising man-made contribution. Weapons testing alone is known to have increased the levels of radioactive contamination in areas between latitudes 45 degrees north and 45 degrees south. In the mid-1960s, the monthly deposition of strontium 90 in the North Atlantic due to weapons testing rose from about 10kCi (a measure of activity related to the Curie) in 1960 to more than 300kCi at its high point in 1964. The highest readings are found in surface waters, although water currents will slowly take the radioactive elements down to the deeps.

Second, liquids discharged from reactor installations are a

daily or weekly occurrence. There are now more than five hundred power-generating nuclear plants around the world. All of them rely on water for various stages in the energy-producing process. In particular, reprocessing plants like Sellafield on the English side of the Irish Sea and La Hague on the French Atlantic coast use vast amounts of water, which is then discharged, with low radioactive content, into the surrounding sea. Nevertheless, even though the radioactive readings are low, the enormous volumes involved are leading to disturbingly high figures for radioactive contamination in those offshore waters.

One study, published in 1982 by scientists from Queen's University, Belfast and the Fisheries Laboratory in Lowestoft on the English east coast, described the Irish Sea as having the highest concentration of radioactive discharges of any area of similar size in the world.[6] Meanwhile, two years earlier about one hundred workers at the Sellafield complex had been taken ill with gastroenteritis after drinking water taken from the nearby River Ellen, which is used to cool the reactors. More recently, scientists surveying beaches on the Isle of Wight near Southampton discovered traces of the radionuclide cobalt 60 in seaweed and shellfish. The source of the contamination was identified as the nuclear installation at Winfrith in Dorset, further along the coast. It was revealed that the installation had been discharging about 300 curies of radioactive waste each year. What was more alarming was the discovery that the plant operators had a licence that permitted them to discharge up to 30,000 curies a year.

Radioactive contamination of the coastal seas can have a direct effect on human health through food products drawn from the affected waters. The Irish Sea, for example, has a significant fishery industry; it also provides an abundant source of the seaweed *porphyra*, which is harvested and transported to South Wales as a prime ingredient of laverbread, a local speciality. Tests on *porphyra* show it to be prone to the build-up of concentrations of radionuclides like ruthenium-106, an element that attacks the tissue of the lower large intestine. Other radioactive elements found in the contaminated seaweed under test – among them strontium 90, plutonium 239 and americium 241 – are known to focus on human bone tissues.

As if this constant stream of radioactive effluent is not sufficiently serious as a threat, some nuclear nations have magnified the danger by dumping canisters of solid nuclear wastes into the oceans. Most countries stopped the practice in 1974; the United States put an end to a twenty-year programme of radioactive dumping in the 1960s. Chief among the governments that chose to continue this dubious practice was the British; by the early 1980s Britain's nuclear waste industry accounted for ninety per cent of the contaminated waste ending up in the oceans. In 1982, for instance, the dumping load contained alpha-emitting nuclides with a total activity of 46.8 trillion becquerels (a unit equivalent to about 27 picocuries, which measure the rate of radioactive disintegration of nuclei in a substance). This figure was expected to jump to about 81 trillion becquerels in 1983.

The dumping ground for European nuclear disposal is an area of the North Atlantic about seven hundred miles north-west of the Spanish coast. It is estimated that between 1967 and 1982 nearly 100,000 tonnes of radioactive waste were dumped in the zone; this tonnage represented the almost incomprehensible figure of 37 million billion becquerels of radioactivity. Although the nuclear industry insists, as it does for onshore dumping, that their disposal methods are failure-proof, the same concerns exist about their efficacy, particularly in view of the known corrosive capacities of saltwater. One report, by Professor W. Jackson Davis of the University of California, raises disturbing issues about the security of canisters used to store hazardous radioactive materials preparatory to dumping them off the coast of San Francisco. Professor Davis alleges – and the US government has apparently not contradicted him – that 55 gallon drums are leaking radionuclides of strontium, caesium and iodine. He insists that the contaminated wastes are not dispersing in the water but are instead concentrating on the ocean floor.[7]

A persuasive confirmation of these allegations has come from the US Environmental Protection Agency, which has reported that levels of radioactivity two hundred times those of ordinary background readings have been found in sediment taken from a dumping area off the coast of California. Meanwhile, another US analyst, nuclear chemist William Schell from Pittsburgh University, has uncovered evidence of considerable radioactivity in rattail fish taken from the dump area of Hudson Canyon near the coastline of New York State. The contamination in question, that of the element americium 241, was caused by a radionuclide not normally found in this kind of fish. Accord-

ing to evidence gathered in preparation for the London Dumping
Convention in early 1983, the nuclear waste office of the US
Department of Energy had admitted that some drums in the
area had imploded.[8]

Hopes that radioactive dumping will cease, and that the
world's water system will be given a valuable breathing space
from this most toxic of all threats, remain precarious. In 1983 an
international moratorium on further offshore disposal of nuclear
waste was agreed. But it was not considered binding by pro-
dumping countries such as Britain and the pressure from other
nations to put an end to the activity have little more than
moral force. In Washington, meanwhile, plans are being inter-
mittently considered that could lead to the oceanic dumping of
contaminated materials remaining from the Manhattan Project
of the early 1940s, together with obsolete nuclear submarines.
The Japanese have made clear that low-level radioactive waste
will be stored deep in the Marianas Trench, five hundred miles
south of Tokyo. The British nuclear industry, with an enormous
reprocessing sector in operation and continual problems from
local residents over the siting of land-based disposal facilities, is
anxious to find a convenient outlet for its rapidly mounting
repository of nuclear garbage. And as with so much of the
world's legacy of deadly wastes, when it comes to convenience,
nothing equals the simple expedient of dropping it into the
water.

7
Poisoned Earth

In the summer of 1983 a young drug addict, George Carrillo, was admitted to the Santa Clara Valley Medical Centre in San José, California. He was suffering from advanced paralysis and was unable to talk. At first, doctors attributed the boy's condition to his history of drug abuse. A few days later they were forced to abandon their diagnosis after a succession of increasingly disturbing events. First, Carrillo's sister was admitted with similar symptoms. She was followed by several other young people with equally serious problems. Their stiff muscles, mask-like faces, tremors and other difficulties would normally lead to the diagnosis of Parkinson's Disease. But further investigation led to a startling verdict.

Analysis showed that they were victims of a chemical called MPTP, traces of which were found in the synthetic heroin that all of them had recently bought from dishonest dealers trading in the backstreets of San José. Alerted to the possible role of this widely used industrial chemical, Canadian scientist André Barbeau decided to study five thousand recent case histories of Parkinson's Disease. He found a direct correlation between the use of certain pesticides – especially paraquat – and the incidence of the illness amongst residents of farmland areas.

Parkinson's Disease has claimed many millions of victims in the twentieth century, amongst them Mao Tse Tung, General Franco and Salvador Dali. But this illustrious list should not divert us from the realisation that our most ancient industry, agriculture, is in danger of turning us into vegetables with the help of its high-tech chemical armoury. Nor should we forget that the strange case of George Carrillo was by no means the first medical mystery involving pesticide poisoning. By no means . . .

In 1981, following reports of deaths amongst workers employed by Dow Chemicals and Monsanto in the United States, the US National Institute for Occupational Safety and Health investigated possible links between these fatalities and the chemicals being used in the plants. The institute uncovered evidence that the deaths were connected to production of the weedkiller 2,4,5-T. The evidence suggested that those exposed to this substance are forty times more likely to contract soft tissue sarcoma, a form of cancer, than are the public at large. In separate research projects carried out in Sweden and reviewed in 1982 by British researchers from the University of Southampton and the Medical Research Council, similar conclusions were reached.

Not for nothing was 2,4,5-T – known more widely as Agent Orange – used in vast quantities by the US military in the Vietnam War as a defoliant. Dropped from the air, its job was to destroy the dense jungle undergrowth that offered cover to Viet Cong guerrillas. Agent Orange did not, however, win the war. And it left Vietnam with millions of acres of poisoned earth that will, for long into the future, leave that desperate country with a legacy of deep-rooted contamination. But Vietnam was only a sideshow; 2,4,5-T had already become the key ingredient of a new weedkiller for farmers elsewhere. And as its awful side effects began to reveal themselves to keen-eyed analysts, the otherwise innocent-looking acronym 2,4,5-T became synonymous with the battle against a different, and more terrifying, kind of chemical warfare.

2,4,5-T kills weeds by speeding up the growth rate of plants to such a point that they collapse under their own excessive weight and die. But the real casualties of this new warfare were to be humans affected by spray drift, direct contact, or by eating foods contaminated by this most powerful of pesticides. The reason is because 2,4,5-T usually contains an impurity called dioxin. Dioxin is widely regarded as the most toxic synthetic chemical known to man; one drop is capable of killing as many as twelve hundred people. It is also the most potent cause of cancer and birth deformities.

The main active ingredient of 2,4,5-T is trichlorophenol, a chemical derived from benzene, a liquid extracted from coal or petroleum. The chemical was first developed in the United States during World War II and by 1950 had become a major weapon for the US agro-industry in its post-war strategy for boosting crop yields that would reap growing profits from the peacetime boom in demand for foodstuffs. In the years that followed, 2,4,5-T was adopted by millions of farmers around the world as a keystone of their efforts to maximise the productivity of their land.

The lethal dioxin found in 2,4,5-T is referred to by yet another acronym, TCDD; it is short for tetrachlorodibenzo-p-dioxin. It is also a further example of the immense complexity that surrounds serious issues of biochemical pollution and makes public awareness and understanding an elusive goal. But, as researchers Judith Cook and Chris Kaufman spell out in *Portrait of a Poison*, an investigation of the dreadful consequences of Agent Orange, understanding the frightening effects of TCDD on living things is an essential prerequisite to understanding the horrors that surround the entire, explosive issue of pesticide pollution.[1]

Scientists have known for many years of the highly toxic impact of TCDD on the skin. Long before the US intervention in Vietnam, workers in a German chemical plant making trichlorophenol were found to have developed a severe skin disease known as chloracne. As with so many aspects of high-tech holocaust, their condition only came to light through investigations at the plant following an accident. More significantly, it became clear that the disease had been prevalent well before the incident took place. But the discovery was made at a time when such issues carried far less weight amongst governments, corporate executives or trade unions. Such episodes, we told ourselves, were part of the acceptable price of industrial activity.

This state of blithe uninterest began to change in the 1970s. In the wake of the Agent Orange offensive in South East Asia considerable research was carried out in an effort to determine the precise effects of TCDD on life forms. The results were highly disturbing. Experiments were conducted, amongst other places, at the National Institute of Environmental Health Science in North Carolina. Doses of dioxin were given to mice every day over an eight-day period. The doses were very small, about one ten-thousandth of a litre. While the mice themselves seemed to suffer no noticeable side effects, the foetuses carried by pregnant mice in the group were horribly deformed. One in three was born with a cleft palate, others suffered serious malformations of the kidneys, enlarged livers and internal bleeding.

Another research team, at Wisconsin University, recorded the effects of varying dosages of dioxin on rats over a two-year period. Two-thirds of the rats died from dioxin poisoning. Those that died had developed tumours in the lungs and liver. Even amongst those on the lowest doses, half contracted cancer. Similar experiments were carried out using monkeys, the closest life form to humans. Again, varying doses – mostly of microscopic proportions – were given, this time to a group of females. All the monkeys in the experiment had problems conceiving. Amongst those that did there was a high rate of miscarriages. The animals continued to abort; they developed bone disorders, gangrene in the toes and fingers, haemorrhages of the heart and lungs and signs of internal wasting. As the experiment neared the end of the third year, the monkeys lost their hair and their faces swelled up. Even those taken off the treatment continued to deteriorate. Most of them died.

Dozens of comparable experiments have been completed at leading research establishments around the world. All have produced similar, equally appalling conclusions about the ferocity of this pesticide in attacking the vital organs and nervous system, with particular consequences for the unborn foetus. One project at Monash University in Australia involved exposing chickens' eggs to very small doses of 2,4,5-T. The chicks suffered noticeable behavioural defects associated with brain damage. Such results are all the more frightening when it is realised that human beings absorb 2,4,5-T three times more easily than is the case for chicks. Indeed, the most telling aspect of the many research findings that relate to Agent Orange is that serious adverse effects occur at extremely low levels of dosage. This is all the more disconcerting in that it is widely known by scientists that humans can be much more sensitive than laboratory test animals to teratogens, the family of chemicals that causes monstrous deformities in unborn babies. Thalidomide, for instance, the pre-natal drug that caused so much tragedy in the 1960s, has one hundred times the effect on human embryos that it has on rats.

Despite these warnings 2,4,5-T is still in use with millions of farmers around the world, particularly in poor countries, and in many places is even available to householders for use on their domestic flowerbeds, vegetable patches and fruit trees. But more horrifying still is the blunt fact that 2,4,5-T is only one of scores of highly toxic man-made products that are sprayed, poured or dropped onto growing things that eventually end up in our mouths. For the exposure of Agent Orange as an agent of destruction did not mark the end of the pesticide era; on the contrary, it coincided with the rapid escalation in pesticide usage around the world. And their toxic toll is not limited to the foodstuffs they are meant to protect. The escalating volume of chemicals employed in agriculture is changing the very make-up of the soil, which in turn has potentially catastrophic effects on the evolution of crop strains. The polluted soil itself poisons the groundwater that eventually ends up in irrigation systems and, more seriously, in domestic water supplies. Just as seriously, their poisonous side effects reap a tragic harvest of death, deformity and bodily damage amongst farm workers – even pilots – who apply them, along with any unfortunate bystanders who are caught in their toxic path as their fine droplets are carried by the winds over the landscape.

The Dirty Dozen and Others

The burgeoning agri-chemical industry, led by the major multi-nationals, has produced an ever-lengthening list of insecticides, herbicides and fungicides to help the late-twentieth-century farmer boost his production and his profits. In Western Europe and North America they have helped create unprecedented surpluses in agricultural production; in poor developing countries they have brought revolution to hitherto poverty-stricken peasant communities. Unfortunately, few have stopped to count the longer-term cost. For while output and farmers' incomes have often risen, the level of worldwide toxic contamination, and hence the scale of global hazard, has climbed dramatically. And the reason is simple: the pesticide revolution has been made possible by the universal use of chemical compounds that are poisonous to humans.

The most infamous pesticides have been grouped together by concerned pressure groups as the Dirty Dozen. All of them have been, or still are, in common use around the world under various brand names:

DDT – an insecticide known chemically as organochlorine. A highly persistent toxicant that accumulates in fat and in mothers' milk. Laboratory tests show that it causes cancer in animals and for humans can lead to damage to the brain and nervous system.

Paraquat – a herbicide also known as bipyridyl. Extremely toxic to mammals if inhaled or absorbed through the skin. Paraquat kills by suffocation with no known antidote. It is also toxic to fish. Banned in many countries, it is still sold in more than a dozen variants across the world.

Lindane/HCH – an insecticide noted for its persistence. Forms of HCH are severely restricted or banned by many governments because of evidence that they are cancer agents. Yet more than one hundred HCH products are known to be on sale in various countries.

The Drins (Dieldrin, Aldrin and Endrin) – insecticides with a disturbing history of official and scientific concern. Banned in Sweden and severely restricted in many other countries, including the United States. Rated by the World Health Organisation as 'highly hazardous', yet cleared by some governments – including Britain – for use in agriculture, horticulture and food storage. Adverse effects range from convulsions to depression; continued exposure causes liver damage. Tests with human cells show these chemicals to cause genetic mutations, while experiments with mice have proved them to be cancer-causing.

Chlordane/Heptachlor – an organochlorine insecticide prohibited by European Community directive and severely restricted by the US government, yet widely available even in some developed countries in earthworm and ant-killer products. A suspected carcinogen.

Pentachlorophenol – another organochlorine insecticide used in treatments for wood and masonry. Classified by WHO as 'highly hazardous' and severely controlled in North America, New Zealand and elsewhere. Can cause damage to the liver, skin and nervous system.

Campheclor – an organochlorine insecticide for long used as a substitute for DDT. Banned in a great number of countries because of cancer risks.

Parathion – a highly dangerous nerve poison banned in many states and condemned by WHO as 'extremely hazardous'. It is thought to account for fifty per cent of all cases of pesticide poisoning worldwide, and eighty per cent of all cases in Central America. One teaspoonful is sufficient to kill through the skin alone.

Ethylene Dibromide – worm killer and fumigating agent, recognised as an extremely potent and long-lasting cancer-causing chemical and mutagen, which can penetrate protective clothing and human skin. Banned in US; other countries are following.

Chlordimeform – like DDT an organochlorine insecticide widely employed by growers of tobacco and cotton. Causes cancer in laboratory tests and leads to stomach and kidney damage. In a celebrated, if alarming stunt the manufacturers Ciby-Geigy sprayed it over children in Egypt.

The list is completed by 2,4,5-T; it is commonly used in agriculture, horticulture, home gardening and forestry, despite the verdict of the US Environmental Protection Agency that 'the quality, quantity and variety of data demonstrating that the continued use of 2,4,5-T contaminated with dioxin presents risks to human health is unprecedented and overwhelming'.[2] It needs to be added that this EPA ruling is only one of many made public by worried official bodies in different countries.

This list, nevertheless, is not exhaustive. There are others that cause equally serious concern, amongst them such pesticides as Captan, Thiram, Dichlorvos and Aldicarb, names that would sound more at home in some space-fiction adventure than in the annals of toxic threat.

● Captan is a fungicide known to cause genetic mutations in tests on fungus, bacteria, rats, mice and human cells.

● Experiments with animals show that Thiram causes mutations, monstrous deformity and damage to the liver, kidney and brain.

● Dichlorvos is cleared by some governments, including the British, for use in home gardens, kitchens and larders, as well as in commercial farming and horticulture. Yet it is acutely toxic and is thought to interfere with the human nervous system; American researchers have suggested it should be handled with care by women of child-bearing age.

● Aldicarb gained notoriety amongst mothers on Long Island in the United States, who became concerned at the forty-six per cent rate of spontaneous abortion that was recorded in areas where water supplies had been seriously contaminated by the pesticide.

And there are many, many more: glyphosate, dichlofluanid, lenacil, cyhexatin, permethrin, azinphos-methyl and a stream of other chemicals with esoteric formulae that are sold around the world under brand names that extol their macho, frontier-beating virtues. Ambush from ICI and Roundup from Monsanto are typical examples. But the other major multi-nationals – Montedison, Shell, Boots, Sumitomo, Bayer, Union Carbide, Dow, Cynamid, Du Pont and others – as well as large nationally focussed companies such as Tata in India, have their own favourites.

Whatever the entry route into the human bio-system, whether through residues on food, groundwater contamination, spray drift or direct contact with toxic substances, either deliberate (suicides are regular occurrences) or accidental, the consequences of pesticide contamination leave no doubts as to the seriousness of the hazard that confronts all of us. Surveys of individual cases reveal a spectrum of short-term adverse effects that range from superficially unpleasant symptoms to severe injury and death. Although insufficient evidence exists for us to reach firm conclusions about the long-term results of such toxic invasion of our bodies, the presumption can only be, as with lead and other ever-present pollutants, that humanity is being steadily poisoned and our biochemical balance radically altered for the worse.

There is mounting evidence, for instance, that large amounts of poisonous pesticides are left on crops as residues after spraying. Even post-harvest cleansing operations do not remove the hazard. A recent research exercise in Britain produced alarming results in this respect. It also added further weight to the observation that sophisticated modern governments can fall prey to terrifying bouts of myopia when confronted with potentially very dangerous situations involving public health. The British government record in such areas as sulphur dioxide, toxic industrial substances, lead pollution, food additives and nuclear waste is extremely poor. On the issue of pesticides it is no better, as an increasing amount of persuasive testimony now shows. For this reason, the British experience is an important reference point that allows us to scrutinise more closely the effects on public health of heavy reliance on toxic chemicals in food production.

Each year more than one billion gallons of pesticides are used by Britain's farmers and vegetable growers. To assess the dangers for the average household, the Association of Public Analysts recently carried out two surveys of pesticide residues on food items bought in busy shops and markets around the country. The first survey used gas chromotography to examine 438 samples of fruit and vegetables. More than a third showed pesticide contamination. One in ten of the fruit samples, and two in ten of the vegetables, recorded levels of contamination at or above the 'reporting limits' set down by the British Ministry of Agriculture.

The cancer-causing HCH, in various forms, was found on watercress, apples, mushrooms, celery, cherries, turnips, onions, cucumber, cauliflowers, and many other everyday shopping basket selections. The nerve poison Parathion was found on mushrooms. Dieldrin was discovered on courgettes; another 'drin', Aldrin, was present in varying amounts on spring onions, mushrooms, watercress and tomatoes. Captan – thought by scientists to be mutagenic, teratogenic, carcinogenic and, by Russian researchers, to cause sexual disorders in test animals – was left behind on cabbages and cauliflowers. Residues of the dreaded DDT were found on blackcurrants, strawberries and lettuce.[3]

The second survey was completed in association with the Ministry of Agriculture, Fisheries and Food. It looked only at the insecticide DDT and its chemical cousins, which are banned in many countries and are widely recognised as cancer-causing in laboratory animals and likely to lead to brain and nerve damage in humans. This most potent of pesticides was banned totally in Britain in 1984. At the time of the government-backed survey, in November 1983, it was already severely restricted to a very narrow band of permitted applications. The survey results, however, included strong evidence that it was still being used for purposes not covered by the regulations, in particular for apples.[4] Such breaches are a regular feature of surveys throughout the world.

The British DDT study analysed 293 samples over five product areas. DDT or its derivatives were found in ten per cent of all samples tested. The report continued: 'Three of the samples contained levels above 0.10 milligrams per kilo which is the maximum residue limit specified by the EEC Directive . . . It is significant that DDT was found in a percentage of each food category tested in spite of the controls over the use of this chemical.'

Illicit use of pesticides is a permanent problem faced by all governments and regulatory authorities. In North America,

Europe (both at the national and the EEC level) and in a host of smaller, often less-developed, countries from Sri Lanka to Peru there are laws and official programmes aimed at reducing or eliminating the reliance on highly toxic pesticides. But there is considerable evidence that such efforts have only limited success. The pressure on farmers and growers to meet production targets and fulfil contracts set by buyers is an ever-present factor; pesticides are a guarantee that harvest volumes are protected, whatever the cost to the public at large in terms of health risk.

The two British studies illustrate the breadth of this risk. Even though there are very strict controls over the kinds of chemicals used and the manner in which they can be employed, set both by the national government and through Common Market guidelines, supermarket shelves and greengrocers' stalls still carry glaring proof that the extreme hazard of pesticide residues remains a daily danger. Few should be surprised, however, at the persistence of Britain's farmers and vegetable growers in continuing to cover their produce with poisons. They are a strong political lobby and have always succeeded in convincing governments to compromise between the interests of the consumer and the commercial goals of the farmer. In 1983, for instance, when the European Commission urged London to ban garden weedkillers containing 2,4,5-T, the British Agriculture Minister at the time, Peter Walker, refused, arguing that his advisory committee on pesticides had recommended that such weedkillers should continue to be sold.

Nothing highlights the escalating problem of pesticide poisoning more sharply than a disturbing report published in Britain in 1985, nearly two years after the Public Analysts and Ministry officials had concluded their work. Although, in view of the permissive approach of British governments towards pesticide restrictions, its revelations should not be entirely unexpected. In *Pesticides: the First Incidents Report*, details of recent cases involving poisonings or other adverse effects were spelt out.[5] The report makes harrowing reading; it contains scores of separate incidents which, taken alone, raise little more than vague sympathy for the afflicted people. Taken together, they represent an incontrovertible mass of circumstantial evidence in support of the contention that Britain is already at the brink.

The report also relates to cases in which contamination has

only occurred on a single occasion, for a short space of time and with only very limited doses of pesticide involved, usually through spray drift. Indeed, all the incidents took place within the one year of 1984. In every episode the consequences have been extremely disturbing. How much more damaging is the constant, long-term exposure to which we are subjected as a result of food contaminated by the pesticide-ridden soil in which it grows, by residues left on the crop after harvest, or by drinking from water supplies polluted by toxic chemicals draining out from the poisoned earth?

The report sets out details of more than one hundred pesticide incidents taking place in twenty-eight counties in England, Scotland and Wales. It is all the more disturbing because British safety standards and regulations have evolved over many years and are regarded, at least by successive generations of civil servants, as highly refined and effective controls over the nation's comparatively small agricultural population. A selection of cases from the report is sufficient to convey the sense of extreme fear and disquiet – and helplessness in the face of official unconcern – that overtakes the unfortunate victims:

● In July 1984 Enfys Chapman, a Welsh-born resident of the English county of Cambridgeshire, was sprayed from the air by a helicopter applying the pesticide Triazophos to a field of peas next to her small-holding. The sprayed droplets were also carried by the wind and fell on her cattle. A number of the cattle became ill and died. Their deaths were attributed to bloat following the loss of use of their back legs. More extensive examinations revealed serious deficiencies of essential minerals, especially selenium, brought about by poisoning, as well as fatty livers. Autopsies carried out by government specialists also showed bone deterioration. Amongst the cattle that survived many became sterile and were destroyed.
But for Mrs Chapman the problems had only just begun. Apart from being within range of the helicopter spray herself, she also spent five days treating her contaminated livestock, thus risking further exposure. She sickened and was admitted to Addenbrooke's Hospital in Cambridge. Mrs Chapman made no improvement; she developed liver problems and became confined to a wheelchair. She also suffered serious nervous damage, finding it necessary since the incident to translate all her thoughts from her native Welsh into English before making decisions or communicating with people. Her eyesight was affected and her memory was dulled. She had, in her own words, become 'a victim of premature ageing'.

- In October 1984 a woman in the county of Essex reported that her daughter had developed an intolerance to fats in her diet. The family lived next to a field that is used to grow peas and wheat alternately. Each year the field is sprayed. In 1983 the daughter had inexplicably suffered from severe lacerations to the face and hands; the other children in the family had suffered similar symptoms. Some of their hens died and others lost their feathers. After extensive tests, doctors diagnosed the daughter as being the victim of Crohn's disease – an inflammation of the intestine, the causes of which are unclear. She is unable to eat fat or meat and some of her enzymes no longer function.

- Little Jake Kearns was even more unfortunate. Being a small baby he was in no position to take avoiding action when employees from a wood treatment company came to apply chemicals in his parents' house in a London suburb. The workmen made very little attempt to limit the spread of chemical vapours, only advising Mrs Kearns of the need to keep the house ventilated at the end of the day, after fumes had invaded rooms being used by her and her small son. Jake became ill and was admitted to hospital, where he was found to be suffering from severe bronchitis. Upon closer examination, the chemicals used in the house were shown to include dieldrin and the anti-rot agent tributyl tin oxide, or TBTO. Both dieldrin and TBTO are known to be poisons. The hospital authorities however, were not prepared to admit the possibility of any link between the toxic fumes and young Jake's sudden collapse in health.

  After being discharged Jake's blood was sampled and sent for analysis. It was found to contain quantities of eight different organochlorine pesticides, widely recognised as highly persistent and proven causes of cancer, nerve and brain damage and other serious conditions in animal tests. Present amongst the eight were dieldrin, DDT, DDE (a pesticide linked to DDT) and chlordane. Only time will tell what consequences there will be for Jake in terms of physical, intellectual and nervous retardation or malfunction.

  A major complicating factor in the investigation of Jake's condition was that the workmen, like many others employed by companies selling household treatments, regularly used their spraying equipment for a succession of jobs involving different toxic chemicals, thus making it extremely difficult to know precisely which chemicals had been used on the day in question. Such a practice could well mean the difference in an emergency between a correct diagnosis of the source of the poisoning and a counter-productive (and possibly fatal) course of medical action.

● The case of Carol Jevey, in the south-coast county of Hampshire, is a salutary example of what victims themselves can do to track down the evidence and prove their allegations. Ms Jevey had a promising police career ahead of her when she contracted chronic insecticide poisoning. She was told that her condition was caused by slow absorption from sprays; it seemed self-evident to her that the source was a grower of strawberries and Christmas trees who used land at the back of her home. But she needed proof.

Ms Jevey decided to carry out her own survey, sending out a questionnaire to hundreds of local residents. The response was extremely helpful . . . and deeply shocking. The survey revealed that some two hundred local people had similar symptoms, all of which were undiagnosed or failed to respond to treatment. Vegetation in gardens had died; pets living in the area around the suspected field had also died. Ms Jevey's dog was diagnosed as having cancer. Indeed, the exercise confirmed that the cancer rate amongst humans in the area was above average. Investigations by conservation groups indicated that the field had been subjected to more than a dozen pesticides including DDT, DDT variants, paraquat, glyphosate and endrin. Ms Jevey was obliged to abandon her career after suffering from the effects of poisoning for six years. So far all her attempts to secure action from the health authorities and other responsible departments to have the site controlled have failed.

● Mary Haybittle, an energetic sixty-eight-year-old resident of a village near Cambridge, was caught downwind in the summer of 1984 when a spraying vehicle applying Hostathion to a neighbouring field of peas came close by. She was taken ill suddenly with dizziness and other unpleasant symptoms, and was unwell for several days. The doctor diagnosed it as a virus. But the woman continued to have difficulty walking and suffered constant stomach pains. She felt, she said, as if her entire nervous system had been attacked. The symptoms have persisted.

In an ominous postscript to her experience, Mrs Haybittle let it be known in a letter: 'When I am well I hope to do a study of school attendance as I am a school governor and have been concerned for some time about the amount of summer illness among the children.'

Even as *The First Incidents Report* was appearing, more alarm signals were going out from every corner of the country. In July 1985 the *Western Mail*, which covers Britain's west and south-west regions, made public that 2,4,5-T was still in widespread use in most parts of Wales. Although banned in many countries, only three local authorities in Wales had seen fit to follow suit.

The report also stated that ninety-seven per cent of grain and vegetables consumed in Britain have been sprayed with pesticides. It also pointed out that there are no controls on the frequency or intensity of spraying, and that crops are sometimes sprayed with a million times the strength of pesticide needed to kill pests.

Meanwhile, farmers in Bonnybridge in Scotland reported a mysterious disaster that had befallen their cattle. One farm lost fifty cows after the animals became caught up in a descending spiral of decreasing milk yields and starvation. Neighbouring farmers suffered similar losses. Nearby was a waste-disposal plant operated by ReChem International and suspicions arose that toxic substances had escaped and found their way into cattle feed. Analysts called in to find causes failed to confirm any readily apparent connection. But they recalled a similar incident in the state of Michigan, in the United States, some ten years earlier. In the Michigan case, dubbed 'Cattlegate' to reflect its status as the most widespread and least reported disaster of its kind ever to affect the western world, the cause of the deaths was pinned down to the accidental invasion of cattle feed by the extremely toxic chemical polybrominated biphenyl, or PBB. The feed was subsequently distributed throughout the state, and more than three hundred cattle were reported to have died.

Breakfast with Death?

Meanwhile, the ReChem chemical incineration plant at Bonnybridge was accused by researchers of allowing dioxins to contaminate milk produced in the area, and thereby of being responsible for cases of rare congenital deformity found amongst babies born locally. The plant, however, was given official clearance in a subsequent report prepared by Professor John Lenihan of the University of Glasgow. Professor Lenihan also decided to speak publicly about his conclusions. His statements have to be considered as amongst the most bizarre ever uttered by a respected academic on this subject.

The professor, in an address to the British Association, dismissed public concern at the discovery of dioxin in milk supplied from Scottish farms as 'a little local excitement . . . There would have been more cause for interest had someone found milk which did not contain dioxins.' Such substances are present wherever organic material is burnt in the presence of trace quantities of chlorine, he continued: 'it is not possible to know whether they do any harm at the levels prevailing in the environment.' It seems only fair to observe that if it is not yet possible to know the precise nature of the risks from dioxin, how can anyone, even a professor, be so adamant that there is no cause for worry?

Other specialists backed Professor Lenihan and attacked ill-informed journalists for their part in fomenting what they regarded as unnecessary public fears. Dr Peter King, general secretary of the British Society of the Chemical Industry, added to the list of villains 'a fifth column of scientists who should know better . . . Dioxin causes chloracne, which is unpleasant, but that is all.' The situation in the United States, he added, was even worse: '. . . an essentially gullible country . . . It is fortunate that penicillin was not tested on guinea pigs because it is lethal to them.'

Such a hostile reaction is not uncommon amongst professions faced with rising popular interest and concern about issues traditionally obscured from the public eye by complicated vocabularies and professional secrecy, whether it be the law, architecture, accountancy or medicine. After all, for expensively trained – and expensively employed – practitioners a monopoly of knowledge is the sole guarantee of their earning power. But the cynical observer can be forgiven for hoping that they will, at least, make their counter-attack watertight. The reference to penicillin, for instance, overlooks the fact that this miracle drug can cause significant adverse side effects in allergic humans, and that in the early days the guinea pigs were the unfortunate patients themselves. It proves the point precisely that all drugs are potentially hazardous to somebody, whatever their hallowed place in the history of medical science.

In any event, it is unlikely that the public will be given adequate information on which to make proper judgements so long as governments protect the privileged position of the medical profession by holding back vital facts. A case in point is the recent refusal by the British government to give researchers access to important information about thousands of toxic pesticides used in Britain. Despite the 'freedom of information' provisions under the new Food and Environment Protection Act, passed in 1985, the Ministry of Agriculture declared it 'administratively impossible' to make available files containing safety data on a large group of older pesticides.

A major concern is that many pesticides approved for general

use more than twenty years ago were subjected to far less
stringent tests than those applied today. The original laboratory
data could highlight risks that are now known to us because of
more up-to-date studies, particularly those dealing with longer-
term adverse effects. But this embargo on old information is
only part of the problem. The 1985 law does not even oblige
government scientists to reveal details of tests on new pesticides
still awaiting approval for sale. Their expert findings will be
made available only in 'exceptional' cases.

Meanwhile, whatever the considered opinions of Professor
Lenihan and Dr King, the fact remains that evidence produced
by the US National Institute for Occupational Safety and
Health, by other high-level research studies carried out since
and by a long list of analyses on dioxin stretching back to the
early work in Germany, suggests a very significant link between
dioxin and cancer. And although we are told by some specialists
that 'it is not possible to know' whether dioxins do any harm at
the levels prevailing in our habitat, when it does become
possible to give a firm opinion the wider public would surely be
very pleased to be informed.

Fortunately, many other countries do not share the British
obsession with secrecy and professional mysticism. And it is in
such countries that some of the most enlightening research work
on pesticide hazards is being produced. A recent project in
Sweden, for instance, has given fresh insight into contamination
of human milk by organochlorine pesticides, a possible causal
factor in abnormal births. Milk samples were collected from
maternity hospitals in five regions of the country, chosen
because of their geographic differences. Analysis showed that all
the milk samples contained traces of DDT, dieldrin, HCH and
other pesticides but that there were variations in the levels of
contamination, with significantly higher levels noted for milk
taken from mothers in the southern parts of Sweden. The
findings of the study pointed clearly to a higher level of pesticide
fall-out in the more intensively farmed regions closer to
congested industrial conurbations like Stockholm and Gothen-
burg. Similar geographic variations were noticed with comparable surveys in Belgium and the United States.[6]

In Denmark in 1982 researchers carried out a six-region
survey. They, too, found traces of DDT, dieldrin and HCH in the
human milk samples taken from fifty-seven donors, though the
regional variations were not so great. To evaluate the health

risks posed to newborn babies by these contaminants the findings were examined by a group of experts set up by the Danish Board of Health, which reported in 1983. The survey also included figures relating to levels of polychlorinated biphenyls, or PCBs, a hazardous chemical compound that finds its way into the human environment through industrial discharges.

The Board of Health conclusions offered little comfort to young parents living in any of the world's chemical-infested zones, whether they be cities or farmland areas: 'The group finds, particularly for PCBs, that there is a low safety margin between the amounts which breast-fed infants might consume in milk and the amounts which have caused toxicity in animal studies.' More frightening still, the Danish figures which so troubled the Board's experts were only a fraction of those found in human milk samples elsewhere in Europe. Levels of dieldrin in the Danish investigation were only half those recorded in comparable British studies conducted two years earlier. And West German researches into PCB contamination of mothers' milk, using a massive sample of two thousand, produced figures two and a half times greater than those for Danish mothers.[7]

Export and Die

Whatever the dangers facing Europe's unborn children, those analysts of dioxin-affected cattle in Bonnybridge, Scotland, could have had no better reminder that the pesticide peril is a global threat of increasing scale. Since 'Cattlegate' in Michigan in the mid-seventies, the rich and literate developed world has made only haphazard progress towards stopping the poisonous chemical contamination of our most precious asset, the land. And whatever limping progress we have made in the highly industrialised countries is more than overtaken by the catastrophe that has been visited on poor developing nations by the wholesale export of pesticide products and technology.

The spread of chemical warfare to the heavily agricultural (usually peasant-dominated) areas of Africa, Asia and Latin America has significantly increased the world consumption of toxic substances. For the past decade most of the growth in world use has been in these regions. Today, world agriculture applies more than 2 billion kilos (more than 5 billion pounds) of pesticides each year, approximately a pound weight for every man, woman and child on the planet. The volume of chemicals used has risen roughly twenty per cent since 1976. Most pesticides used by farmers in the developing countries are imported. Western Europe, with its strong ex-colonial links, accounts for two-thirds of the total, nearly five times the volume exported by the United States. The superficial reasons for this vast trade are the laudable ones of seeking to achieve improved crop yields and less disease in societies long plagued by pests that attack both humanity and the foodstuffs they depend on for survival.

About one billion people in the warmer latitudes are exposed to the risk of malaria. By debilitating the local farming population, this disease is itself a major factor in reducing levels of output and preventing effective husbandry. But pests in general also lead to lower crop yields. Estimates suggest that at least one-third of potential harvests are lost because of insects, weeds and fungi. Although other problems such as unequal land ownership, ignorance and lack of proper infrastructure are major contributory reasons, it is self-evident that little can be achieved in the long run unless pest damage is eliminated or dramatically reduced. Indeed, it is recognised that pesticides, together with better farming methods, have been important elements in the almost revolutionary transformation of food production in many regions. Increases of two hundred per cent in crop yields are not uncommon.

But, as researcher David Bull records in his indictment of the pesticide trade, *Pesticides and the Third World Poor*, this reasoning cannot obscure the immensity of the hazards that have been inflicted on unsuspecting communities by the introduction of pesticide technology.[8] Most citizens of developing countries are poor and live in rural areas close to the soil. Their level of education and their grasp of basic technological concepts is rudimentary. These factors in combination make calamity an inevitable and frequent companion.

Pesticide poisoning in developing countries is estimated by the World Health Organisation and others to be running at the rate of nearly four hundred thousand cases a year, with ten thousand deaths. This is about one-half the world total, even though poor countries only account for one-sixth of global consumption. The causes of this appalling death toll are varied. The farm workers who mix and apply the chemicals are in danger, not least through drifting spray. The protective gloves and clothing recommended by pesticide manufacturers are rare – and prohibitively expensive – commodities in societies that boast per capita incomes of $300, only one-tenth the level enjoyed by the subsidised farmers of the affluent nations. The equally poor labourers who work in local factories making up the chemical batches are also seriously at risk through exposure. Two-fifths of poisonings are believed to result from accidental contact while working with toxic preparations in chemical plants or in the fields. Other cases arise through accidental drinking, and by the contamination of containers used for the storage and transport of water or food by families or middlemen.

But other cases of poisoning have resulted from sequences of events which could happen in any country, rich or poor, where pesticides are in widespread use. A particularly terrifying example, reported by Bull, involves the practice of applying pesticide dressings to seeds that can be used not only for planting but for eating in their existing state. Cooking and eating such seeds directly is an extremely hazardous step, as villagers in Kerala in southern India can testify. In 1958 about a hundred people died after eating wheat that had been treated with parathion, one of the Dirty Dozen. Subsequently, more than two hundred and fifty villagers died in the north Indian state of Uttar Pradesh after a similar experience, this time with wheat contaminated by a derivative of the highly persistent, cancer-causing HCH insecticide.

Both tragedies fade into insignificance, however, when compared to the horrors of the Pink Death that came to Iraq during 1971 and 1972, when imported wheat and barley seed treated with methyl mercury fungicide was distributed in various farming districts. The seed arrived too late for planting in many areas and warning labels on the sacks – some of them printed in English or Spanish – were unclear or went unnoticed by local families unfamiliar with pesticide precautions. As a result the treated grain was either eaten by local inhabitants or fed to their animals. Official figures from Baghdad put the death count at 459 with another 6,100 permanently affected by mercury poisoning, one of the most serious forms of toxic metal contamination. Later investigations in the country by journalist Edward Hughes produced a massively increased estimate of around one hundred thousand poison victims, of whom six thousand died.[9]

Most cases of fatal pesticide poisoning in peasant areas,

however, occur with nothing more than few days of private mourning by relatives and neighbours to mark the sad event. Few ever grasp the broader pattern of pesticide-induced suffering that now claims as many casualties as a major armed conflict. More to the point, few Third World citizens are even remotely aware of the longer-term consequences for their communal health of daily exposure through soil contamination and chemical residues on their food. For just as the more affluent consumers of the old industrial world have for some years been buying pre-packed chemical pollution off their supermarket shelves every day, so the bustling rural markets of Nigeria, Mexico and Thailand now offer produce tainted by the same toxic applications. There is one serious difference: the poor world is only beginning to apply, in considerable and ever-increasing quantities, the poisons that are being outlawed by governments in North America and Europe. The poisoning of Third World earth has just commenced.

Already the signs point in an ominous direction. A survey of vegetables in Kenya reveals that forty per cent of those examined contain residues above the officially acceptable level. Livestock feed made from cotton seed is found to be contaminated by highly toxic aldrin and dieldrin. Studies of vegetables on sale in Sri Lankan markets have identified the widespread presence of pesticide residues; on rice the quantities of dieldrin and heptachlor were found to be above the tolerance levels set by accepted medical standards. A research project amongst patients in the capital, Kandy, showed that DDT contamination of their fatty tissues reached as high as 102 parts per million; the world average is only 5 to 10ppm. One reason could be the practice of Sri Lankan and Indian growers of spraying their produce with pesticides just twenty-four hours before delivery to the markets.

A key factor producing this escalation in pesticide usage in developing countries is the breakdown of the delicate natural balance brought about by the chemicals themselves. Until the arrival of the toxic sprays, pests were kept under limited control by the flourishing cohorts of benign insects and other wildlife that attacked and eliminated the unwanted species. But the coming of chemical warfare took heavy toll of these pests and in doing so removed the natural food sources on which the farmers' helpmates relied for survival. Hence Nature's own correcting mechanisms were seriously distorted. In the short term the benefits were clearly visible in much-increased local output. But in the long term the pests would re-establish their presence. The farmer would be forced to apply even heavier measures of chemical death. And so the spiral of pesticide overkill turns sharply upwards.

The development of resistance to pesticides by the organisms they are meant to kill is the central predicament faced by millions of food producers across the world, whatever the prevailing political or social system. But its consequences have been most severe in less developed countries where chemical weaponry has been introduced into hitherto untainted agro-systems. A typical case study is the cotton belt of Nicaragua in Central America.

Cotton became an important local crop in the 1950s. But its introduction accelerated the concentration of land ownership and the use of capital intensive technologies. This process was further intensified under the dictatorship of the Somoza regime. It also needs to be remembered that cotton, of all crops, lends itself most easily to the use of machinery, hybrid seeds and chemicals. More than any other agricultural product, cotton production is dependent on vast quantities of pesticide, with more than twenty-five per cent of world insecticide usage being devoted to this one crop.

Nicaragua was quickly caught in a self-tightening vice of chemical poisoning. The cultivation of cotton increased the rate of topsoil erosion; the displaced topsoil filled the streams with silt in the rainy months and poured dust into the air in the dry season. Repeated planting of cotton steadily depleted the soil of essential nutrients; ever-increasing amounts of fertiliser were called for to maintain crop yields. Meanwhile, fertiliser and herbicide pollutants ran off into the rivers and contaminated the water system. And to make matters worse, the amount of insecticides applied by cotton growers rose disastrously. By the beginning of the 1960s growers were applying lethal pesticides such as DDT and methyl parathion as many as twenty-eight times in a single growing season, or roughly once every four days. They were applied by aircraft; according to people resident in the country at the time, the entire cotton region reeked of toxic chemicals for the whole year. But the pesticide onslaught was becoming counter-productive; as the insects developed resistance to this chemical attack, crop damage began to increase. Yields started falling. And the consequences of Nicaragua's pesticide overkill became all too apparent.

The US government banned imports of beef from the country because of unacceptable levels of DDT present in the meat. A survey carried out by the World Health Organisation revealed that levels of DDT in human breast milk in the cotton areas were forty-five times greater than the safe limit. A study completed in 1980 reported that human fat tissue of Nicaraguans carried sixteen times more DDT than the world average. And from the farming areas came tragic evidence of widespread pesticide poisoning. During the years of peak cotton production, more than three thousand field labourers were poisoned annually, many of them fatally. Even malaria returned to Nicaragua to claim thousands more victims, as mosquitoes developed resistance to the chemicals being heaped onto the land. During the 1970s, the incidence of malaria reached the highest level ever recorded in Nicaraguan history. In the two years between 1968 and 1970 the malaria count jumped from just over seven thousand cases to more than twenty-eight thousand. Only the overthrow of the Somoza regime, the break-up of a concentrated land ownership system and the creation of rudimentary ecological repair programmes stemmed the tide of a potentially nationwide disaster, for the moment at least. For a return to pesticide-intensive farming would certainly resurrect the spectre of toxic genocide.

But the example of Nicaragua was to be repeated all across Central America and in cotton-producing regions of Africa. The spiral of pesticide dependency took most Central American areas to the point where fifty per cent of cotton production costs were those related to the control of pests. Meanwhile the number of major pests rose from three in the early days of pesticide use to eight by the early 1970s; by then it had become common in many parts of Central America to spray forty or fifty times in a season.

The African experience is best illustrated by events in the cotton region of Gezira in the Sudan, where tenant farmers plant a total of some 2 million acres, including secondary harvests of food crops. Pesticides were brought in during the 1940s and their use escalated sharply as the Sudanese government pressed for ever-greater foreign exchange earnings. In 1946 some 600 hectares of cotton were sprayed. By 1950 the figure had reached 53,000; by 1974 it was nearly 250,000.

The now familiar pattern of pesticide overdose began to set in. By the start of the 1980s Gezira's cotton farmers could look back

on a troubled decade in which production costs had risen fourfold while yields had all but halved, ironically to levels of output
attained pre-war, before the pesticide revolution took hold.
Certain pests, meanwhile, had developed strong resistance and
were now flourishing. One of them, the whitefly with its sticky
excretions, was rendering much of their crop unfit for mechanical processing. And experts from the United Nations have concluded that whitefly resistance may be so entrenched that the
pest is now 'beyond effective chemical control'. Put more
bluntly, Sudan's cotton belt may well be trapped in a cycle of
irreversible and terminal decline, with traumatic effect on the
local economy.

But the cotton farmers of Africa are not an isolated case.
Many analysts predict that rice production in many parts of the
developing world may well follow the same self-destructive
path. In many areas of Asia, for example, vital rice harvests are
under threat from the brown planthopper. Pesticides are being
used to eradicate the problem but are instead acting to disturb
the long-established natural balance of local ecosystems. Apart
from seemingly inevitable by-products in the form of human
poisonings and more generalised health dangers, other pests,
hitherto only marginally important, are expanding their
domain. Only a long and energetically directed re-education
programme amongst peasant farmers – and a severe reduction
in pesticide usage – can hope to avert an agricultural disaster of
incalculable proportions for rice-dependent cultures in places
like India, Malaysia and Sri Lanka. Here, too, the minutes are
ticking away.

Meanwhile, the pesticide danger threatens all of us from
every direction, employing the element of surprise to maximum
effect. Every time we take a country walk, or enjoy the sunshine
in a quiet suburban garden, or sit down for a meal, we need to
ask the question: am I at risk? Certainly, watermelon lovers in
California, Oregon, Washington State and Alaska will ask that
question every time their thoughts turn to their favourite fruit.
In July 1985, several hundred people in these western US states
were poisoned after eating watermelons contaminated with
aldicarb sulphoxide, a pesticide similar to the substance that
caused so much anxiety amongst those Long Island mothers
troubled by the abnormal number of spontaneous abortions
happening in their area.

Ten million watermelons, one-third of California's crop for the year, had to be destroyed. Union Carbide, the manufacturers of the pesticide in question, attempted to avoid blame by criticising growers for 'flagrant misapplication of the product'. The event took place just one week after the publication of a report by a US government agency pointing out that about two and a half thousand Californians can expect to die each year over the next decade as a result of cancers caused by exposure to toxic chemicals. And it took place only seven months after the same Union Carbide saw over two thousand people die, and a quarter of a million more injured, when its plant at Bhopal in India leaked deadly gases onto the surrounding neighbourhood.

California and Madhya Pradesh: two states half a planet apart but united by a common thread of tragedy. A poisoned earth, in both the East and the West, seems already to be exacting its terrible revenge.

8
Staff of Life?

Doctors in Italy were recently confronted with a puzzling and disconcerting phenomenon that defeated ready explanation. A number of baby boys began developing breasts. A series of tests led to the conclusion that the infants were reacting to residues of growth-promoting hormones contained in canned veal-based baby foods in common use with Italian families. The synthetic hormone in question, diethylstilboestrol, or DES, was illegal in Belgium, the country where the veal had originated, but the ban did not extend to meat for export.

The episode brought into sharp focus the wilful adulteration of foodstuffs that has become a key feature of efforts by many food-processing companies to increase market share and boost profits in a highly competitive industry. These efforts do not stop at hormone injections, used in this case to speed up the growth cycle of calves so as to yield more meat earlier than Nature would otherwise dictate. Modern food technology has also created chemicals and processing techniques to preserve, colour, flavour and disguise the products that fill our shopping baskets. And we, the consumers, are the ones who pay the price. Never before has our daily bread been so impregnated with foreign substances. Many of them are hazardous to our health (on others the scientific verdict is unknown). And each mouthful we take brings us one step closer to biochemical disaster.

Food is, of course, made up of chemicals that occur naturally. For centuries, it has been common practice to add others to improve taste or to act as a preservative. Salt, honey and oil were typical throughout ancient history. Colouring agents such as saffron, annatto (a fruit dye used in cheese) and cochineal (made from the dried bodies of Mexican insects) have been in use for hundreds of years. Spices and herbs have earned themselves an unrivalled status as an essential tool in food preparation.

There was, too, a long tradition of improper practices. Illicit adulteration, meant to deceive the buyer, was a not infrequent occurrence until quite recently: water added to milk to increase its bulk, alum mixed in with flour to help produce a whiter loaf, vinegar diluted with sulphuric acid. Beer was bulked out by adding *Cocculus indicus*, the poisonous dried berry of a climbing plant found in parts of India. Arsenic sulphide was put into Bath buns to give them their yellow colour. Batches of tea were made heavier by mixing in ash leaves that had been browned on hot copper plates. Red lead was introduced into cheese. Most of these activities were fraudulent; many were seriously hazardous. But not until the second half of the twentieth century has the food we eat fallen prey to a bombardment of chemicals and high-tech processing methods that has transformed our diet into a terrifying array of potentially toxic ingredients.

Imagine a traditional Christmas dinner somewhere in the Western world, sometime in the late 1980s. It is prepared, as always, in keeping with the style of Victorian England captured in the pages of Charles Dickens' novel *A Christmas Carol*. There is but one departure from the text. The celebratory turkey is injected with water to make it appear plump; the water is likely to contain traces of toxic chemicals which, if ingested in large doses, would prove fatal. Emulsifiers have been added to help blend the water with the fat in the meat. Flavourings have also been injected into the bird to enhance its otherwise dull, mass-produced taste. The mixed peel in the Christmas pudding has probably been coloured with a selection of coal tar dyes. The Christmas cake has been baked with flour containing chemical additives that may not even be mentioned on the packet, at least not in straightforward terms. The chocolate biscuits, trifles and potato crisps that complete the picture are brim-full with artificial sweeteners, preservatives and colourants. It is a Christmas dinner fit for a seminar on toxicology. And it is being enjoyed in millions of homes.

It could just as easily have been a Thanksgiving celebration in Wyoming or Tennessee. Or, with a few changes of menu, a wedding party in Sydney or Singapore. Indeed, there need not be a celebration at all; in the industrial nations, where food has become a gift from technology, every mealtime is an occasion for doubt. If the food ingredients used, whether packaged or loose, frozen or 'fresh', are supplied by a modern food-processing company they are likely to contain chemicals that were unheard of a hundred years ago. Many of these chemicals are either toxic or likely to produce an allergic response.

Today more than three thousand five hundred additives are in common use by the world's food industry. More than ninety per cent of them have no nutritional value at all. Most of them shelter behind esoteric scientific names: ethyl 4-hydroxybenzoate, dodecyl gallate, potassium hydrogen L-glutamate and sodium 5'-ribonucleotide. To the lay person they mean nothing, even though their effects on the human biochemistry can be extremely serious. The four just mentioned, for example, are dangerous to asthmatics and to people sensitive to aspirin; specialists recommend that they should not be used in food or drinks likely to be given to babies or young children. Yet the first additive on the list, ethyl 4-hydroxybenzoate, is typically found as a preservative in fruit juices, dessert sauces, jam, salad cream and flavouring syrups. The others are used regularly in condiments, potato waffles, frozen croquettes and other food items.

But this is only to touch the surface of the rapidly spreading problem of food additives. The unprecedented growth of consumer purchasing power since the end of World War II has fuelled a massive expansion in convenience foods. New food products, from oven-ready pizza to synthetic cream, from alphabet soup to low-calorie squash, have poured out of the research laboratories and into the freezer cabinets and display areas of supermarkets and local stores. These new products would not have been possible without the sophisticated techniques and chemical components that modern science has put at the disposal of the food-processing industry.

Additives were already in use, on a minor scale, by the middle of the nineteenth century in order to help meet the burgeoning demand of quickly growing urban centres. Copper sulphate was added to vegetables to enhance their green coloration. Formalin was put into milk to give it the longer life needed to supply large urbanised populations. The same industrial revolution that had promoted this drift to the cities also developed the new chemicals essential to the rise of a high-tech food-processing sector. After a slow start the transition to a man-made diet accelerated sharply, assisted by the technological discoveries of war and a post-war surge in general prosperity.

At the end of World War II there were fewer than a thousand

different food items on offer to everyday shoppers. Now there are more than ten times as many. At least seven thousand of them have been processed. Today, seventy-five per cent of the average daily food intake of citizens living in the developed world is the product not of the land but of sophisticated techniques that use a wide range of chemicals to turn natural raw materials into perfect-looking food objects with appealing brand names. This shift to chemically controlled foods has generated a one thousand per cent increase in the use of additives since the mid-1950s. Currently, the amount of additives absorbed in a year by a typical Western consumer is the equivalent in weight to a family-size sack of potatoes. Market surveys point to an ever-increasing dependence by food companies on their profit-promoting chemical aids, despite the emerging (though very limited) interest in 'health foods'.

There has been a massive growth not only in the number of chemical compounds but in the kind of uses for which they are employed. At the end of the nineteenth century some fifty additives were available to the food companies; today there are seventy times as many. They are added to food products to perform one or more of at least one hundred different functions: as propellants, bleaches, solvents or anti-foaming agents, for instance, as well as to prolong shelf-life, intensify flavours or give stronger colour. With few exceptions these functions are necessary to comply with the commercial needs of distributors and retailers, whose business survival depends on having products that can maintain their freshness and customer appeal far beyond the timetable set by Nature.

Take, for example, the problem of preserving egg yolk. Food scientists recommend the addition of sodium sulphite, a synthetic substance that also acts to keep down microbes. Few people would be aware that the most common use of sodium sulphite is for 'fixing' photographs. Nor would many be aware that sulphites of all kinds are potentially dangerous to asthmatics. In other areas of food processing, calcium and magnesium salts are used to keep fruits and vegetables crisp. Research suggests that calcium polyphosphates could block vital enzymes, causing disorders of the digestive system. Potassium hydroxide is used in cocoa products as a base, to increase their alkaline properties or reduce acidity. Yet the caustic nature of this chemical is so marked that unless it is heavily diluted it will produce immediate burning in the mouth, throat and stomach;

the membranes that line the internal tracts become swollen and detached. The victim suffers from vomiting, pain and shock.

Meat products are widely adulterated in order to disguise their appearance or add to their finished weight. Sausages and pies, for instance, are often made from parts of the animal that would horrify customers if the truth were known. So the truth is disguised by chemistry. Thus, manufacturers will make use of the rectum, testicles, spleen and udder and make the resulting mixture palatable by the addition of the flavour enhancer monosodium glutamate. Yet monosodium glutamate is recognised as the cause of a condition referred to as Chinese Restaurant Syndrome because of the reliance of Chinese cooks around the world on this synthetic taste-creating agent.

Sufferers from the syndrome are overtaken by heart palpitations, dizziness, nausea, weakening of the upper arms and pains in the head and neck. In many countries monosodium glutamate is prohibited for use in foods intended for babies and young children. Provided, that is, they are not offered any of the take-away Chinese dishes so popular with millions of modern families, or indeed the one hundred and one meat products that also contain the substance. Other food items that rely on monosodium glutamate for their distinctive flavour include packet snacks, chilli sauce, frozen potato waffles and dried soups. How many parents dutifully keep these things away from their cherished but ever-hungry little ones? How many parents even know that they should?

Since it is not in the interests of food manufacturers to raise public fears about their products, most people remain ignorant of the risks they might run every time they open a can of potatoes or mix a cup of cocoa. In most countries food companies are not obliged to give detailed information about the chemicals and other additives that are being used. More to the point, they are not required to publicise the adverse effects their products may have on specific groups of consumers who, by reason of age or disability, face a far greater danger. Some additives are even suspected of having mutational effects on yet unborn consumers, through contamination in the womb during the months of gestation.

Those risks arise at the very earliest point in the manufacturing cycle. The operatives who work in the food-processing plants themselves are surrounded by hazardous substances, not to mention the invisible threat that constantly awaits them in the

form of pesticide residues on the fruit and vegetables delivered
to the factory or chemicals present in meat, poultry or offal.
Here, too, most food manufacturers have been less than active in
eliminating these risks. And government agencies usually
support them, adopting the reasoning that if the chemical
agents are approved for use in food they must be safe in the
congested confines of the working environment. Yet the medical
record is filled with case studies of additives causing health
havoc in the workplace. To quote just two examples:

● People handling sweeteners, flavourings and food colourings at soft
drinks facilities have developed serious skin ailments. Rashes
broke out on their hands and rapidly spread up their arms to the
neck and face. Rubber gloves were issued to provide protection, but
the rise in the skin temperature of their hands opened the pores and
exacerbated the irritant effect. At one soft drinks plant in the
English Midlands an outbreak of dermatitis caused in this way has
persisted indefinitely. As one woman employee, with no previous
record of skin disorders, put it: 'dermatitis is bad but I hate to think
what these additives are doing to my lungs.'

● In factories making seasonings for meat products large amounts of
phosphates are used. Polyphosphates are commonly relied on to
bind extra water to processed foods. But when sacks of phosphates
are tipped into mixing bins the air fills with a highly irritant dust.
Workers caught by the dust suffer continual nose bleeds. They are
doubly at risk if soya flour is used as a carrier for additives; dust
from soya flour is known to cause occupational asthma. It is not
uncommon in such plants for employees to suffer from stomach
ulcers, without knowing the precise cause among the several
pollutants that fill their lungs and digestive tracts.

Sweet Reason

Such cases are just one small part of the evidence linking certain
additives to serious diseases, either in the workplace or – by
logical extension – through long-term ingestion via the daily
diet. In the United States, scientists now suspect that food
chemicals like nitrates are major causal factors in cancer.
Another additive, the artificial sweetener called cyclamate, has
been put in doubt by a report published in Washington recently
by the US National Academy of Sciences' National Research
Council.[1]

Cyclamate, a substance thirty times sweeter than ordinary
sugar, was widely used in North America until 1970 and

classified by the Federal Drug Administration as being 'generally recognised as safe'. All that changed in 1969, when scientists employed by the FDA reported that rats given large doses of certain sweeteners became more prone to cancer of the bladder. In 1970 cyclamate was banned by the US authorities. Many other countries followed this lead. But as the trend towards low-calorie foods and soft drinks climbed steeply through the late seventies, manufacturers focussed their attention once again on the unique properties of cyclamate. In 1984, after representations from Abbott Laboratories, the makers of the sweetener, a committee set up by the FDA ruled that cyclamate was not, after all, a cancer-causing agent.

This verdict held sway until the National Academy of Sciences took another look. Their report, published in June 1985, disputed the FDA finding. The National Academy experts concluded that while cyclamate may be classed as safe when used on its own, when mixed with saccharin, another artificial sweetener, it may cause cancers. A particular risk identified was that of cancer of the bladder. But the more significant part of its verdict concerned the effect of additives when used in combination with others.

Saccharin was itself classified by the National Academy research council in 1978 as a low-potency carcinogen in animals. According to the research council's latest conclusions, mixing it with cyclamate could produce a sweetening substance that raised even higher the risk of serious adverse effects. In the words of the council's 1985 report: 'If reintroduced, cyclamate would probably be used by large numbers of people. Thus, even if cyclamate were found to exert only a weak carcinogenic effects, its use would alter risk in millions of people.'

The new report unwittingly highlights three significant issues that can only increase the degree of anxiety that surrounds the debate on additives. First, it demonstrates the inconsistency of opinion amongst the scientific fraternity on key questions of additive safety. The lack of agreement about the risk levels attached to cyclamate and other artificial sweeteners is also found with many other additives. Second, by suggesting that ordinary consumers may be at risk from small amounts of synthetic sweeteners in foods or drink, the report implies that workers in food-processing installations or laboratories handling these substances in bulk are under considerably greater threat. Again, this danger applies to many other manufacturing environments where quite different bulk chemicals are being handled. Third, the National Academy conclusions endorse a suspicion that is giving increasing cause for alarm amongst analysts of additive side effects. The suspicion is that it is not individual chemicals acting alone but combinations of additives, or of additives reacting with natural ingredients present in foods, that pose the most serious hazards to human health.

This fear about the 'combination effect' of additives arises out of research work with hyper-allergic children and other vulnerable groups; so far the results are suggestive rather than conclusive. The same cannot, however, be said of many individual chemical agents used in food. For these a mounting catalogue of surveys, research projects and case studies point inexorably to the judgement that they are toxic hazards for the human body. These hazards are invariably those related to above-average incidences of cancer.

Many researchers have already drawn our attention to the strong correlation between cancer and abnormal factors in the surrounding environment. A growing consensus amongst analysts is that cancer is caused by the interaction between an individual's genetic make-up and his or her physical, social and economic environment. This would help explain the wide variations in cancer rates between differing social groups, different occupations and even between people living in separate regions of the same country. In developed countries it is common to have higher percentages of the most serious cancers among semi-skilled and unskilled workers than amongst people from more affluent backgrounds.

Some types of cancer are so clearly linked to a particular kind of job that governments have identified them as special cases for medical compensation. One example is cancer of the liver brought on by constant exposure to vinyl chloride monomer. Bladder cancer is extremely common among workers affected by aromatic amines in chemical dyestuffs and rubber production. The world's food industry, however, is understandably reluctant to admit that the chemical compounds used in their processing activities could be remotely hazardous to the people who swallow them. To this end, industry spokesmen reject the immense body of research based on animal tests as being irrelevant to the issue of cancer risks for humans.

This view is not shared by specialists who have devoted time and expertise to the subject. The International Agency for

Research on Cancer, a Geneva-based institute associated with the World Health Organisation, made known its verdict in a report on chemicals and human cancer published in 1982: 'It is reasonable for practical purposes to regard chemicals for which there is sufficient evidence of carcinogenicity in animals as if they presented a carcinogenic risk to humans.' Denials from the food industry are countered by a stream of laboratory test data linking various chemical additives with cancer in animals. Many of them are present in food items we eat every day:

Hazardous Eating?

Selected additives suspected of causing cancer in animals

Additive	Function	Typical Food Products
Sunset yellow	Colouring	Hot chocolate mix Marzipan Packet soups Yogurt whip Sweets
Carmoisine	Red colouring	Packet jellies Packet cheesecake mix Brown sauce Savoury mixes Prepacked Swiss roll
Amaranth	Red dye	Packet soup Packet cake mixes Liquid vitamin C Canned fruit pie fillings Gravy granules
Brilliant blue	Blue colour	Canned processed peas
Diphenyl	Preservative	Treatment of skins of oranges, lemons, grapefruit etc
Hexamine	Preservative	Marinated herrings and mackerel Provolone cheese
Sodium nitrite	Preservative and curing salt	Cured meat products Pork sausage Bacon Ham, tongue Frozen pizza
Butylated hydroxyanisole or BHA	Antioxidant (stops fats becoming rancid)	Biscuits Raisins Cheese spread Soft drinks Margarine

Additive	Function	Typical Food Products
Carrageenan	Emulsifier and thickener	Ice cream
		Desserts
		Pastries
		Milk shakes
		Infant formula
Sodium carboxy-methyl cellulose	Thickener and stabiliser	Canned potato salad
		Frozen mousse
		Tomato sauce
		Cottage cheese
		Diet orange squash

SOURCE: M. Miller, 'Danger! Additives at Work' (The London Food Commission, 1985)

The list covers only a fraction of the many dozens of additives linked with cancer in test animals. There are others that are already strongly suspected of being carcinogenic for humans as well. Among them are: carbon black, used to colour fruit juices, jams and jellies; mineral hydrocarbons, commonly used to polish, glaze or seal food products such as dried fruit, cheese rind and chewing gum; sulphuric acid, talc (or French chalk, a release agent), ethyl alcohol and ethyl acetate (these latter being used as solvents in various processing activities). There is already considerable disquiet about their more widely recognised adverse effects, irrespective of suspicions about cancer. Excessive dosages of mineral hydrocarbons, for instance, can lead to anal seepage and irritation. Carbon black is banned in the United States because of serious misgivings about its safety, including a potential link with cancer. Studies have linked carbon black with cancer in humans through skin contact and inhalation.[2]

But cancer is only one of the extreme risks posed by these compounds. A great number of them are also believed to be the cause of genetic damage to reproductive cells (mutagenic) that can be passed on to future generations, or of direct damage to the foetus already in the womb (teratogenic). Here again, the evidence relates to genetic disorders and foetal deformities observed amongst laboratory animals, but it can be no less disturbing to pregnant women entrusted with the responsibility of eating wisely during the months prior to delivery. The list includes additives already mentioned as being carcinogenic, such as carmoisine, amaranth, hexamine and sodium nitrite. There are many others:

Hazardous Motherhood?

Selected additives suspected of being mutagenic in animals

Additive	Function	Typical Food Products
Red 2G	Red colour	Sausages Cooked meat products
Caramel	Brown colour; flavouring agent	Biscuits Pickles Soya sauce Scotch eggs Chocolate dessert
Brown FK	Brown colour	Kippers Smoked mackerel
Sulphur dioxide	Preservative; antioxidant	Canned fruit salads Beer, wine, cider Dried vegetables Powdered garlic Frozen mushrooms

Selected additives suspected of being teratogenic in animals

Additive	Function	Typical Food Products
Amaranth	Red dye	Packet soup Packet cake mixes Liquid vitamin C Canned fruit pie fillings Gravy granules Packet trifle mix Quick set jelly mix
BHA	Antioxidant (stops fats becoming rancid)	Biscuits Raisins Cheese spread Soft drinks Margarine Sweets Fruit pies Beef stock cubes Savoury rice Butter
Carrageenan	Emulsifier and thickener	Ice cream Desserts Pastries Milk shakes Infant formula Cake decorations Biscuits Blancmanges Cheeses Salad dressings Alcoholic beverages

Additive	Function	Typical Food Products
Monosodium glutamate	Flavour enhancer	Packet snacks Pork pies/sausages Flavoured noodles Quick soups Frozen potato waffles

SOURCE: M. Miller, 'Danger! Additives at Work' (The London Food Commission, 1985)

To complete the list such items as saccharin, caffeine, nitrous oxide, aspartame (another sweetener) and sodium acetate should be added. Together with substances that also appear under the headings for carcinogens and mutagens, the full list of food additives suspected of being teratogens comes to more than twenty.

Nor are these suspicions based simply on the ill-informed doubts of non-specialist pressure groups anxious to prove their case. To take some of the last-mentioned examples, the scientific pedigree of the critical evidence is unimpeachable. The concern over the food dye amaranth is supported by painstaking research carried out by the Soviet analysts Shtenberg and Gavrilenko and published in the learned journal *Voprosij Pitaniya* as far back as 1970. Worries about the teratogenic effects of caffeine were set out in an article by P. E. Palm and others which appeared in *Toxicology and Applied Pharmacology* in the late 1970s.[3] The possible risks associated with the artificial sweetener saccharin have been highlighted by a number of research projects, including those by D. Stone and others reported in *Nature* in 1971,[4] and by Lederer and Pottier-Arnoud, whose findings were published in *Diabete* in 1973.[5]

Indeed, the medical journals are replete with case studies and research conclusions providing a vast body of adverse testimony from experts:

● The risks of stomach cancer from ingested talc (used to dust tins and trays to prevent food from sticking) were described by Wolff and Oehme in the *Journal of the American Veterinary Medicine Association* in 1974.[6] Cancer of the lung and lung membranes has also been traced back to contact with talc.

● In 1984 the *American Journal of Epidemiology* carried an article identifying a link between sulphuric acid in the workplace and cancer of the larynx.[7] Sulphuric acid is sometimes used illicitly in food and beverages.

- N. I. Sax, in his book *Cancer Causing Chemicals*, elaborates on the hazards of carbon black, an additive used in fruit juices, jams and jellies.[8] Though carbon black is obtained naturally from the burning of plant material, the US government has placed it on the prohibited list. There is no such restriction in Britain.

- As long ago as 1975, the EEC Scientific Committee responsible for food recommended striking the colouring agent yellow 2G (a synthetic coal tar dye) off the permitted list for fear of its toxic qualities. It is still in widespread use.

- Another colourant, patent blue V, recently lost its World Health Organisation ADI rating – the letters stand for Acceptable Daily Intake – because of lack of data confirming that it is safe in food. This additive, too, is still commonly used by food manufacturers around the world.

It is noteworthy, in any event, that most of the colouring additives are considered toxic enough to merit very low ADI ratings from institutions like WHO and the UN Food and Agriculture Organisation. By way of comparison, the current recommendation on acceptable daily intake for the thickening agent carrageenan is 75 milligrams per kilogram of bodyweight. For quinoline yellow, used in such foods as Scotch eggs and smoked haddock, the ADI is 0.5mg/kg; iron oxides, added to give extra colour to such things as salmon and shrimp paste and packet cake and dessert mixes, also have an ADI of 0.5. Red 2G rates just 0.1, while ponceau, another red colour additive used in a variety of packet cake mixes, seafood dressings and canned fruits, merits a rating of only 0.125.

If we are to assume, as logic demands, that ADI ratings are a rough guideline to the relative toxicity of a chemical compound, then colouring agents need to be placed at the very top of the list. Indeed, many colourants are already outlawed by certain health authorities. The EEC, for instance, has withheld approval for the use of a wide range of synthetic food dyes including riboflavin, yellow 2G, red 2G, brilliant blue FCF, brown FK (until recently used as a constituent of Marks & Spencer smoked kippers) and chocolate brown HT. The EEC disapproval, however, does not necessarily prevent their use in imported food and drink products, and certainly cannot eliminate illicit practices; the temptation for manufacturers to ignore official proscriptions is very great, particularly when they come from a much criticised, supra-national institution. Needless to say, any visit to a country where food regulations are more lax will expose the traveller to an increased level of hazard.

The weight of learned opinion on additive dangers is not only immense but highly persuasive in raising reasonable doubts about the longer-term consequences of putting chemicals into food. In most countries such 'reasonable doubts' would be sufficient in a court of law to win the verdict. Limited steps have been taken by some countries, supermarket chains and manufacturers to curb the more self-evident dangers, but both companies and politicians draw back from the prospect of more drastic action that may harm profits, jobs and votes.

Facts of Life

The law-makers in some countries can argue, in any case, that considerable progress has been made. In the United States manufacturers have for some time been required to carry details on their labels of the chemical ingredients contained in food and drink products. Since January 1986 the twelve member states of the European Community are also obliged to apply labelling laws related to additives (though some companies have been doing this for several years), although more recent members such as Spain and Portugal enjoy a lengthy period of adjustment. Looked at broadly, these regulations convey a sense of responsible monitoring and control of the complex world of processed food. A closer scrutiny reveals disturbing shortcomings.

To begin with, the laws call for nothing more than a brief, clinical reference to the additives used. In Europe the new rules dictate that labels now have to carry either the 'E' number or the actual name of the ingredient used. In neither case is there a duty to offer any indication of the possible toxic effects associated with a particular additive. Unless the shopper in question has a university degree, or the equivalent, in chemistry or a related subject, the details on the label will mean nothing. Shoppers with the time and resources to secure a copy of one of the information pamphlets made available by various EEC governments will be rewarded for their diligence by pages of chemical references which disclose nothing of the potential hazards of chemical ingredients appearing on the labels of food items they have purchased.

It might even be asked whether such new regulations will

make any real difference to the level of risk. The European Community has issued scores of directives on food additives since 1962, yet these have not prevented the problem of food adulteration from escalating steadily over the ensuing quarter century. And the much-heralded 1986 rules on labelling were not designed to apply to flavourings. Indeed, they laid down no requirements controlling the composition of flavours, except the general expectation that foods shall be safe.

This loophole would seem to confer privileged status on a number of additives long considered to be suspect. Monosodium glutamate, the key factor in Chinese Restaurant Syndrome, is one of them. Potassium hydrogen L-glutamate is another; it is linked to adverse effects that include diarrhoea, vomiting and abdominal cramps, and is considered harmful to people with impaired kidneys. It should not be given to babies under twelve weeks old. Sodium guanylate is another flavour enhancer; it is prohibited in or on foods that might be fed to babies or young children and to adults suffering from conditions that result from disorders in the creation of uric acid, such as gout.

But there is an even more disconcerting weakness in the emerging pattern of additive regulations, a weakness indirectly pinpointed by the loophole connected to flavourings. It flows from the fact that labelling regulations, apart from giving no information about possible adverse effects (that range from blurred vision to cancer), tell us nothing about the higher levels of risk faced by particular groups of consumers. This failing is especially disturbing in relation to infants and young children.

The more observant reader will have noticed that infant formula figures in the list of products containing carrageenan, an emulsifier and thickener shown in tests on animals to be cancer-causing. It is not an isolated case. Many of the products containing additives that are linked to cancer, foetal deformity and genetic mutation in animals would be regular favourites at any children's party. They include ice cream, jellies, milk shakes, sweets and biscuits, as well as cakes and the marzipan that covers them. These chemical ingredients appear in children's food for the simple reason that they are contained in processed products and mixes that inevitably end up on a child's plate. This absurd contradiction between regulations and realities exists across the entire spectrum of additive rules. The same sodium guanylate that is prohibited in many countries for foods intended for babies and young children is a prime constituent of potato crisps – a staple item for many youngsters.

This anomalous situation has been vigorously explored by groups representing parents of children classed as hyperactive in their efforts to understand, and possibly cure, the condition that has transformed their offspring into intolerable and unpredictable 'monsters'. Hyperactive infants sleep as little as two or three hours a night, are excessively boisterous, and invariably suffer from eczema or asthma or both. Cot rocking and head banging are common symptoms; attempts to calm them down are unsuccessful. As they grow older their level of over-activity increases to the point where physical injury can result. They have trouble with intellectual functions such as speech, have difficulty with their balance and suffer problems with learning even if their IQ is high. Hyperactive children are also prone to excessive thirst, and to disorders of the respiratory system. Unfortunately, their parents have gained very little help from the medical establishment. Meanwhile, they become social outcasts as well as mental and physical wrecks.

Until recently, hyperactivity in children was seen by most doctors either as an unwelcome, but temporary, aspect of childhood – a form of 'naughtiness' – or as a symptom of mental retardation. Many doctors still refuse to accept hyperactivity as a distinct and diagnosable complaint, just as many doctors do not recognise the existence of pre-menstrual tension except as a semi-pejorative term to describe psychosomatic fancies. Ironically, where PMT is diagnosed by a sympathetic doctor it is sometimes mistaken for what is, in fact, the adverse effects of additives, particularly in food-processing plants where 'women's problems' are a more convenient explanation for recurrent ill health among the work force.

There is, nevertheless, a fast-growing record of case studies that points to a direct connection between hyperactivity in children and additives in food. The work of an American doctor, Ben Feingold, has isolated a group of additives that are thought to be significant causal factors.[9] Chief among them are artificial colourings, flavourings, the preservative sodium benzoate (and related preservatives), and the antioxidants BHT and BHA. Many of these also appear in the lists of suspected carcinogens, mutagens and teratogens. A diet based on Feingold's conclusions has been developed for use by the parents of hyperactive children. It clearly eliminates most processed foods and drinks that are brightly coloured and sharply flavoured. Ironically these would include an item such as concentrated blackcurrant juice, for many years highly regarded by parents as a source of valuable vitamins for their growing infants. Also falling within the prohibited category are fruit jellies, chocolate biscuits, sweets, fruit pies, barbecue sauce, freeze drinks, dessert sauces, glucose, pickles, chewing gum, salted peanuts, potato crisps, dry breakfast cereals, most packet convenience foods and many, many more.

The Feingold diet also recommends avoiding all foods containing salicylates, a family of aspirin-like substances. A large number of people of all ages are allergic to aspirin; they will also react to foods that contain salicylates. In some cases, these are present naturally in food rather than as an added ingredient. Included in this category are almonds, apples, apricots, blackberries, cherries, cucumbers, currants, gooseberries, and other commonly available fruits and vegetables. But the food industry has also found it necessary to produce synthetic salicylates; they are used to flavour such childhood treats as sweets, ice cream and soft drinks, as well as finding their way into cake mixes that eventually appear on the table at teatime.

Ben Feingold has attracted very limited support from the medical authorities; diets, like allergies, are invariably considered as grey areas of medicine, to be classified alongside faith healing and extrasensory perception as 'interesting' but not serious. Yet a vast literature – both scientific and informal – has accumulated on the subject of hyperactive children and the seemingly miraculous results that have followed the elimination of specific additives.

A major source of data on these successes is the network of parents' action groups that have grown up to help resolve the problem of hyperactivity. Such groups are firmly established in North America, Britain and some other parts of Europe. One claim is that as many as one in five children is a victim of hyperactivity. There are cases of infants who are hyperactive even in the womb. And the collective experience of these groups is that hyperactivity is closely linked to certain food additives, and that a switch to diets without these additives produces remarkable changes for the better in the affected children.

One case revolved around apples, oranges and tomatoes – precisely the food items that thoughtful parents might build into the dietary habits of their families. For several years the baby daughter in one household never once slept continuously through the night, waking up repeatedly with a raging thirst and aggressive, unruly behaviour. The problem was attributed to salicylates and action was taken to eliminate these from her food intake, both in their natural form in fruits and vegetables and as synthetic additives. The girl's behaviour was transformed.

Another young girl had never slept properly for five years, waking constantly complaining of thirst; she was continually troubled by diarrhoea and outbreaks of eczema. The problem was traced to salicylates in orange – whether as squash, orange colouring or the natural fruit itself – and to artificial colouring agents and preservatives in cooked meats, bacon, sausages and chocolate. In another instance, a boy of twelve had been 'signed off' by his psychologist after years of terrible behavioural problems; again the cause was related to salicylates in certain fruits, in this case raspberries, and to artificial flavourings and colourings.

There are thousands of similar cases reported by parents throughout the industrial world who have adopted the Feingold theory (and those of other specialists) and applied it to their own disturbed children with surprising results. While individually they may not represent earth-shattering medical events, looked at as a mass phenomenon evident in many different cultures and geographical zones across the world, they represent an overwhelmingly convincing argument.[10]

Far more disconcerting is evidence that suggests a link between food additives and damage caused to babies while they are still in the womb. One example is the artificial sweetener aspartame, already mentioned as having a doubtful record in animal tests. Researches have led to the discovery that a large number of people have a body chemistry that prevents them from metabolising one of the two main ingredients of aspartame, an essential amino acid called phenylalinine. The condition is known as phenylketonuria and an estimated four million people in the United States alone are thought to suffer from it. If the sufferer is also a pregnant woman, there is a risk that the much higher levels of phenylalinine in her system will produce a baby with defects such as microcephaly (an abnormally small head), mental retardation and a damaged nervous system.[11]

Studies in Finland, meanwhile, indicate that women working in food processing have a greater risk of spontaneous abortion, as well as an above-average chance of giving birth to a baby with musculo-skeletal malformations and to children who succumb to cancer before they reach the age of fifteen. This latter danger was found to be especially true of women working in the bakery trade.

While these are obviously extreme cases involving consistent, heavy exposure to toxic substances, it is nevertheless also true that they refer to the very same chemicals that end up in our food. And many young women of child-bearing age will, over the years, have absorbed considerable amounts of these chemicals through their diet. A recent estimate in Britain, for instance, has put the intake of additives at roughly five and a half pounds a year for every man, woman and child in the country, or the equivalent of twenty-two aspirin-sized tablets every day.[12] In 1955 the annual intake was only one-quarter this much. How can we be sure that this fourfold increase has not pushed our future generations into the shadow of toxic catastrophe? Alas, only time will tell.

Time will also bring us new and more inventive additives to supersede the crude chemical concoctions that currently determine the colour, taste and shelf-life of our food. The laboratories of the food-processing giants are busily at work in the search for the flavours and cosmetics that will help them win market share in the twenty-first century, even before we fully understand the risks posed by additives currently in use. The burden of research has so far concentrated on only a small group of the three and a half thousand substances in regular use by the food industry. Enzymes, processing aids and flavours – more than three thousand in all – have barely been considered, even though flavourings are recognised as very suspect.

Yet the search for the ultimate additive continues. A major area of spending is on the development of colourings that can replace the much-criticised azo dyes that have been the foundation of artificial food colours since the nineteenth century. Many of them, like yellow 2G, amaranth, red 2G and ponceau, appear regularly on the lists of substances that have connections with cancer, genetic mutation or foetal deformity. Hence, scientists in Japan are working on 'natural' colours developed from plant cell tissue culture and fungi. Elsewhere, biotechnologists are developing a new breed of flavour-enhancers based on an enzyme that is added to meat to promote the flow of glutamic acid.

The truth is, however, that these are no more 'natural' than any of their counterparts in the additive armoury. They are at best 'nature identical'. They rely on the same synthetic or artificial processes, including the stimulation of unnatural flavour-enhancing reactions within meat, fish, fruit and vegetables, that attends the use of existing additives. More to the point, the testing procedures used by food-processing companies to verify the safety of such 'natural' additives are no more certain than methods currently employed, which are themselves less than satisfactory for a number of vital reasons.

Tried or Tested?
The range and complexity of testing procedures applied to food additives are equalled only by the lack of precision that surrounds them. The key question is whether tests on animals under controlled, short-term laboratory conditions give any clear guidance as to whether a particular additive is or is not safe. A growing body of opinion is convinced that such short-term testing procedures are inadequate. The misgivings fall into four areas:

● Are the tests themselves carried out thoroughly? The answer to this question depends on such variables as the quality of laboratory practice in the institution conducting the research, the abundance or lack of resources devoted by a company or government department to the task, and the relevance or efficiency of the testing methods in producing the right information. It comes down to fundamental issues such as the exact size of dose to be used in tests. Is that dose, administered over a controlled period of time, a realistic guide to possible human side effects resulting from lifetime consumption?

● Are conclusions reached after studying the results on animals necessarily of value to an assessment of the human risk? The classic and tragic case of thalidomide proves beyond any doubt that there is no such thing as the perfect animal test; in this instance thalidomide was subsequently found to produce serious adverse effects on an obscure breed of New Zealand white rabbit. By this time, however, thousands of mothers had given birth to hideously deformed babies.

● Are the testing procedures applied to additives able to identify the 'cocktail effect' from mixing additives together in the random way that will occur in normal eating patterns? The answer to this is in the negative, if only because of the sheer size of the problem. The permutations offered by several thousand additives in a vast range of different processed food products would defeat even the most sophisticated computer, even if it possessed the power to unravel the secrets of unpredictable human biochemistry. A typical meal in a normal household in a developed country will contain as many as sixty separate additives, all mixed together by the digestive process.

● What political, administrative or commercial factors are involved? Have they interfered with, or blocked, the research effort on a particular substance or group of substances? Much of the research work on additives is carried out in secret. Government departments entrusted with food safety also consider the effects on the food industry of any sudden changes in safety regulations.

This last point, with its spirit of compromise, produces strange anomalies, especially in conjunction with the other factors. An example widely used is that of bread. Though by tradition it has been sanctified as the staff of life, modern baking has borrowed comprehensively from the chemical industry. Preservatives are used to make the loaf last longer; a common favourite is propionic acid. Though preservatives in bread are banned in some countries (Portugal and Luxembourg are examples), the majority of governments have done nothing to eliminate them. Oxidising agents may be used, including azodicarbonamide, benzoyl peroxide and cysteine. Again, some countries have outlawed these additives, among them France, West Germany, Switzerland, Portugal and Italy; but in most countries bakers have a relatively free hand. Emulsifiers like lecithin and stearyl tartrate are introduced. Colouring agents are mixed in to give an attractive, wholesome appearance; caramel is one such agent, though animal tests have shown it to be a possible mutagen. Then there are anti-caking agents, acids and salts to promote reactions in yeast, as well as release agents in the form of mineral oils or magnesium stearate that prevent the dough from sticking to food-processing equipment.[13]

The striking fact about this chemical breakdown of modern baking technology is not the large number of additives commonly used, but the lack of agreement amongst apparently sophisticated governments as to what should be permitted in bread and what should not. The same is true of frozen vegetables. While countries like Belgium, Canada, Finland, France, Israel, Italy and others have prohibited the use of anti-foaming agents such as dimethylpolysiloxanes, a form of silicon, they are allowed in Britain and elsewhere. Preservatives like ethyl, methyl and propyl hydroxybenzoate are banned for frozen vegetables in Austria, Finland and Spain, but used regularly by food companies in many other parts of the world. The Austrian, Finnish and Spanish governments have a point: the hydroxy-benzoate family of preservatives is known to be dangerous to asthmatics and aspirin-sensitive people, and could with good reason be added to the list of additives not allowed in foodstuffs given to babies or young children.

National differences on additive rules are even greater in the contentious area of artificial colours. These differences are all the more disturbing considering the weight of expert opinion ranged against their use. In Norway all artificial colours, principally azo dyes, have been banned since 1978 because of the mounting evidence of colour-induced allergic reactions. Not so in the United States, where seven artificial colourants are permitted, or in Britain (one of the most permissive countries) where a total of seventeen artificial colouring agents are allowed. Nearly all countries permit the use of ponceau 4R, amaranth, carmoisine and sunset yellow, even though they are suspected of being carcinogenic and, in some cases, mutagenic in animals.

The Bitter End?
The world food industry is locked into an ever-increasing spiral of technological processes that rely on chemicals and other man-made ingredients. Even the development of 'nature-identical' and other sophisticated additives will not change the methods, or the commercial imperative, that have given us food products that would not have been out of place in Aldous Huxley's *Brave New World*. Tight profit margins in the highly competitive retailing sector demand new food concepts that can reduce costs or boost earnings. This competition is made even more fierce by the static condition of the food business in most Western countries; to win customers it is necessary to steal them from rivals by offering cheaper or more appealing products. The key to achieving this objective is new food technologies that allow the manufacturer to cut production costs by utilising cheap or waste ingredients, synthetic substances, and more water to give increased 'value-added' – to the company, at least.

The marketplace, meanwhile, is dominated by a small

number of immense corporations and retailing chains that have
grown powerful on the back of the high-tech food revolution.
They have carried that revolution beyond the developed countries into the vast, populous markets of the newly industrialising world. Their very existence is based on the continued growth
of the processed-food industry. To dismantle the technological
armoury that has made them big is to tempt commercial
disaster. Quite to the contrary, the new investments and product
ranges that underpin today's food corporation will be expected to
yield profits until well into the next century. Food-processing
machinery, and the products that it creates, cannot function
without the chemicals and other synthetic elements that have
become so essential a part of this latter-day alchemy.

A vital component in the alchemist's cupboard is the ability to
substitute inferior food ingredients for high quality ones, and
use additives to disguise the fall-off in taste and nutritional
value. Even more profitable is to omit the natural ingredient
altogether and replace it with a synthetic alternative. An
example is that of the artificial cheese and tomato flavourings
used in pizzas. According to a recent report on the additive issue,
one US manufacturer of synthetic tomato flavours wished to
leave no doubts about the commercial gains that can come from
using science rather than Nature: 'Cooked, ripe tomato flavour
in either dry or liquid form . . . is recommended for use in soups,
sauces, dips, salad dressings and convenience foods . . . one
pound [of artificial flavouring] replaces the flavour and aroma of
between 1,200 and 1,600 pounds of tomato juice, at a cost of
$5.'[14]

But manufacturers are equally aware that their processed
products should look genuine, as well as taste real. There will
therefore be more emphasis on colouring agents in the years to
come; industry forecasts see this as a major area for future
exploitation. An important consideration is that supermarket
shelves do not betray any variations in product appearance; an
even, predictable colour is the objective.

The march of chemical adulteration will continue hand-in-
hand with the growth in 'natural' product categories. Health-
conscious shoppers will be dismayed to discover that very few
'natural' items on sale at their local supermarket could be made
without the help of additives. Low-fat yoghurts, for instance, are
likely to contain a variety of flavourings, emulsifiers, colours
and preservatives. Even vitamins, a mainstay of diet for many

thoughtful people, deserve a second look. Vitamin C, for example, is not only to be found in tablet form for daily dosage. It is also used as an antioxidant to stop fats deteriorating and to prevent cut fruits from turning brown. Yet research shows that large doses of vitamin C may cause diarrhoea and dental erosion. An intake above ten grams a day could lead to kidney stones.

A far more alarming prospect, however, is the possible use of irradiation techniques to alter Nature. It is widely known amongst food scientists that irradiation is a powerful weapon for killing pests, delaying the ripening cycle of fruit, preventing the sprouting of vegetables, and holding back the micro-organisms that can cause food to perish. And it has had an erratic history of official enthusiasm followed by condemnation since it first emerged from the nuclear industry as a food-processing option. Now, with business pressures mounting, irradiation is once again in vogue.

The technique first appeared as far back as 1916, when Swedish scientists experimented by irradiating strawberries. But more active interest developed during the 1950s, with a major research project funded by the US Department of Defence. The first commercial efforts were made in 1957 by German food technologists for the sterilisation of spices being used in sausages. Soon afterwards the technique was prohibited by the German government. The first government to give an official blessing to irradiation was the Soviet Union in 1958; it was subsequently used by Soviet farmers to treat potatoes and grain.

Since the 1960s there has been a steadily growing interest in irradiation for a range of food-processing functions. It was used, for example, by US companies to sterilise canned bacon; the US government (which classes it as an additive) withdrew its approval for this process in 1968 after doubts were raised over possible side effects and the inadequacy of testing procedures. But over the past few years more than thirty separate governments around the world have allowed, or are actively considering, the irradiation of a total of about three dozen products sold for ordinary human consumption.

Those governments are supported by expert opinion at the highest international level. J. van Kooij, Head of the Food Preservation Section of the UN Food and Agriculture Organisation, writing in the *Bulletin of the International Atomic Energy Agency* in June 1984, praised the new technique as a godsend that would help preserve the one-quarter of world food production that is lost after harvesting each year because of spoiling, particularly in the less developed regions: 'People in such countries are accustomed to buying fresh food for immediate consumption at home. They would welcome any new technology which would keep food fresh for a longer time.' The FAO has gone further; it has disseminated considerable amounts of informational material to UN member states extolling the virtues of irradiated food. In doing so, it has helped create an enormous potential market for exploitation by the major food companies.

It is hardly surprising that food manufacturers are enthusiastic about the benefits of irradiation. To begin with, it is a fairly accessible technology that involves using large doses of ionising radiation to stimulate changes in food. In simple terms, radiation is directed at the target at levels that break down the molecular structure, so as to generate charged particles called ions. These ions can then be directed to produce chemical reactions in the surrounding material. These reactions can, in turn, have a range of effects on any organisms that are present; one result could be longer storage life for the food in question, producing considerable financial gains for growers, processors and retailers.

The technology is widely available throughout the industrial world, with about thirty irradiation plants either built or planned. Many of these plants have been used for sterilising medical supplies or similar tasks, but they can easily be converted to be used with food products. But while it may have its attractions for the food industry, certain aspects of irradiation give cause for alarm. The more obvious one is that irradiation of living organisms, people included, is almost always damaging. Clearly, no government would allow irradiation processes to be conducted without proper safeguards, but there are areas where public concern is bound to emerge if the practice becomes widespread.

And public fears are unlikely to be allayed by some of the more eccentric schemes dreamt up by scientists over the years. One suggestion, published in a British government report in 1955, was that radioactive waste from nuclear power stations could be used as a source for food irradiation. As it is, favoured radiation sources among many specialists are cobalt 60 and caesium 137, both created as waste by-products during the manufacture of nuclear weapons and the generation of energy.

A first area of concern relates to monitoring techniques. Specialists say there is no accurate way of detecting whether food has ever been radiated, how often it has taken place, or to what level. This will call for extremely strict rules about monitoring systems and labelling. Can the food industry maintain such high standards, especially when it has found it difficult to act responsibly in the comparatively simple area of ordinary additives, acting only at the insistence of governments and even then in a less than enthusiastic manner?

Second, high energy irradiation can create radioactivity in the material being bombarded. Above an energy output of between 10 and 15 million electron volts, significant levels of radio-activity can be generated. Trace metal compounds in the food might be made radioactive. Thus, there is a vital requirement that irradiation plants have failsafe methods of guaranteeing that levels do not exceed that 10mev limit. Is this a realistic guarantee when seen against the background of public unease about all things 'radioactive'? And what would happen if there was an unobserved fracture or other accident affecting the plant?

All this, of course, ignores the very high risks that will face food workers employed in irradiation facilities. Here again the official position in most countries is confused, with outdated safety limits still applying in many cases. In Britain, for example, employees are permitted to absorb up to 5 rems of radiation per year, a rem being a measurement of the biological damage inflicted by radiation. This is ten times the level permitted for ordinary members of the public, although the reason for such a marked difference is unclear. Why, in other words, should a person face a ten times greater risk of radiation-induced disease merely because he or she has a particular kind of job? The same logic would dictate that if a bus driver is ten times more likely to die in a road accident because the bus he is given to drive is unsafe, there would be no need to redesign the bus to eradicate its dangerous features.

Just as important, the 5 rem limit is itself suspect. It was set down in 1957, since when it has become apparent to many experts that it is unacceptably high. To reduce the level of health risk to match that in a safe industry the limit should, they argue, be reduced to 0.5 rem per year. Unfortunately, even this limit could be dangerously high. But once built into a future generation of irradiation facilities it will become, like so much in the nuclear industry, a sacrosanct figure. Either way, it seems, workers in the irradiation sector will find themselves alongside all their counterparts in the additives business. Their bodies will act as unwilling experimental specimens, testing with large, short-term doses the same substances or processes that reach the general public in small doses over a longer span of time.

Another area of anxiety is the precise dose of radiation imparted to a food product. In simple terms, how much energy has been deposited in the food as a consequence of irradiation processes? And here the facts are even less reassuring. The traditionally accepted unit for measuring radiation doses is the rad (now being replaced by the Gray, a much larger unit). By way of a yardstick, a visit to the X-ray clinic will involve exposure to approximately 0.01 rad. The average dose from background radiation present in the air is about 0.1 rad in any twelve-month period. Food irradiation processes are likely to involve doses up to one million rads, or one hundred million times greater than the dose delivered by an X-ray machine. The regulations currently operating in France, to take just one example, do not require companies to submit any data on toxic side effects if they are applying for clearance for irradiation processes using up to this one million rad level.[15]

The higher the level of dose the greater the changes occurring in the food itself, including unwelcome ones. For instance, irradiation is very destructive of vitamins, especially A,C,D,E and K. Some of the B vitamins are also severely damaged. The exact degree of damage depends on dose levels and on the kind of food involved; the rule is that the more complex the food the less likely it is to suffer major vitamin destruction. Unfortunately, the simple foods are often the most valuable; fruit juices and fresh fruit, for example, are the most vulnerable.

As with so many facets of the high-tech holocaust, the most serious negative effects would be felt by low-income families. While affluent people may be able to purchase more nutritious food, poverty tends to be reflected in poor eating habits with a heavy reliance on cheap packaged-food products. These are precisely the products that would emanate from the irradiation plants if, or when, the manufacturers decide to adopt the process on a large scale.

Practically all the arguments supporting irradiation of food stress benefits that are of value chiefly to manufacturers; there would be few gains for the average consumer, and several areas of loss. For most products, refrigeration will still be needed; if the packaging is damaged during storage there is just as great a risk of contamination, even if the product has been irradiated. Vitamins will have been destroyed. Changes to the consistency of the outer skin in fruit and vegetables could lead to easier bruising and less palatable produce. The ripening process itself may have been interrupted by irradiation to remove pests; the result is an apple or a pear that may be pest-free, but is not yet ready to eat. A recent American study revealed that of twenty-seven fruits subjected to irradiation only eight were improved by the process. The somewhat absurd conclusion prompted by the tests is that most fruits are damaged more by irradiation than they are by the fungi that occasioned its use in the first place.[16]

Another problem is that irradiation changes the aroma of many food products. Researchers refer to the 'wet dog' smell of meat after high doses are delivered, and to the 'typical irradiation flavours' that develop in a large number of other food items. This may offer even greater encouragement to manufacturers to fall back on their vast catalogue of more orthodox additives in an attempt to recreate lost characteristics. Among the substances likely to be used are sodium nitrite, diphenyl, sodium sulphite and BHA. All four are suspected of causing cancer and genetic mutations in animals, and possibly in humans.

Hence, a commonly available irradiated product on the supermarket shelves of the future might be a tasty-looking piece of beef. But outward appearances will be deceptive. Before reaching the display area from the slaughterhouse it would have been dipped in a solution such as sodium tripolyphosphate, a chemical that also serves as a cleansing agent to remove greasy slime from walls. Then the meat would be film wrapped, refrigerated at 0–5°C and irradiated with a dose of up to 200,000 rads, before being shipped under cold conditions. Other additives may have been used to provide greater appetiser value. By following a preparation process along these lines, the shelf-life of the beef would have been increased to about three weeks. And the trusting shopper will take it home in the firm belief that modern technology had delivered a natural freshness and nourishment that amply repaid the handsome price.

That same trust is open to considerable abuse by unscrupulous or negligent manufacturers and retailers. For the chemicals and processes that have created the modern food industry also increase the risk of buying food that has been improperly stored or displayed beyond its safe time limit. Additives, and the high-tech packaging methods that come with them, offer encouragement to food suppliers to rely on science rather than common sense when judging whether a product has perished. Often they may be wrong. Preservatives and vacuum-sealed packs do not guarantee shelf-life indefinitely; even in the short term they are only effective if the correct storage procedures are followed. Additives can have the unexpected result of making suppliers lazy about caring for the food that we buy from them.

This could well be the reason for the rapid rise in cases of food poisoning that has occurred in recent years. Throughout Europe, public health statistics have been overwhelmed by an escalation in incidents related to contaminated food. Fittingly, one of the countries with the worst record is Britain, where regulations on additives are amongst the most permissive to be found anywhere in the industrialised world. In 1979 considerable official concern was expressed at the figure of 14,597 cases reported in England alone during that year. In 1980 the figure dropped, but the improvement was short-lived. In 1981 the number of cases leapt by just under ten per cent. In 1982 it rose again by 9.7 per cent. The authorities comforted themselves with the knowledge that they were still below the 1979 peak; then food poisoning took on all the characteristics of an epidemic. In 1984 the number passed twenty thousand. At the beginning of the 1970s the annual total was no more than eight thousand. Investigations linked the many thousands of cases to a variety of causative agents. Chief amongst them were the different forms of salmonella.

But a more surprising trend within the British example is the steep increase in reported cases of campylobacter, a food-borne disease that does not strictly qualify as a poisoning. For this reason, most incidents involving campylobacter do not appear in the statistics alongside salmonella. Scrutiny of the relevant data, however, reveals a dramatic growth in gastrointestinal infections traced to this organism. In 1984 the total was nearly twenty-one thousand. The figure for rotaviruses, a major cause of gastroenteritis in children and infants, was more than five thousand six hundred, nearly two and a half times what it had been seven years earlier. Cases involving shigella, a bacteria that is a contributory cause of dysentery, were double what they had been at the beginning of the 1980s.

The fundamental cause of this explosion in food-related infections is not known. There may not be a single explanation. In one episode the origins of a local salmonella outbreak were traced to milk supplied by a nearby dairy farm. In another, the evidence pointed to a batch of sausage meat. The lesson, nevertheless, seems clear. The additive revolution and its associated technological advances in packaging and storage have not been accompanied by an advance in food hygiene. On the contrary, the advent of chemical foodstuffs has made us more ready to take hygiene for granted. It has also contaminated our diet and taken us several steps further away from wholesome eating. In doing so it has opened up yet another abyss, one that confronts us every time we sit down at the table. And the plans being made by an ambitious food industry for our mealtimes in the future offer little reason for optimism.

9
Doctors of Death

In his book *The Diseases of Civilisation*, author Brian Inglis issues one of the most striking condemnations ever published in the twentieth century. In this age of miracle medicine, Inglis turns his wrath on doctors: 'If nominations were called for to select THE disease of our civilisation, the one with the most familiar symptoms in our time . . . it would be the one which has come to be called iatrogenic: illness caused by medical treatment.'[1]

To assist them in the task of healing, modern doctors have been armed with the products of a rich and powerful drugs industry. Together they make a frightening, often lethal, combination. And the victim is the internal environment of the patient. In an era of rapidly growing pollution of our external surroundings, an equally serious threat now overshadows our own biochemistry. Its trade marks are deformity, bodily deterioration and death. A major factor in this threat is the ever-expanding armoury of pharmaceutical preparations made available to the physician. Created to cure us, too many of them succeed in doing the exact opposite.

Not that there is anything new about the risk of being cured to death. The term iatrogenesis, from the Greek meaning 'caused by medical treatment', is as old as Hippocrates. But, as Inglis records, it was not until this century that the concept took on real meaning when it was discovered that sulpha drugs (widely used to counter a broad range of infections) induced clearly observable adverse reactions in patients, ranging from mild discomfort to death. In the single year of 1937, more than one hundred US citizens died after being given a sulpha preparation.

Unfortunately for humanity, the appearance of such adverse

effects was not to become a reason for prohibiting the use of specific pharmaceutical treatments. After all, revolutionary breakthrough drugs such as penicillin and other antibiotics were, from the beginning, attended by a consistent incidence of negative results in patients, sometimes proving fatal. Health authorities across the world accepted this toll of reactive conditions and fatalities as the cost of medical progress. Or, to be more precise, they accepted it as the inevitable consequence of encouraging a rapidly expanding international drugs business. In time it was to seem clear to more discerning minds that the borderline between profits and human well-being was becoming dangerously blurred.

The rise of the modern pharmaceuticals industry has indeed been exceedingly fast, even by today's standards of high-speed technologically based new product development. In fact, like its counterpart in pesticides, this massive worldwide industry has emerged almost entirely since World War II. In the 1930s, when those pioneering sulpha drugs were in circulation, it would have been difficult to list more than three dozen synthetic drugs then available on the everyday market. Amongst them were mass-produced painkillers like aspirin and phenacetin that had been produced by German researchers in the nineteenth century. Even as recently as the late sixties, a survey in the United States of the two hundred most widely dispensed drugs showed that less than twenty of them had even existed before the start of World War II. Now the total number of drug variants at the disposal of doctors exceeds twenty-five thousand.[2]

This enormous growth in the drugs armoury has turned physicians into prescribing machines, dealing with patients by writing out orders for pills, lotions and ointments. By the mid-seventies it was estimated that two thousand million prescriptions were being written every year in the United States alone, a fifty per cent rise in just ten years. In France the increase had been closer to two hundred per cent. A UK study conducted in 1969 showed that more than half the country's adult population, and almost one-third of its children, were taking some kind of medication every day.[3] More important, three-quarters of the drugs being used by British patients questioned in the survey had been obtained by repeat prescriptions; the local doctor had abrogated all responsibility for monitoring the progress of the patient's condition. In other studies on British medical practice, it was discovered that people were still taking certain drugs on repeat prescriptions even though the last session with their doctor was as long as five years before.

As with so many other issues raised by the gathering storm of the high-tech holocaust, a key factor in the trend towards excessive reliance on pharmaceutical devices is the demands of consumers themselves. In the same way that food additives have become a crucial weapon with the food-processing companies in their efforts to satisfy customer requirements for tastier, more attractive, longer-lasting foods, so patients have grown to regard drug prescriptions as an essential part of the curative process. A study of the British pharmaceutical market completed in the 1970s revealed that more than forty per cent of the country's population would feel cheated if they were not given a prescription on their next visit to the doctor.[4] In a research project covering five hundred households in the town of Hartlepool, in north-east England, families were asked to search their cupboards for pills and potions. The search yielded forty-three thousand items, one-third of them drugs for the treatment of emotional or nervous conditions. The scenarios of the future sketched out by Huxley, a world built on the sedative properties of the mind-deadening drug Soma, were not, after all, so far-fetched.

A second important factor is that once those pills and potions have been prescribed, there is very little control over the means by which they are administered. To begin with, doctors themselves are required to keep abreast of a spiralling flow of new or improved products, most of them energetically marketed by the manufacturers; a pile of increasingly complex technical literature comes through the mail every week. All this places a considerable burden of information overload on the ordinary family doctor. The possibility of ill-informed, or even dangerous, prescribing has become a permanent feature of today's medicine. And once the ailing visitor has left the surgery, or the physician has left the bedside, the implementation of the chosen treatment is usually left to the individual concerned.

Often this is the beginning of a journey into the medical unknown. Many doctors prefer not to know what happens to their patient after the diagnosis and prescription process is completed. One medical practitioner, quoted in a scientific journal on the subject, summarised the feelings of thousands of his colleagues around the world: 'When you've worked hard in an attempt to find a rational and scientific answer to a patient's problem, it's not very nice to think that they may go off and ignore or forget your instructions so that the whole thing comes to nothing. It's like making a nice new shiny car and seeing it smashed up fifty yards from the factory.' There couldn't be a more telling illustration of the new mood of the medical profession; they have become an industry every bit as high-tech and automated as immense mass-production operations turning out cars, hi-fi and computers.[5]

Thus it is that drug products are unleashed into a market-place that has all the outside appearances of a carefully monitored, professionally organised system geared to the curing of the sick. In reality it is haphazard and misleadingly chaotic; at the centre of this vortex of risk is the patient, not least because of his or her own ill-informed actions – or non-actions. Several studies have indicated, for instance, that roughly fifty per cent of the patients put on courses of psychiatric drugs do not actually take them. Old people are particularly prone to bizarre activities involving drugs, especially because the drugs themselves are often prescribed in the first place to treat conditions of mental vagueness or emotional instability. As a result, the patients often carry around with them an assorted baggage of pills of no real relevance to their current condition; they may even represent a lethal threat if taken to excess.

Specialists at a teaching hospital in London's East End tell of the case of an old man, admitted to the wards, who was found to be carrying a bottle of digoxin tablets (a powerful cardiac tonic) prescribed for him some years earlier. It was his practice to take a few of the tablets whenever he felt below par. Other elderly patients known to the hospital were found to carry their various pills mixed together in a single bottle. At medicine time they would simply shake out the correct number of pills and swallow them, irrespective of the particular combination that ended up in their stomachs. One seriously ill arrival had a selection of digoxin, thyroxine (a hormone preparation for thyroid conditions), potassium, a diuretic and a hypnotic in her bag. She knew she had to take five pills at particular intervals. On the day in question she tipped out five tablets, all of them digoxin, and swallowed them; she was admitted with digoxin poisoning. As a professor at the hospital put it: 'It is a kind of pharmaceutical Russian roulette.'

By 1980 the world consumption of pharmaceutical products had reached $76 billion annually; since then the figure has climbed steadily. A major factor in stimulating this phenomenal rate of growth was the creation of systems of socialised medicine in many parts of the developed world. These systems removed the financial constraints on prescribing, and in doing so removed any barriers to untrammelled expansion of the world pharmaceutical industry. Inevitably, it was to be the world's rich nations that were to account for the major share of this massive yearly spending. Indeed, per capita expenditure on pharmaceuticals quickly came to be regarded as an important index of prosperity, so close was the correlation between a nation's affluence and its habit of drug purchases.

Recent figures show that nineteen of the world's most prosperous countries – with a combined population of less than 700 million, out of a global total of some five billion – consume nearly two-thirds of the drugs sold on the world market. The level of spending per individual on pharmaceutical preparations in a West European or North American community is many times greater than in any region of the poor developing world. One survey estimates such spending in the richer industrialised nations to be above $50 per head per year; in the poorest countries it is less than 75 cents.

In keeping with this rich-poor divide, the world pharmaceutical industry is dominated by a relatively small group of companies from a handful of advanced economies. Thus, nearly three-quarters of global production is controlled by corporations headquartered in Western industrialised countries; about one-fifth is located in collectivised economies, chiefly in Eastern Europe. Little more than one-tenth of world pharmaceuticals are produced in the poor developing areas. With this concentration of production in the rich world goes control over the research and development that gives determining power over the future in terms of new products. At the beginning of the 1980s the twenty-five biggest drug companies – all of them either American, West European or Japanese – were spending between them more than $3.5 billion a year (in 1979 money) on R&D, or more than the entire gross national product of many poor countries. This mammoth expenditure helped generate an ever-rising tide of wonder drugs, miracle preparations and placebos. It also helped bring closer the prospect of a pharmaceutical surfeit that could transform the world into a drugged dependency, prey to the vagaries of scores of tested-but-not-tried formulae.

Pharmaceutical Roulette

Since the early post-war years, in the days when the pharmaceutical boom was barely measurable, there have been warnings about the potential havoc that can be caused by global overdose. The possible side effects of many of the newer products being introduced onto the market were widely appreciated. As early as 1931 it was recognised that amidopyrine, a widely used painkiller, could destroy the white blood cells that protect the body against infection; it could, in some circumstances, even kill. A study cited by Inglis, *Side Effects of Drugs* by L. Meyler, was published in 1952; it set out in graphic detail the disturbing record of suffering already attributable to recently unveiled preparations.[6] One category that came in for especial criticism was the new family of cortisone-based products known as corticosteroids, which acted through simulating natural hormones.

Prescribed for conditions such as rheumatic complaints, unfortunate patients suffered a wide range of deeply unpleasant consequences: some lost their resistance to infections, others grew extremely obese, while male patients lost their hair and female patients began to grow beards. Other patients developed diabetes after following a course of the much-heralded treatment. The drug manufacturers simplified the name to 'steroids' to shake off negative consumer associations, but failed to escape the adverse judgement of a US Senate Committee in 1961, which threw light on both the side effects produced by these drugs and on the considerable efforts employed by the companies to obscure the unpalatable facts from the public.

The Senate Committee report, pulled together by the campaigning energy of Senator Estes Kefauver, became a touchstone of concern about this vast new source of human danger. Amongst the most disturbing revelations was that the antibiotic chloramphenicol, widely promoted as an effective treatment against common infections of the lung and stomach, had now been recognised as the cause of serious side effects, among them aplastic anaemia, a disease of the bone marrow that can be fatal. A study published in 1963 pointed out that in some prescribing situations more people were dying as a result of the side effects of chloramphenicol than were actually being saved.[7]

The Kefauver evidence was only the beginning of a series of case histories that cast new, and terrifying, light on the considerable risks inherent in the post-war boom in medicines. By far the most tragic of these case histories began with glowing testimonials about the quality and effectiveness of the new product. In the words of an article published in 1960 in one of the world's leading learned journals on pharmacology, the drug was 'a new sedative hypnotic drug which produces no toxic effects when administered orally to animals in massive doses.'[8] The drug referred to was thalidomide.

The thalidomide story is well covered in the literature of medical tragedies. But this does not detract from its status as the most powerful illustration of the pharmaceutical roulette wheel at play. The outline of its tragic progress is a model of how professional etiquette and scientific rigour can be beaten by the sheer immensity of the problem of assuring that drugs are safe for humans. The developing and testing of thalidomide (intended for use with pregnant women to reduce pre-natal discomfort) prior to its release onto the market were as thorough as prevailing standards could ever have demanded. Yet still the roulette wheel turned against the patient, with horrific consequences, though in this case with a difference: it was thousands of unborn babies still in the womb who were to suffer the consequences.

Between 1956 and 1961 medicines containing thalidomide were in common use around the world. In some countries, principally Germany, Japan, Sweden and Britain, its use was followed by a mounting number of cases of congenital deformity that had no precedent in recorded medical history. Yet there had been no indications in years of exhaustive testing procedures that any such adverse effects could possibly occur. The animals on which tests were carried out ranged from mice and rats to cats and rabbits, as well as on isolated tissue taken from guinea pigs. And the tests gave no hint of tragic things to come. Quite to the contrary, the early tests produced almost no negative findings at all.

First synthesised by a Swiss pharmaceutical enterprise in 1954, thalidomide was subsequently adopted by a German drug company; both were driven by the prospect of the healthy profits awaiting any venture that could produce a new and better way of calming the nerves and promoting sleep. Both were disappointed at the seemingly neutral effect induced by their experimental compound. Almost by chance, whilst testing thalidomide preparations as an anti-convulsant for epileptics, the German firm discovered that it did, indeed, act as a powerful hypnotic drug, ideal for combating sleeplessness. During 1960 it became the most popular sleeping pill in Germany, with a low price tag and easily available over the counter without any need for a doctor's prescription.

Indeed, as John Elkington notes in *The Poisoned Womb*, at first the new pill lived up to its reputation as a benign potion. Would-be suicides found that even after large self-administered doses they were still very much alive. The manufacturers mixed it with aspirin and other preparations in order to market it for a variety of conditions, ranging from simple colds to migraine and asthma. In liquid form, it became Germany's No 1 baby-sitter; hospitals used it in vast amounts as a means of calming children prior to carrying out tests on brain functions. And from Germany thalidomide spread out into a promising world market.

But the German company, Grunenthal, that had developed the product had never carried out tests to see whether thalidomide was a teratogen – whether it could cause malformations of foetuses in the womb. Though its marketing literature suggested that the company had tested the drug on pregnant women, no such work had ever been carried out, either on pregnant women or on animals. Grunenthal (the name, ironically, means 'Green Valley' and conjures up images of rural peace) maintained that such tests were not normal practice at the time, a claim that did not stand up to an examination of methods used by many other pharmaceutical companies to identify any reproductive dangers. It would soon become apparent that such dangers were most emphatically present in the Grunenthal product.

The terrible consequences that afflicted many thousands of babies born to mothers who had used thalidomide-based sedatives gave a new phrase to the medical dictionary. Thalidomide syndrome – more properly known as phocomelia (literally 'seal-limbs') – became synonymous with pharmaceutical roulette run riot. The condition is clearly visible to anyone who encounters one of its tragic victims: a seriously malformed body, with arms and feet attached directly to the trunk, giving what the medical books describe as a 'seal-like appearance'. The more extreme cases had no limbs at all. Other side effects included large reddish marks on the body, flattened noses, missing ears, paralysis and deformed or malfunctioning internal organs.

The thalidomide saga was an essay in the failure of testing procedures. But it was not an isolated instance of this phenomenon: throughout this assessment of toxic hazards to the human race, ranging over dangerous food additives, radioactivity, toxic chemicals and poisonous metals, the stumbling block preventing the reaching of firm conclusions has invariably been a lack of consensus about testing methods and interpretation of test results. In the case of thalidomide, there was such stark inattention to lessons coming from the laboratories that if there were no other drug-related tragedies in the entire span of twentieth-century pharmaceutical endeavour, this one alone would suffice to sustain a charge of monumental negligence.

To begin with, Grunenthal was in some degree correct in saying that its researches followed normal industry guidelines. As one specialist, published in the British medical journal *The Lancet*, put it in 1962: 'As testing for teratogenic effects is not part of standard pharmacological screening procedure, experience in this field is very limited.' In fact, no tests had been done with thalidomide on pregnant animals of any species before the drug was marketed anywhere in the world. Yet even when experiments and analytical studies did raise doubts about the apparently ideal characteristics of the new compound, the profession failed to sound the alarm.

There is much evidence that thalidomide was known from the earliest moments to have a dark side; there was simply no mechanism by which this evidence could be marshalled into one powerful attack on the commercial edifice of the pharmaceutical industry. The welcoming phrases of the statement quoted earlier (in fact from the *British Journal of Pharmacology*), extolling the virtues of 'a new sedative hypnotic drug which produces no toxic effects', takes on different meaning when judged in the wider context in which it appeared. The analyst in question continued: 'This lack of toxicity may be due to a limited absorption.' In other words, the animal tests could well have been neither adequate nor inadequate as measures of the hazard; they were irrelevant, since the animals used in the experiments were not receiving sufficiently high doses to produce a statistically valid reaction.

Meanwhile, an earlier report on the drug, published in the

British Medical Journal in 1958, suggested that thalidomide had an anti-thyroid effect when taken in higher doses. Suspicions should also have been aroused by the forceful observations made by Dr Frances Oldham Kelsey of the US Food and Drugs Administration. Dr Kelsey argued that since the foetus is different from the adult female in its reactions to pharmaceutical inputs, there should be convincing evidence that thalidomide had been thoroughly tested to cover this area of potential risk. Despite considerable efforts on the part of various companies to produce convincing data to eliminate such doubts, including by Grunenthal's own chemists, none could ever be presented. As a result, thalidomide was prohibited from direct sale in the US market and American mothers were spared the ravages of phocomelia, though there were to be cases where deformed babies were born to women who had obtained variants of the drug whilst overseas.

In the meantime, the flow of negative comment from the scientific community continued. In 1960 the *British Medical Journal* carried an article entitled 'Is Thalidomide To Blame?'; in it, a number of cases were described in which users of the drug were suffering from peripheral neuritis, a condition of the nervous system producing tingling sensations of the skin and limbs. In more extreme instances, the article continued, permanent damage could be done to the peripheral nervous system. Other research highlighted the importance of timing in assessing the deforming effects of a drug; in foetal deformity this meant administering the suspect drug at a precise point in the development of the embryo, when the limbs and organs are being formed. Such a factor makes even more difficult the task of identifying through laboratory tests the exact link between a chemical compound and any teratogenic consequences for the unborn baby.

Most damning of all, however, was the revelation that a pharmacologist working for one of the major distributors of the drug, the British company Distillers, had identified certain toxic effects as early as the first months of 1959, yet had been overridden by his employers. Dr George Somers had discovered that a liquid variant of thalidomide destroyed the Distillers' claim, used in its marketing material, that the drug was completely without toxic side effects and that there appeared to be no indication that even massive doses could be fatal. Yet Dr Somers' findings were kept from the public, even after reports began to accumulate that long-term users were exhibiting symptoms of sensory disturbances and other adverse reactions.

Several years after the discoveries in Distillers' laboratories had placed a question mark over an entire category of thalidomide-based compounds, many of them were still in general use. In West Germany, for example, the official reaction to the spreading rumours, formalised in April 1961, was to make such compounds only available through prescription. Bearing in mind the considerable popularity of sedative-type products amongst the medical profession by this time, this action was hardly likely to reduce the dimensions of risk by any appreciable margin. By the end of 1961, meanwhile, about five thousand cases of thalidomide syndrome had been reported around the world.

Take-off to Oblivion

There was one major benefit from the tragedy of phocomelia. As Elkington summarises it: 'Thalidomide and its effects on human reproduction gave teratology, the study of birth defects, an enormous boost.' But this was just one facet of the ever-increasing problem of pharmaceutical roulette. The experience with thalidomide occurred at a relatively early stage in the drugs revolution. Since then the world market in pharmaceuticals, and the number of products being pushed onto that market, has exploded. In the ten years after the German authorities took their first, faltering steps to control thalidomide, the international trade in drug products went through an unprecedented take-off in revenue and profits.

A typical example is that of Ely Lilley, one of the top dozen drug multinationals. In a survey of the company, published in 1971, an industry analyst summed up the staggering rate of change that had characterised the pharmaceutical sector in a few short years: 'Ely Lilley & Co is ninety-six years old; in terms of growth it took seventy-five years to reach the first $100 million sales level, fourteen years to reach $200 million, four years to attain $300 million, only two years for $400 million and little more than a year for $500 million.' By 1980 Ely Lilley & Co had a turnover of $1.2 billion and through the eighties have continued the strong upward surge, part of a worldwide expenditure worth approaching $100 billion on a product list that contains some twenty-five thousand therapeutic substances.[9]

This upward surge, by the simple law of averages, could only serve to increase the danger of producing another rogue drug. It would not be long before another case of foetal deformity hit the headlines. One of the therapeutic substances developed independently of thalidomide was also meant for pregnant women, a morning sickness drug sold in the US market under the name Bendectin, and in some other markets as Debendox. First introduced in 1957, when the facts about thalidomide were yet to become widely known, Bendectin was to be used by more than thirty million women before a federal jury sitting in Orlando, Florida, in March 1980 ruled that the drug had caused the arm and chest deformities suffered by the small son of Mrs Betty Mekdeci. Despite approval by the US Food and Drug Administration and by health departments around the world, the evidence of the Mekdeci case, and of hundreds of other deformed infants in the United States and elsewhere, now pushed these official approvals into tragic relief.

Expert witnesses, including a specialist who had come to prominence during the thalidomide hearings, described their misgivings about the suitability of the drug for pregnant women; one expert defined Bendectin as 'a low-grade teratogen', capable of causing injuries such as those seen in Mrs Mekdeci's five-year-old child. Despite the findings of an advisory panel, set up by the FDA after the trial, that Bendectin could not be directly linked to birth defects, the broader picture remained unconvincing. To begin with, the panel recommended that the drug be used only with more explicit labelling details that cautioned doctors and pregnant women against unnecessary and excessive use. And two individual studies cited by the panel left a 'residual uncertainty' about the drug being associated with congenital heart defects and cleft lips and palates.

Whatever the precise outcome of the Bendectin affair (there were to be further court victories by aggrieved parents, followed by reversals on appeal), another nail had been driven into the coffin lid of trust about the safety of pharmaceutical products. This massive industry is a cousin of the global fraternity of chemical producers that have done so much to contaminate the planet and our own insides with toxic pesticides, industrial agents and high-tech additives for the food-processing companies. And as with these other purveyors of pollution, the pharmaceutical sector has grown immense by treading a narrow line between profit-seeking expediency and the health of the general public – the drug producers, along with the rest, inviting us to assist them in the hazardous exercise of exploring the margins of human tolerance to substances that are foreign to our biochemistry. In this endeavour they have enlisted the willing help of the medical profession. As George Bernard Shaw wrote in *The Doctor's Dilemma*: 'All professions are conspiracies against the laity.' In the particular domain of medicine, it sometimes appears as a conspiracy against our own long-term health.

Bendectin and Debendox apart, there have been many episodes reminiscent of thalidomide since this apparently benign mixture of chemicals began to reap its sorry harvest, though since that harvest was comprised of monstrously deformed infants none of the later tragedies has captured such a central place in the public conscience. Humanity has also become hardened to the various dangers of living in the late twentieth century, including the risks of taking medical preparations. Familiarity, rather than breeding contempt, has bred complacency. And to compound this tendency there is the most worrying aspect of the high-tech holocaust, which runs through this narrative as a dismaying leitmotiv, namely that thousands of single casualties caused by chemical mayhem, ranging from foetal deformity to death, which occur over a lengthy period of time, rarely generate the level of public outrage that results from one, sudden catastrophe involving a smaller number of victims. The thalidomide story breached that convention, putting public support behind a direct assault on the commercial enterprises who were to blame. But the thalidomide case was an exception.

A review of the news columns of the past decade will reveal that the roulette wheel of pharmaceutical fortune is turning faster than ever. Drugs are still killing, deforming and damaging people; the steadily growing output of the pharmaceutical companies is ending up as packaged and branded chemical magic, ready to be poured, popped, inhaled or injected into an unsuspecting human bio-system . . . but let the buyer beware. In their book *Cured to Death*, Arabella Melville and Colin Johnson survey the lengthening list of recent medical case histories involving drug abuse at the hands of doctors who have prescribed the wrong product (or too much of it) for their trusting patients, or have given wrong advice in an attempt to rectify a drug-induced crisis.[10]

One patient they describe is Mary Wilkins, a young Welsh

woman suffering from excessive strain due to family problems. After a visit to her doctor, and from there to a consultant, she is given, amongst other medications, a new 'wonder drug' designed to slow the activity rate of the heart. Within weeks the patient is suffering from heavy periods, dizzy spells and bouts of blindness. After months of uninterest on the part of those treating her, and following an attack of total blindness, she succeeds in securing a meeting with her doctor, which results in the withdrawal of one of the pills. But the symptoms persist over the next two years; her eyesight continues to deteriorate, her skin becomes inflamed, she has ringing in the ears. By the third year the young woman is unable to sleep, even with the assistance of sleeping pills. She is afflicted by stomach pains and soreness in the nose and throat . . .

Later diagnosis suggested that the steady collapse of this young woman's health was due to the prescribing of tablets containing practolol, a substance developed by ICI to help treat stress without negative effects on the heart and bronchial system. And while practolol – sold in Britain under the brand name Eraldin – proved to be in some ways an advance on earlier medications, it also showed itself to be extremely troublesome when administered to reactive people. All this was unsuspected despite the most rigorous checks by the manufacturers and various medical watchdogs. More alarmingly, there was little data on the possible long-term effects of taking the drug. Five years after her course of practolol-based medication had begun, Mary Wilkins had lost about thirty pounds in weight, while her stomach had become abnormally enlarged. Her local doctor advised her that she was pregnant, a diagnosis that she knew to be impossible. Referred to the nearby hospital, she underwent a hysterectomy, with a fibrous ball the size of a large grapefruit being removed. The growth proved not to be cancerous.

Mary Wilkins' condition did not improve. Shortly after her operation, and some seven years after the start of her treatment for nervous strain, she was diagnosed by a consultant as having multiple sclerosis, a diagnosis that was subsequently withdrawn. Meanwhile, this young woman, twenty-seven years old when she took her first practolol pill, had been reduced to the condition of a chronic invalid, dependent on a walking frame and able to sit upright only with the aid of a surgical collar. By this time drugs containing practolol had been banned for sale in her country.

The case of Mary Wilkins was one of many linked to practolol. It was voluntarily withdrawn by ICI in October 1975, but not before an estimated seven thousand victims had succumbed to its destructive powers. On the other side of the world, meanwhile, another biochemical catastrophe was in the making, this time involving products containing clioquinol, a compound developed to treat stomach disorders of the kind commonly experienced by travellers.

One country that took to the drug on a comprehensive scale was Japan, where it became the norm to recommend dosages that were considerably higher than in most other parts of the world. This higher dosage was to expose millions of Japanese to a terrible fate. By 1970 suspicions began to emerge that clioquinol might be linked to a growing incidence of a condition known as subacute myelo-optic neuropathy, which produces symptoms ranging from stomach pains to paralysis and blindness, in extreme cases followed by death. It took six years for the manufacturer, the Swiss company Ciba-Geigy, to admit that there might be a connection between their drug and the steadily mounting toll of human misery. By this time more than ten thousand Japanese had contracted the disease, with over one thousand of them dying (some through committing suicide to escape the horrors produced by the medication).

The mid-1980s were to have their own share of pharmaceutical misfortune. One instance involved the anti-depressant drug Merital, withdrawn early in 1986 after eight patients had died and a growing number of people under treatment had begun to complain of side effects. Since some half a million individuals had used the drug since its introduction by the German company Hoechst in 1977, the final reckoning of its biochemical effects is yet to be made known. A second drug, Psyton, incorporating the same active ingredients as those in Merital, was also withdrawn. Hoechst estimate that fifteen million patients in eighty-two countries have been treated with the two drugs during their period of availability.

The medical history of the recent past is filled with similar examples of drugs that have survived the most exhaustive testing, only to wreak havoc and death when put to use. Often, as with the case of Japan and clioquinol, tragedy results from local variations in dose levels. In other circumstances, it is the consequence of concealment by the manufacturer of negative test reports, or negligent prescribing by doctors who are aware of suspicions surrounding a particular product. The following episodes are largely taken from Britain, though they involve drugs produced by major multinational companies. The setting could, in fact, be anywhere in the affluent developed world, where the first instinct of a growing number of physicians is to counsel patients to keep taking the tablets:

- In November 1983 the US Food and Drug Administration is condemned as negligent by a Congressional committee for its decision to approve the anti-arthritis drug Opren. In 1982 the drug (also known as Benoxaprofen and Oraflex) was withdrawn in Britain following reports that more than sixty people had died after taking it. By the time the Congressional rebuke was issued nearly eighty people had died, and an estimated three thousand eight hundred were reported to have suffered side effects. The committee also revealed that the manufacturers, the boom beneficiaries Ely Lilley, had failed to report several deaths linked to the drug. In the summer of 1985 lawyers representing people claiming damage after using Opren revealed that they had evidence that the manu-facturer, and even government departments, ignored laboratory data casting doubt on the safety of the drug.

  The lawyers, with scientific support, said that the recommended maximum dose was twice that of levels found to be safe in studies with laboratory rats; that the length of the clinical trials and the numbers of people involved were inadequate; that important information on side effects to the skin when exposed to the sun were played down, or ignored altogether. And by using the US Freedom of Information Act, lawyers also discovered documents from the US Food and Drug Administration that said 'the data does not allow us to make a definitive evaluation of the safety and efficacy of Benoxaprofen (Opren).' The same data, incidentally, was taken by Britain's Committee on the Safety of Medicines as the basis for issuing a licence for the drug in March 1980.[11]

  Meanwhile, in August 1985, the Ely Lilley management admitted that they failed to tell the US authorities about deaths amongst patients using the drug in Britain during the two years from when it first went on sale there to its approval in the United States. The cases included the jaundice, kidney failures and deaths of five elderly patients who had been using Opren. Lilley did not pass on this evidence to the Food and Drug Administration until 10 May 1982, three weeks after the FDA had issued its approval. Shortly after the US launch the product was hastily withdrawn in both countries. The US Department of Justice subsequently brought a lawsuit against Ely Lilley and its former chief medical officer.[12]

- US drug producers were not to be alone, however, in attracting tough government action against pharmaceuticals aimed at the lucrative market for arthritis sufferers. Within a month of that Congressional announcement, British Health Minister Kenneth Clarke moved to prohibit another anti-arthritis medication, called Flosint, after learning that seven people had died and another two hundred and ten were suffering adverse effects. Flosint, made by the Italian-based multinational Farmitalia Carlo Erba, had by this time been given to more that seventy-five thousand patients in Britain alone. A company executive had meanwhile revealed that the drug had been given to about four and a half million patients around the world over a six-year period, with no apparent side effects, though yet again it was reported that the company's own research had given cause for concern about serious and toxic effects of the drug. Flosint was the fourth arthritis preparation to be prohibited by the British authorities in little more than a year, along with Zomax, Osmosin and the much-criticised Opren.

• Early in 1984, it was revealed in a private survey by a market research group that despite the withdrawal of drugs such as Flosint after official pressure, doctors were continuing to prescribe them at an alarming rate. The survey disclosed that British medical practitioners (most of them working in the private, non-state sector) were writing about one thousand prescriptions a month for withdrawn drugs in this category, in defiance of the official ban, on the grounds that no other drug would suit their patients' special needs. Under British law, pharmacists are legally bound to supply a drug covered by a doctor's note; there were still large supplies of the banned products in storerooms and dispensaries around the country. Just as alarming is the discovery that doctors are often seriously lax when it comes to reporting cases of adverse reactions to specific drugs, a highly disturbing tendency since doctors are a vital source of hard information about drug side effects. A survey of British practitioners for 1982 revealed that the government watchdog body, the Committee on the Safety of Medicines, received only 11,240 reports from doctors on adverse reactions, under an arrangement set up in 1964 after the thalidomide tragedy. The Committee estimated that it should have received about a quarter of a million reports.[13]

• By February 1984 the British health ministry was studying an enormous dossier dealing with the hazards of yet another category of drugs, this time painkillers based on butazone. It was believed that products containing this compound were responsible for at least fifteen hundred deaths in Britain alone, one reason being their considerable popularity amongst doctors, who at one point were issuing more than one million prescriptions a year. British drug

safety officials had become alerted to the potentially hazardous
nature of butazone after documents leaked from the Basle head-
quarters of the manufacturers, Ciba-Geigy, showed that the
company knew of 1,182 deaths around the world linked to the drug.
More than a third of the deaths were due to blood disorders. Other
causes of death included internal bleeding, perforated ulcers and
leukemia.

The leaked Ciba-Geigy documents led to an international
reaction. Israel and Norway immediately banned the sale of
butazone products; the West German government restricted
their use to the particularly painful condition of arthritis of the
spine. The US authorities took steps to control its availability.
But the episode is illustrative of the seriously flawed mechanics
of drug development and approval across the world. As a result,
humanity has been adopted by the global pharmaceutical
industry as a vast community of guinea pigs, with the added
bonus that in this instance the guinea pigs pay in advance for
the privilege of acting as experimental specimens.

Nor is there any sign that major drug companies like Ciba-
Geigy, the fourth largest in the world, are becoming more open
about test results that raise doubts about the safety of their
products. At the end of 1985, Ciba-Geigy executives admitted
that the company had falsified safety data on a total of forty-six
antibiotic and other drugs given to the Japanese health
authorities, one of the largest-ever incidents involving false
documentation. A key omission was failure to perform vital tests
ascertaining the shelf-life stability of the drugs. It was a matter,
as the head of Ciba-Geigy in Japan openly accepted, of being
caught out: 'We strongly recognise our ethical and social
responsibility and, upon a serious self-examination, we wish to
express our deepest apologies,' said company president Paul
Dudler. The contrite words could hardly reassure the Japanese;
in 1978 Ciba-Geigy made payments totalling more than $150
million to Japanese victims of its drug clioquinol. The company,
meanwhile, had every reason to appear penitent: the Japanese
market for their products is worth more than $500 million a
year in sales.

But the Ciba-Geigy experience is but one more example of
the lack of any international standards about safety checks and
the release of laboratory results. A telling illustration of the
weakness of testing procedures is that only a few countries
demand that all new drugs be tested for their ability to cause

genetic damage, and through this their ability to cause cancer. This might be considered a surprising oversight in view of the considerable evidence that has built up in recent years, linking chemicals in general and certain compounds in particular to genetic mutations and tumours. Researches on the one subject of the contraceptive pill have yielded considerable statistical support for the argument that long-term use raises the chances of contracting serious diseases. In a typical Western country the incidence of breast cancer, for instance, has risen by about twenty per cent since the pill was introduced in the 1960s. This rise has been accompanied by a significant rise in cervical cancer.

These statistical facts were nevertheless not to be reflected in any new international regime of screening rules for new drugs. Not until 1985 did governments in Western Europe, for example, need to take steps to legislate for such a blanket test procedure, and only then because of the need to comply with forthcoming EEC regulations. Meanwhile, the drug companies continue their search for even more products, with even better profit margins, in the knowledge that there is no such thing as a totally safe drug and that the ultimate test of the safety of a product will take a full human lifetime to apply.

As if these risks are not serious enough, many pills contain additives that are also used by the food companies and are known to be harmful to allergic persons. The yellow dye tartrazine, for one, is commonly employed as a colouring agent, even though it can cause bronchial asthma and skin rashes if swallowed by sensitive patients. Yet there is rarely, if ever, any national regulation that obliges drug manufacturers to disclose details of any synthetic colouring agents or flavourings that have been used.

Testing by Numbers

Even the most vociferous resistance to a pharmaceutical product, backed by reputable international institutions, will fail against a determined manufacturer keen to capture a share of a promising world market. The contraceptive injection Depo Provera was one such product. Refused a licence in the United States because of fears that it had cancer-causing properties, the drug was identified in a recent report from the World Health Organisation as likely to double the risk of cervical cancer if used for more than five years. The WHO report, based on data collected from more than eight thousand women using the contraceptive in Kenya, Mexico and Thailand, reached a blunt conclusion: 'The doubling of risk in women who used [Depo Provera] for five or more years is of potential concern.' Despite this warning the injection was launched in Britain, where there was no official ban, in the hope that use of it in a developed country would create confidence amongst doctors and patients in less developed regions of the world, where simple contraceptive devices are desperately needed and where the drug has already been given to millions of women.

An added benefit of a launch in a major West European market would be to put pressure on the US authorities, so as to secure a reversal of their prohibition. British patients could hardly have been reassured by the list of possible adverse effects described in a leaflet published by the manufacturers at the insistence of the British Department of Health. They included heavy and irregular bleeding, backache, weight gain and depression; women were advised that they might not regain their fertility for up to two years after their last injection. In the meantime, sales of Depo Provera in the low-income, high-population societies of Africa, Latin America and Asia continue to mount.

Such a sales strategy should come as no surprise; a common thread in the defining of the high-tech holocaust is the vulnerable condition of the world's poor countries. This is equally as true of the world pharmaceutical industry as it is for every other component of the worldwide toxic threat. Because of the less sophisticated administrative systems that prevail in poor nations, and their lack of experience in applying complex regulatory laws, these territories represent vast, untapped markets for the drug manufacturers in which there are few barriers to the sale of products that have been outlawed by governments elsewhere. Thus have these poor nations become the dumping ground for hundreds of medicines that have been scrutinised by watchdog agencies in the rich world, and found wanting.

The catalogue of exploitation makes unpleasant reading. Dangerous drugs such as anabolic steroids being sold to mothers in underdeveloped areas as cures for malnourished infants, despite a well-documented case linking them to liver disease. The massive offloading on poor economies of ingredients used to make tranquillisers and sedatives, without proper provision to prevent misuse in countries where medical supervision and prescriptions are rare. It was this offloading that prompted the International Narcotics Control Board to warn world governments recently that the menace of drug abuse 'had reached unprecedented proportions', with the illicit trade in synthetic and psychotropic (mind-affecting) drugs overtaking cocaine and heroin as the new threat.

One recent study on the marketing of pharmaceutical products in less developed countries highlights the flourishing trade (worth more than $200 million a year) in drugs offered as a means of increasing the body weight of infants, a major concern in areas afflicted by malnutrition. One such product is Periactin, made by the US-based Merck, Sharp and Dohme. Its promotional literature stresses the value of Periactin in promoting 'natural weight gain for the growing child; for the adolescent who is underweight; and for the convalescent who needs a good appetite'. The US authorities were not impressed by such claims; Periactin had been barred from the US market since 1971 because of lack of adequate evidence that it served any useful purpose. Another weight-gain drug mentioned in the report as being sold widely in poor countries was Mosegor, manufactured by the Swiss company Sandoz. It was promoted as offering 'significant' weight increases in nine patients out of ten. Travellers from those poor regions to Europe would have been confronted with a somewhat puzzling fact had they paid a visit to a local pharmacy. They would have discovered that in Europe the same product has carried the brand name Sanomigran; it is sold as a cure for migraine.

Comparable stories abound of the double standards that are being applied to the world market for drugs. One instance is Eraldin, the practolol-based medication that caused so much trouble before being withdrawn from the British market. Yet even after the decision to withdraw Eraldin had been taken, visitors to medical centres like the KCMC hospital in Moshi, Tanzania, would have found that supplies of the suspect product were still arriving from ICI.[14]

The exploitation of markets in poor countries takes two forms: the heavy promotion of medications that are non-essential and expensive, diverting precious income away from the purchase of useful drugs, and the sale of products that have been prohibited or controlled in affluent countries because of doubts about their safety. The first category, which includes vitamins, tonics and cold cures, has burgeoned in recent years as the multinationals having stepped up their attack on areas with large and quickly growing populations.

In her book *Bitter Pills*, Dianna Melrose cites a study of Nepal which points out that of two thousand different drug products found to be on sale in the country, about seven hundred and thirty, a third, were tonics. Specialists say that a handful of simple and inexpensive formulations based on iron and vitamins could replace this immense array of impressively packed preparations. In North Yemen nearly one-fifth of all pharmaceutical imports were vitamins and tonics; only 1.3 per cent of the total was spent on drugs to cure three of the serious diseases most common in the region – malaria, bilharzia (a worm infestation) and tuberculosis. A recent survey in Sri Lanka revealed that more than fifty per cent of local production (mostly controlled by large international companies) was concentrated on vitamins, soluble aspirin and cough remedies. As the survey observed: 'They were elegantly presented, heavily promoted and used by the affluent ... swallowed by the well-nourished who did not need them. The under-nourished could not afford to buy them.'

But the sale of non-essential drug products in poverty-stricken markets is, at worst, a form of robbery. It is the sale of suspect drugs, prohibited elsewhere, that raises the far more disturbing prospect of injury and death through irresponsibility. And the accumulating evidence indicates that, as with pesticides and hazardous chemical processes, the poor world is becoming the dumping ground for risks that have been outlawed in more advanced societies. Eraldin is one of many examples. Lomotil with neomycin, manufactured in Europe, can be bought easily over the counter in certain developing countries as a treatment for diarrhoea. It rarely carries information counselling caution when used for children, even though the World Health Organisation and national health authorities in developed countries advise against using neomycin for treating diarrhoea. More serious is the sale of anti-diarrhoea preparations based on clioquinol, the compound that caused acute suffering amongst more than ten thousand Japanese in the 1960s and is now banned or strictly controlled in many parts of the world. Invariably, the drug is sold in foil strips with inadequate or non-existent instructional information, even though it is widely recognised by medical specialists that doses over a certain level, or prolonged usage, of clioquinol-based products are dangerous.

Another suspect product category is anabolic steroids; they are deemed by expert opinion to be inadvisable for children, with evidence of a link with tumours of the liver. Yet they have been commonly sold in developing countries, with heavy promotional material extolling their virtues for helping under-fed infants to gain weight. In Bangladesh the Dutch company Organon sold their anabolic steroids with the advertising slogan 'Growth in every drop, strength in every tablet'. Inside the package was a leaflet which contained uncompromising advice: 'Causes no fluid retention and is free from harmful effects on liver . . . The raspberry flavoured liquid administered in drops is especially meant for younger children and infants.' A similar preparation, Anapolon, made by ICI, was sold as 'the potent, safe anabolic agent' and as ideal 'for children underdeveloped or debilitated as the result of illness or malnourishment'. The growing concern over anabolic steroids, however, was enough to convince Swiss drug producers Ciba-Geigy, in April 1982, to withdraw their product Dianabol worldwide.

No doubt other pharmaceutical manufacturers have changed their marketing strategies in the developing world as a result of increasing pressures against the sale of certain kinds of drugs. But other suspect products will take their place. Disease and the fears of poor parents over the health of their children is a recipe for big business, particularly in markets ruled by the most rudimentary monitoring systems and a chronic shortage of trained personnel. The attitude of many major drug producers on this issue was summed up in remarks attributed to the managing director of a multinational subsidiary in Bangladesh: 'We are businessmen first. First of all we want profits . . . we are oversensitive about reports from WHO. Restrictions on drugs and pesticides imposed in the US and Canada should not be applied in our country because our people are ethnically and biologically different from others.'[15] Perhaps he knows a secret.

10
The Odds Grow Short

In June 1983 Mr B. A. Semenov, the Russian head of the Department of Nuclear Energy and Safety at the International Atomic Energy Agency summed up his pride at the safety planning that surrounded the building of the nuclear plant at Chernobyl in the Soviet Ukraine: 'A serious loss-of-coolant accident is practically impossible.' In March 1986 the US edition of the publication *Soviet Life* carried a nine-page article on the Chernobyl installation; it appeared under the headline 'Total Safety'. As history now records, over the weekend of 26–7 April 1986 Chernobyl was the scene of the world's worst nuclear accident, after cooling water leaked into the graphite core.

As the water reacted chemically with the graphite, hydrogen gas was produced. Gas pressure buckled the fuel rods at the heart of the reactor and the core began to heat up. Then the top of the core was blown off by the mounting build-up of gas; hydrogen mixed with the outside air and exploded. Radioactive debris was scattered over the Ukraine countryside for distances of more than a mile; horrifyingly, it was later revealed that six days were allowed to pass before 30,000 people from the nearby town were evacuated, having by then been exposed to exceptional levels of radiation. Radioactive clouds were meanwhile carried up into the atmosphere, to be borne by prevailing winds many thousands of miles into Scandinavia and eventually into countries on the Mediterranean and North Sea, to Japan and the USA.

In 1975 a ten-volume report published by the US Atomic Energy Commission concluded that a nuclear accident serious enough to kill seventy people could only happen once in a million years of a reactor's life. On the Tuesday following the disaster at Chernobyl, a correspondent in Kiev of the news

agency United Press International, after contacting hospitals
and other sources in the vicinity, reported that the immediate
death toll had been approximately two thousand. But a blanket
of official secrecy had by then descended over the incident; it is
unlikely that the world will ever learn the full truth. Meanwhile, a week later the reactor core at Chernobyl was still
burning; it was known that a large expanse of the Ukraine
countryside was devastated and that several thousand people
had been seriously irradiated, probably fatally.[1] Vast areas of the
European continent were affected by unprecedented levels of
radioactive fall-out. Foreign airlines in Moscow made passengers travelling from the Kiev region change their clothes
before being allowed to board their aircraft. Across Europe
samples of milk, water supplies and vegetables were collected
for examination by worried environmental authorities, and in
some cases destroyed.

More to the point, the US Atomic Energy Commission had
been proved wrong. Or, at least, they should have made it clear
that the million-to-one disaster referred to could just as easily
happen at the beginning of their million-year time span. The
odds are growing short.

The secrecy and official ambiguity that surrounded the accident at Chernobyl is not a peculiarly Soviet trait. Incomplete
facts, confusion and misleading statements have become the
staple diet of the nuclear industry. Only four weeks before the
incident in the Ukraine there was an explosion, followed by a
leak of radioactive gas, at a nuclear power station at Dungeness
on the Kent coast of England. News of the event, however, was
not made public until a month later, when newspaper journalists cross-examined officials after being given information from
other sources. The explosion, which caused a rupture in a by-
pass system nine inches long and two inches wide, led to the
release of about 110 pounds of mildly radioactive gas. No
casualties resulted, at least not in the human sense. As in warfare, in the growing battle between humanity and an increasingly defensive nuclear fraternity, the first casualty was truth.

The high-tech holocaust, however, is no secret to the many
millions of people around the world who have suffered, or still
suffer, from its consequences. Whether caused by toxic chemicals, food additives, pesticides, poorly tested drugs, polluted
water, heavy metals or radioactive debris from a town like
Chernobyl, the effects are real. Nor is its grasp limited to the

well-publicised incidents of the nuclear industry, or to intellectually challenging hazards selected by research scientists in the leading medical establishments. The high-tech holocaust is invading every aspect of everyday life and death.

One less-publicised daily hazard is an inevitable facet of living in the age of the machine: the hazard of vibration. Wherever an engine turns, or wheels roll, or the laws of Nature are defeated by man-made mechanisms such as aircraft or ships, there is vibration. To the casual ear and eye it is a relatively innocuous accompaniment to the wealth-creating process. But vibration can kill. As recently as 1969 a fifty-nine-year-old road driller died from gangrene of his fingers caused by the vibrations of a pneumatic tool. In a typical working life involving vibratory tools, a man will be exposed to the equivalent of 45,000 hours of vibration; medical research shows this exposure to be linked to higher levels of hernias, piles, backache, dead fingers and disorders of the digestive system, bladder, breathing, genitals, muscles and bones, as well as to varicose veins. Vibration has also been shown to have an effect on the central nervous system and on the nervous activity of the brain.

Like so many other aspects of the high-tech holocaust, the danger from vibration can come as no surprise to well-informed physicians. Before World War II a series of studies highlighted the problem of gangrene, dead finger and nystagmus, a shaking movement of the eye. In 1945 medical officers at the Ford Motor Company reported dead hand amongst seventy-five of their workers operating polishing equipment. In the same year Dr Donald Hunter, the grand old man of British industrial medicine, found alarming results amongst men in the shipbuilding industry: dead hand was discovered in sixty-two per cent of riveters, seventy-one per cent of fettlers and seventy-five per cent of caulkers. In 1946 researchers at the Chrysler Corporation reported that 112 out of 1,000 vibratory tool operators in the aircraft sector were affected by dead fingers.

The occupations most at risk do not distinguish between social groups. Helicopter pilots and chain-saw operators, bus drivers, and warehousemen using fork-lift trucks are all equally exposed. A research project completed in 1970 showed extremely high incidences of dead finger in a wide range of jobs. Amongst clinchers and flangers in the car industry 73 out of 100 were found to be afflicted; for foundry grinders the rate was 86 out of 100, for foresters using chain saws the figure was 89 out of 100.[2]

A cousin of vibration is noise, possibly the most pervasive of all twentieth-century visitations. And, as with vibration, we have learned to live with noise, despite its damaging impact on life, limb and nervous system. Studies show that industrial civilisation endures greater noise levels than ever before, with few signs of respite in the foreseeable future. The most significant single source of noise in the modern environment is road traffic.

The basic unit of measurement for noise is the decibel; most measurements use what is known as the dB(A) scale, which takes into account differing sensitivities to some noise frequencies as against others. The consensus of governments in the developed world is that the upper limit of acceptability is in a range between 70 and 80dB(A). In 1977 the European Economic Community adopted 80dB(A) as a long-term goal for vehicles; some governments are attempting to apply a 73dB(A) limit for some motorcycles. Occupational hygienists would like to see 80 dB(A) as the maximum for exposure in the workplace, while specialists agree that the first signs of hearing loss in susceptible individuals may be detected after extended exposure to levels in excess of 80dB(A).[3]

Local variations in road conditions can affect decibel readings considerably: on a wet road surface, for instance, the level of tyre noise can rise by as much as 10dB(A). In any event, most heavy vehicles are permitted to produce readings some way above these limits. Not surprisingly, the evidence shows that the battle against traffic-induced noise is being lost in most parts of the industrial world. This fate will almost certainly overtake the less developed countries as their process of industrialisation brings millions of poorly maintained trucks, buses and passenger cars onto the roads; in the bustling conurbations of Asia, Africa and Latin America the decibel levels are already close to breaking point.

According to a recent research survey, noise conditions in the more affluent countries are deteriorating by the year. It has been estimated that in the OECD countries – the developed Western economies – about fifteen per cent of the population, or about 100 million people, are exposed to noise levels above 65 decibels. Approximately fifty-five per cent of the population in these countries, some 400 million inhabitants, are exposed to noise levels above 55 decibels. And these figures do not refer to noise emanating from aircraft or the workplace. Forecasts in several OECD countries show that if stringent abatement policies are not implemented the situation will remain serious or even worsen. In France alone, says the survey, the annual damage arising from traffic noise totals more than two billion francs, or roughly $300 million, without including the true costs to the community of cardiovascular diseases and other illnesses brought on through noise-induced stress.[4]

Many of the less-publicised hazards, however, fail to make the headlines because they are hidden from the general view. How many Londoners know of the work of the 'fluffers', the poorly paid gangs of women who descend into the tunnels of the Underground system after the last train stops to dust the tracks and clean the ceramic points? Yet the dust on the Underground tracks is not just dirt; it contains high levels of silica and asbestos, which is released from insulation materials, brake linings and other working parts on the carriages. Both these substances cause progressive and incurable lung diseases. London Transport have found levels for both dusts to be above the government-recommended maximum to which workers should be exposed.[5]

And how many schoolchildren, householders or employees in offices and workshops realise the danger that lurks in the fluorescent lighting tubes above their heads? Until the mid-1970s volatile liquids called polychlorinated biphenyls, or PCBs, were used in light-tube capacitors. Hundreds of millions of them were installed in schools, kitchens and workplaces over the years. Yet during their expected life-span of up to fifteen years, one in five of them may leak before it fails. PCBs (contained in some of the more dubious pesticides) are known to damage the skin and liver; as they build up in the environment they pose a highly toxic threat to fresh-water animals. If leaking fluids enter the sewage or drainage system, further dangers will present themselves.[6] The problem is not the first instance where criticisms have been directed at the fluorescent strip. In 1980 the British Lighting Industry Federation set up an inquiry into the effects of fluorescent lighting on health after researchers suggested that the brightly glowing tubes could be linked to heart disease, cancer and other serious health problems. The inquiry yielded little by way of concrete findings, but its work was soon overshadowed by the escalating worries over leaking PCBs.[7]

Even the ultimate high-tech environment of the computer

user is causing increasing concern. According to a report commissioned by IBM, there is a possible connection between visual display units and birth defects because of radiation from high levels of electrical current. The research report, produced by Professor Arthur Guy of the Bioelectromagnetics Research Laboratory in Seattle, Washington, after work involving tests on chicken embryos, reached a carefully worded, but alarming, conclusion: 'Though it is highly unlikely that there is any relationship between birth defect clusters and VDU emissions, the clinical work . . . does indicate that there could be a relationship.'[8] A more recent report from the British Health and Safety Executive reaches an equally ambivalent conclusion, this time about the connection between VDU work and miscarriages: 'Higher levels (of miscarriage) have been reported amongst groups of VDU operators, but investigations show that they are not peculiar to VDU work.'[9]

Doubts are being cast, too, on the safety of workers who produce the memories that form the heart of data-processing systems. Silica, the raw material of silicon chips, is ever-present in the air of high-tech workshops; inhaling or ingesting it is widely known to be as hazardous as taking in asbestos. And the danger is not limited only to the silicon workplace. According to California health officials, miscarriages and birth defects have occurred in one Silicon Valley community at a rate two to three times higher than normal, as a result of an industrial accident. The cause, say the officials, was contamination of the water supply by toxic chemicals leaking from a plant manufacturing semi-conductors. The chemicals, solvents called trichloroethane and dichloroethylene, had been stored in an underground tank just 2,000 feet from a drinking-water well serving the district. Both chemicals are linked to nerve, liver and heart damage, and to birth defects. After the water source was changed the incidence of birth defects declined.[10]

The risks are all about us; they seem to accumulate in a spiral of toxic confrontation. The British National Radiological Protection Board reports that the biggest source of radiation to which Britons are exposed is radon, a radioactive gas given off by the naturally radioactive metal radium, which is present in traditional building materials; it accounts for one-third of the annual average dose for people living in the country. The Board may have to revise its conclusions in the wake of the disaster at Chernobyl and a series of accidents at British nuclear sites such as Sellafield and Dungeness, for their contribution to general background levels of radiation must have been considerable. But whatever the reactions of the Board, the very existence of radon in our habitat must have come as a total surprise to all but a specialised few.[11]

And so the tally of biochemical dangers steadily mounts. Open any newspaper or popular science magazine; yet another concern will be identified. In January 1986, a decade after the alarm was raised over the risks from aerosol sprays, the British journal *New Scientist* carried the following news item: 'A frequent ingredient in hair spray, methylene chloride, causes cancer in mice and may soon be banned by the US government. But the chemical will remain in decaffeinated coffee.'[12] Another publication contained details of a study from the United States that suggests that the modern American male produces less than half the sperm produced by the average male fifty years ago. One possible cause, says Dr Ralph Dougherty of Florida State University, is the presence of a flame retardant, Fyrol FR2, used to cut down fire risks in foam furniture. Other scientists around the world have discovered high concentrations of PCBs – the same chemical leaking from millions of failed fluorescent tubes – in semen samples. Other chemicals known to have adverse effects on male fertility include dibromochloropropane, a soil fumigant, and chlordecone, a pesticide for long ranked second only to dioxin as the most toxic of toxins.[13]

Pushing Back The Future

There are signs, of course, that humanity is fighting back. But the prospects of reversing the welling tide of toxic danger this side of the year 2000 are slender. To begin with, it now seems clear that the self-regulating, self-cleansing mechanisms of the earth's ecosystem are losing their capacity to cope. The drift towards contamination overload seems inexorable, even in the face of ambitious efforts to slow its momentum.

The example of Lake Biwa in Japan is a telling one. In the early 1970s Japan was being engulfed by industrial contamination. In those days, warnings of photochemical smog were sent out on three hundred days of the year in Tokyo; five thousand victims of atmospheric pollution were being recorded each year in the Japanese capital alone. Through official and corporate endeavour, at immense cost to industry and the community, air pollution was cut dramatically; smog alerts were reduced by nearly two-thirds. But today, at Lake Biwa, the signs point to another sad chapter in the breakdown of environmental purity.

Japan's largest lake, some 674 square kilometres in area, is being killed by pollution as the population moves into new satellite towns in the region, from Osaka and Kyoto. The tragic consequences are summed up in a recent narrative on the fate of Lake Biwa: 'The resulting effluent pouring into the lake, coupled with acid rain from the huge industrial areas nearby, is now rapidly turning it into a graveyard. Attempts to cut the input of phosphates, by banning the sale and use of phosphate detergents, began in 1980 but came too late; it is unlikely that the lake water will show major improvement this century.' Similar problems now beset other watercourses in the country. Surveys of water in various wells show that some sources are tainted by cancer-causing chemical compounds at up to six hundred times the level regarded as safe by the World Health Organisation. About one-third of Japan's drinking water comes from underground sources.[14] And Japan is not alone.

This losing battle is not for lack of official recognition of the seriousness of Planet Earth's precarious condition. A stream of books, international conferences and action programmes testifies to a growing awareness. From as long ago as 1962, with the publication of Rachel Carson's book *Silent Spring*, there has been no shortage of evidence of the deteriorating situation of the countryside, and the wildlife it once supported, because of the chemical warfare now waged by farmers in the interest of better yields. The United Nations Conference on the Human Environment, in Stockholm in 1972, represented a landmark in international acceptance of the growing threat. In 1973 the nations of the European Economic Community adopted their First Action Programme, with the aim of taking radical steps to avert environmental collapse. In the United States the work of the Environmental Protection Agency and other bodies has raised public knowledge of the hazards that surround them, and has thereby helped strike out in a new direction.

But such actions are not enough. Governments alone cannot change the habits of industry, nor replace public apathy with informed interest, criticism and vigilance. As much was admitted by the EEC eleven years after that First Action Programme, when it reviewed progress towards a cleaner, safer Europe: 'What has been done – substantial though it is – is clearly not enough . . . We have not so far even begun to tackle the much more fundamental question of whether – and for how long – human beings and ecosystems can continue to accept the total pressure placed upon them by the increasing use of chemicals.'[15]

The cause of that ever-mounting pressure is man's insatiable desire to manufacture, to innovate and to enjoy the fruits of industrial growth. The key to that growth is technology in all its forms – in energy, materials, chemical compounds, packaging and processing methods, information handling, genetic engineering. These technologies produce waste and by-products, as does humanity itself. Together they comprise the equation of toxic hazard that is the causal foundation of the high-tech holocaust. Only by controlling and changing that equation can eventual disaster be avoided. And this will demand a new understanding amongst wealth-makers, waste-makers and consumers.

A critical first step forward is to establish a climate of open business. The tradition of liberal politics is based on the simple maxim that the truth shall set you free. Yet two centuries of industrial history have evolved in conditions that have allowed the corporation, and the research centres and specialists that it finances, to find new technologies, products and processes, to maintain a monopoly over industrial secrets. It is this monopoly that prevents the public from knowing the full extent of the dangers they face. Access to this information is crucial if the consumer, who ultimately makes the market that finances the corporation, is to exercise control over the kind of ecosystem that is developed in the future. We need a Freedom of Information law to make industry more accountable as urgently as we need such a law for our governments.

Second, it is essential that we convert the growing interest in environmental issues – as manifested by the steady attraction of support for Green parties in most political systems in the developed world – into a more acute recognition of the bio-chemical threat that confronts us. For more than a decade, public awareness has focussed on the challenge to wildlife and the countryside, on seal culling, whaling, rain forests, the disappearing species of the animal kingdom. This awareness must now be turned to the pursuit of survival for mankind.

Perhaps the worldwide horror and alarm at the unprecedented nuclear disaster at Chernobyl will be the turning point. In its wake public awareness was taken to new heights and one can only hope that this will lead to an effective concern about all the other perils that surround us in our high-tech world. For what is certain is that if the scale of the assault on our bodily well-being is not reduced, but instead continues to accelerate at the speed witnessed over the past quarter-century, then humanity will itself become the species facing a slow, but inexorable, journey to extinction. We have, perhaps, five years to make the choice.

Notes

Chapter 1
1. *New Scientist*, 28 November 1985
2. *International Herald Tribune*, 14 August 1985
3. 'The Historical Roots of the British Clean Air Act, 1956', Lord Ashby and Dr M. Anderson in *Interdisciplinary Science Reviews* Vol 1 No 4, 1976
4. David D. Doniger, *The Law and Policy of Toxic Substances Control: A Case Study of Vinyl Chloride* (Johns Hopkins, 1978)
5. 'Oncogenic Response of Rat Skin, Lungs and Bones to Vinyl Chloride', 31 Cancer Research 516, 1971; cited in Doniger 1978; ibid
6. Memorandum from Cesare Maltoni to the Members of the European Cooperative Group for the Experimental Bio-assays on Vinyl Chloride Carcinogenicity (undated); cited in Doniger 1978; ibid
7. Doniger 1978; ibid
8. Ibid
9. *New Scientist*, 13 June 1985
10. *Nature*, 28 March 1985
11. *Environmental Health* Vol 92 No 1
12. John Elkington, *The Poisoned Womb* (Viking, 1985)
13. *Ambio* Vol 12 No 2. [*Ambio* is the Journal of the Royal Swedish Academy of Sciences]
14. Elkington, *The Poisoned Womb*
15. Ibid

Chapter 2
1. John Elkington, *The Poisoned Womb* (Viking, 1985)
2. D. Bryce-Smith and R. Stephens, *Lead or Health* (Conservation Society, 1980)
3. 'Lead, Behaviour and Criminality', *Ecologist* Vol 4 No 10
4. Bryce-Smith and Stephens, *Lead or Health*
5. Ibid
6. *The Guardian*, 13 May 1982 and 7 July 1982
7. The Road Research Laboratory Supplementary Report 660
8. L. N. Davis, *Frozen Fire* (Friends of the Earth, San Francisco, 1979)

Chapter 3
1. *The Observer*, 10 March 1985
2. Rosalie Bertell, *No Immediate Danger* (The Women's Press, 1985)

3. Ibid
4. *New Scientist*, 9 May 1985
5. Bertell, *No Immediate Danger*
6. *Biological Effects of Ionising Radiation*, US National Academy of Science (National Academy Press, 1980)
7. Bertell, *No Immediate Danger*
8. Shorthand transcript of evidence given by Mr G. Wedd to the Sizewell B Inquiry
9. Ibid
10. Ibid
11. Robert Jungk, *The New Tyranny* (Warner, New York, 1979)
12. Robert Jungk, *Brighter Than a Thousand Suns* (Penguin Books, 1970)
13. Bertell, *No Immediate Danger*
14. Fred Miller, 'Safety Problems and Government Regulations in the US' in *The Urban Transportation Of Irradiated Fuel*; Ed: J. Surrey (Macmillan, 1984)
15. Central Electricity Generating Board, 'The Transport of CEGB Irradiated Nuclear Fuel'; ibid
16. Fred Miller, 'Safety Problems and Government Regulations in the US'

Chapter 4

1. Steve Elsworth, *Acid Rain* (Pluto Press, 1984)
2. Address to the annual congress of the International Union of Pure and Applied Chemistry, Manchester, September 1985, reported in *The Times* 14 September 1985
3. 'Acid Rain', a Friends of the Earth special report. See also *Acid Rain: A Review of the Phenomenon in the EEC and Europe*, published by Earth Resources Limited for the Commission of the European Communities, 1983.
4. B. Ullrich, 'Effects of Accumulation of Air Pollutants in Forest Ecosystems', in *Acid Deposition: A Challenge for Europe* (Karlsruhe, EEC 1983)
5. John McCormick, *Acid Earth* (Earthscan, 1985)
6. Ibid
7. Ibid

Chapter 5

1. 'Survey of Copper and Zinc in Food', Food Surveillance Paper No 5 (HMSO, London 1981)
2. Ibid

Chapter 6

1. R. B. Clark, *Marine Pollution* (Clarendon Press, Oxford 1986)
2. Ibid

3. *New Scientist*, 16 July 1981
4. *New Scientist*, 25 July 1985
5. *The Gaia Atlas of Planet Management* (Pan Books, 1985)
6. *The Irish Times*, 8 July 1982
7. *Ambio* Vol 12 No 3–4, 1983
8. Ibid

Chapter 7

1. Judith Cook and Chris Kaufman, *Portrait of a Poison* (Pluto Press, 1982)
2. Ibid
3. The results were published in *Journal of the Association of Public Analysts* 22, 1984
4. Ibid
5. Friends of the Earth, London 1985
6. *Ambio* Vol 12 No 1
7. *Ambio* Vol 13 No 4
8. David Bull, *Pesticides and the Third World Poor* (Oxfam, 1982)
9. Ibid

Chapter 8

1. *New Scientist*, 13 June 1985
2. Ibid
3. P. E. Palm and others, *Toxicology and Applied Pharmacology* Vol 144, 1978
4. D. Stone and others, *Nature* Vol 231, 1971
5. J. Lederer and A. Pottier-Arnoud, *Diabete* Vol 21, 1973
6. A. Wolff and F. Oehme, *Journal of the American Veterinary Medicine Association* Vol 164, 1974
7. C. Soskolne and others, *American Journal of Epidemiology* Vol 120 No 3, 1984
8. N. I. Sax, *Cancer Causing Chemicals* (Van Nostrand Reinhold, New York, 1981)
9. Dr B. Feingold, *Why Your Child is Hyperactive* (Random House, 1975)
10. Susan Lewis, *Allergy? Think about Food* (Wisebuy Publications, 1984)
11. John Elkington, *The Poisoned Womb* (Viking, 1985)
12. Lewis, *Allergy? Think about Food*
13. M. Miller, 'Danger! Additives at Work' (The London Food Commission, 1985)
14. Ibid
15. J. van Kooij, 'Food Irradiation Makes Progress', *Environmental Health* Vol 93 No 7
16. Tony Webb, 'Food Irradiation in Britain?' (The London Food Commission, 1985)

Chapter 9
1. Brian Inglis, *The Diseases of Civilisation* (Paladin, 1983)
2. A. Melville and C. Johnson, *Cured to Death* (Secker and Warburg, 1982)
3. *New Scientist*, 23 May 1974
4. Ibid
5. Ibid
6. L. Meyler, *Side Effects of Drugs* (Amsterdam, 1966)
7. Inglis, *The Diseases of Civilisation*
8. *New Scientist*, 23 May 1974
9. A. Melville and C. Johnson, *Cured to Death*
10. Ibid
11. *New Scientist*, 25 July 1985
12. *New Scientist*, 29 August 1985
13. *Daily Mail*, 29 March 1986
14. A. Melville and C. Johnson, *Cured to Death*
15. D. Melrose, *Bitter Pills* (Oxfam, 1982)

Chapter 10
1. *The Observer*, 4 May 1985
2. *Vibration*, British Society for Social Responsibility in Science (London, 1977)
3. A. J. Rowland and P. Cooper, *Environment and Health* (Edward Arnold, London, 1983)
4. *Ambio* Vol 13 No 1
5. *The Guardian*, 10 August 1979
6. *The Guardian*, 15 August 1983
7. *The Observer*, 8 June 1980
8. *The Financial Times*, 17 June 1985
9. 'Working with VDUs', Health and Safety Executive (London, 1986)
10. *The Financial Times*, 18 January 1985
11. *The Financial Times*, 30 April 1980
12. *New Scientist*, 23 January 1986
13. *The Guardian*, 23 May 1985
14. *Nature*, 16 May 1985
15. 'Ten Years of Community Environment Policy', Commission of the European Communities, March 1984